Petersen's Safety Supervision

Third Edition

Petersen's Safety Supervision

THIRD EDITION

Dan Petersen

with

Kyle Dotson and Dave Johnson

American Society of Safety Professionals, 520 N. Northwest Highway, Park Ridge, IL 60068
Copyright © 2020 by American Society of Safety Professionals
All rights reserved. Published 2020.

American Society of Safety Professionals, ASSP, and the ASSP shield are registered trademarks of the American Society of Safety Professionals.

Limits of Liability/Disclaimer of Warranty
While the publisher and authors have used their best efforts in preparing this book, they make no representations or warranties with respect to the accuracy or completeness of the contents of this book, and specifically disclaim any implied warranties of merchantability or fitness for a particular purpose. The information is provided with the understanding that the authors are not hereby engaged in rendering legal or other professional services. If legal advice or other professional assistance is required, the services of a qualified professional should be sought.

Managing Editor: Rick Blanchette, ASSP
Editor: Cathy Lombardi
Text design and composition: Cathy Lombardi
Cover design: Janet Chen, ASSP

Print ISBN: 9781885581051
E-book ISBN: 9781885581068

Printed in the United States of America

29 28 27 26 25 24 23 22 21 20   1 2 3 4 5 6 7 8

Library of Congress Cataloging-in-Publication Data
Names: Petersen, Dan, author. | Dotson, Kyle, author | Johnson, David, author.
Title: Petersen's safety supervision / Kyle Dotson, David Johnson, and Dan Petersen.
Other titles: Safety supervision
Description: Third edition. | Park Ridge, IL : American Society of Safety Professionals, 2020.
 | Revised edition of: Safety supervision / Dan Petersen. c1999. | Includes bibliographical references and index. | Summary: "Petersen's Safety Supervision discusses the various aspects of supervision in the occupational safety and health (OSH) field. The book espouses the concept of human and organizational performance. Rather than being an esoteric look at high-level theory, this text aims to define reality--what's going on, what works, and what doesn't work in safety supervision. Chapters examine the supervisor's job, the dynamics of supervision, key safety and health tasks, various techniques that work--coaching, investigating incidents and root causes, hazard identification, today's safety and health philosophy, industrial hygiene and health, and safety leadership at the executive level"-- Provided by publisher.
Identifiers: LCCN 2019056273 (print) | LCCN 2019056274 (ebook) | ISBN 9781885581051 (hardcover) | ISBN 9781885581068 (adobe pdf)
Subjects: LCSH: Industrial safety. | Supervision of employees.
Classification: LCC HD7261 .P48 2020 (print) | LCC HD7261 (ebook) | DDC 658.3/82--dc23
LC record available at https://lccn.loc.gov/2019056273
LC ebook record available at https://lccn.loc.gov/2019056274

Table of Contents

Preface to the Third Edition   vii
Preface to the Second Edition   xi
Introduction: Safety and Health Influences   1

PART I: Defining Supervision
Chapter 1. The Supervisor's Job   13
Chapter 2. The Dynamics of Supervision   33

PART II: Navigating the World of Safety and Health
Chapter 3. The Safety and Health Job   71
Chapter 4. Key Safety and Health Tasks   89
Chapter 5. Accountability   115
Chapter 6. Leadership   133

PART III: Techniques That Work
Chapter 7: Coaching   151
Chapter 8: Hazard Identification and Mitigation   167
Chapter 9. Incident Investigations and Root-Cause Analyses   185

PART IV: Stepping into the Future
Chapter 10. The New Realities of Safety and Health   207
Chapter 11. Today's Safety and Health Philosophy   227
Chapter 12. Industrial Hygiene and Health   245

PART V: Appendices
Appendix A. Executive Safety Leadership   259
Appendix B. The "New View" of Safety   265
Appendix C. ANSI/ASSP Z10.0-2019
   Occupational Health and Safety Management Systems   273

Index   277

Preface to the Third Edition

The writings of Dan Petersen in the field of safety management transcend decades of change in American organizational management theory. "I think we could be going back to the 1970s, when the concentration was on management and accountability. Also human factors concepts. We could be going down that route where we build into the organization an environment that takes into account the human factor, the human element. The idea is to not build traps into the workplace. This isn't new."

Dan said this in an interview with Dave for his magazine, *Industrial Safety & Hygiene News*, on June 26, 2003. As usual, Dan was ahead of the curve. In essence, what he describes above is what's known today as HOP—Human and Organizational Performance, perhaps the most sophisticated safety management model being practiced (Petersen 2003).

In that same interview, Dan said, "People are always screwing up for good, logical reasons. It's universal. We make environments that make it logical to screw up."

HOP is a risk-based operating philosophy that recognizes error is part of the human condition and even the best employees make mistakes. Organizational systems and processes greatly influence employee actions and the likelihood of success or failure. HOP provides an understanding of how work gets done; considers the context in which employees must cope with hazards; assesses an organization's capacity to identify and respond to risk; and improves employee engagement, work quality, system reliability, and overall operational performance.

Dan nailed the heart of HOP 16 years ago.

This third edition of Dan's *Safety Supervision* is a full 21 years after the second. The first edition was published in 1976 for the American Management Association. The second edition was published in 1999 by the American Society of Safety Professionals (ASSP, formerly the American Society of Safety Engineers). In his preface to the second edition, Dan wrote, "Everything has changed since [1976]. . . . In some cases there is pure chaos—nobody is running the show."

Dan could easily be talking about today's fast-paced, unpredictable business life. That's Dan's uniquely prescient nature, what makes him a founding father of modern safety and one of its greatest thought leaders. His thinking is timeless. In 2003, he described a safety model (HOP) that was the subject of special conferences, presentations, books, and articles in 2018 and will be for years to come. In 1999, he characterized the work environment that exists 20 years later.

This is why a third edition of *Safety Supervision* is justified. Times have changed, supervision has changed, the economy—the context and reality of work—has changed. Dan said it in the 2003 interview (Petersen 2003): "Define reality. What's going on here? What works and what doesn't work?"

That's the goal of this book. The third edition of *Safety Supervision* aims to define reality, what's going on, and what works and doesn't work in safety supervision. Many of Dan's approaches to safety absolutely still apply and are practical, valuable, and as relevant as ever. For example, he said in the 2003 interview: "Get involvement. Get employees on their own doing things the way they think it should be done." Today we call that engagement.

The third edition updates terminology, including use of nongender-specific "he and she" references in place of the first and second edition's use of "man," "key man," "foreman," and "he." (Here again, Dan was ahead of the times. In the second edition in 1999 he wrote, "Although the discussion uses the masculine forms of pronouns, the author's intent is gender inclusiveness, and the reader may substitute "she," "her," etc., as appropriate. We have also endeavored to use more current terms in the third edition (for example, incident rather than accident).

Parts of the third edition have been reorganized into chapters on coaching, leadership, new realities, today's safety philosophy, and entirely new text written by Kyle and Dave on industrial hygiene and health.

The third edition drops the three appendices from the second edition. Appendix A on supervisory self-appraisal and Appendix B on stress tests are limited since today you can google these tests and come up with hundreds of tools. Appendix C of the second edition has been deleted, as supervisors today have myriad new laws to follow, far more than supervisors had in past decades. You are better advised to seek specific references for current regulations applicable to your specific jurisdiction.

This third edition adds three new appendices. Appendix A is an article by Dan and Kyle on executive leadership, published online for *Professional Safety* (Petersen and Dotson, 2006), and based on a conversation they had with Dan in 2006, shortly before he passed away at age 72. Appendix B is an overview of the "New View" of safety. Appendix C summarizes the ANSI/ASSP Z10.0-2019 *Occupational Health and Safety Management Systems* standard.

References have been extensively updated. We've examined new sources, new information, and new research that in many ways validate Dan's original approaches to safety supervision. In a few select cases where Dan's work is no longer applicable to a world of work that has indeed changed, the editors left a bit of Dan's original work on the cutting room floor.

Certainly, most of the third edition text is Dan's original writing, which in many cases remains lightly edited. There is no need for any major course correction. After all, this is the man who 17 years ago in the interview with Dave said, "Safety is about one-to-one interactions—supervisors to managers, supervisors to workers, managers to workers. Safety is about these interactions happening every day. It's people looking out for each other. That's how safety is achieved." That's as true today as it was then.

Dan Petersen was born in 1931 in Omaha, Nebraska (human interest fun fact: the Sage of Safety, Dan Petersen, and the Oracle of Omaha, Warren Buffett, were childhood friends). Before Dan died in 2007 in Arizona, he had received in his lifetime just about every honor and award of significance that exists in the professional occupational safety and health management field. He was a Fellow of the ASSP and national vice president of ASSP. He authored 18 books, filmed numerous videos, lectured extensively, and wrote a small library of articles. Perhaps more importantly, in his work in private industry for insurance companies, and as a very independent-minded consultant, Dan used his EdD dissertation ("Human Error Reduction and Safety Management") and his PhD ("Organizational Behavior and Management") to pivot occupational safety away from the realm of engineers and inspectors, machine guards and physical conditions, and toward recognizing and addressing the human behavioral and organizational cultural aspects of safety.

Dan anticipated the increasing impact of work on stress and mental well-being. Never one to mince words, he said (Petersen 2003), "I've never seen the number of pissed off and angry people working in companies." He might as well have been describing social media and the great divides in our American public today. He also anticipated the potential irony of technology advancing yet distracting from the timely human correction of unacceptable human conditions. "We need safety people spending less time on the computer and more time on the floor," he said. Dan foresaw that an overreliance on technology could "destroy relationships, those close interactions."

This classic safety management textbook is as relevant today as ever. We believe the wisdom and practical interventions of Dan Petersen deserve a wide, diverse audience among new generations of safety professionals and organization managers learning and practicing today and in the future. It is an honor to present to you the third edition of Dan Petersen's *Safety Supervision*.

Respectively,
Kyle Dotson and Dave Johnson

REFERENCES

Petersen, Dan. 1999. *Safety Supervision*, 2nd ed. Des Plaines, IL: American Society of Safety Engineers.

Petersen, Dan. 2003. "Charting Your Course." Interview by Dave Johnson. *Industrial Safety & Hygiene News*, Sept. 2003.

Petersen, Dan, and Kyle Dotson, 2006. "Executive Safety Leadership." *Professional Safety* web exclusive.

Preface to the Second Edition

Many years ago I wrote *Safety Supervision* for the American Management Association (AMACOM). When I did that in 1976, the world of safety was a quite different place. It was still largely before OSHA's influence became pervasive, and it was in an era where we believed that the supervisor was the "Key Man" in safety, as Heinrich taught us.

Everything has changed since then. OSHA is here and the supervisor is no longer perceived as the "Key Man" in safety. In some organizations there are no supervisors, or they may be referred to as "Team Leaders" or "Facilitators." In some, the so-called supervisor is not a member of management but is really a member of the union. (What is his/her role?)

So the whole concept of "safety supervision" appears to have changed. Or has it? Do workers today have no supervision—no bosses? In some cases, yes: in some companies team management has led to high-performance operations. And it usually works very well. But most of the time it is not quite that simple or pure. Supervisors are now team leaders—a mere title change—since decisions are still made above. In some cases there is pure chaos—nobody is running the show. And, in fact, in most cases there has been little change—workers still are supervised by bosses as they always were. For all of our wonderful talk about participation and involvement, in the majority of organizations there still exists a boss, or a boss structure—from top to bottom—from CEO to worker, and in that structure there is always a crucial link—the worker to his or her direct boss. By whatever name, that person is a supervisor.

This book is about that person—that one person who connects the hourly employee to the organization—the supervisor. In the Army we called him a sergeant, and he was the only person that made it all work. In industry we used to call him a foreman—and he got the same results—he made it all work.

In the Army, I was a lieutenant—one of the most worthless positions—without the sergeants I would have been ridiculous; at least I think I knew it at the time, and they (the sergeants) saved my ——— over and over. In industry, the first-line supervisors make the organization run, when the organization allows them to. When the organization uses that position only as a training ground, with constant churn, the only hope is that they have good enough employees to run the operation in spite of the situation.

This book is dedicated to two first-line supervisors that I knew well, and who were just as typical as the ones who saved me in the Army:

- my dad, JP, in the Omaha packing houses;
- my father-in-law, AB, at Northwestern Bell (then a part of the AT&T system).

In 1996, VNR published three revisions of books I had previously written: *Human Error Reduction & Safety Management*; *Safety by Objectives—What Gets Measured and Rewarded Gets Done*; and *Analyzing Safety System Effectiveness*. As I was revising these, I also was revising this book, *Safety Supervision*. We postponed publishing this revision—three was enough for one year. However, we referred to *Safety Supervision* several times in the other revisions, particularly in *Safety by Objectives* and *Analyzing Safety System Effectiveness*, since *Supervision* was intended to be a companion piece to the other books. The later two revisions were aimed at management—how to set up systems to hold people accountable for their performance—for doing things regularly, proactively, to control losses.

I am constantly asked in seminars after discussing accountability, "Accountable to do what?" This book describes some options, and what supervisors might actually do which will result in fewer accidents and injuries. In the other books accountability systems are discussed, this book suggests some actions that supervisors (or teams) might be held accountable to do.

Dan Petersen

Introduction: Safety and Health Influences

This book is directed at you, the front-line supervisor responsible for managing individuals who don't manage others. If executives and middle managers are going to require specific safety and health activities from you—and they should—what exactly are you going to do to satisfy these responsibilities? The following chapters spell this out.

Hopefully you have been given flexibility and the opportunity to provide input to determine which safety and health-related tasks and activities you agree to take responsibility for. As you fulfill these responsibilities, those who report to you will recognize your commitment—that you hold safety as a core personal value. But it all starts with you setting the example. Perform those tasks and activities on a consistent, daily basis.

The supervisor's role is multifaceted.

You are the link between management and the floor, the line, the workforce in any manufacturing or service organization. To the workforce, you are management because of your daily contact "at the sharp end" (Flon 2016)—where the work gets done. You are responsible for three key integrated values of any company: production, quality, and safety and health (Spencley 2015). Also, you are charged with communicating, instructing, planning, scheduling, prioritizing, problem-solving, and dealing with emergencies. All in an atmosphere that today is time-crunched, deadline-driven, often chaotic, unpredictable, and filled with characters, surprising motives, and company politics. Plus, making decisions as system complexity and uncertainty increase today is a challenging task to accomplish (Colombo 2019, 18–37).

With today's emphasis on engaging workers, as a supervisor you are also expected to build relationships and teams, coach, motivate, converse one-on-one, listen, give feedback, provide recognition when deserved, and administer discipline and corrective action when warranted.

All of this requires leadership. A leader who is both technically competent—knows the tasks that need to be done (standard operating procedures)—and possesses good people skills, which include actively caring about your people as individuals who have lives outside of work. This "actively caring" certainly includes the safety and health of your direct reports (Geller 1991, 607–612).

So what might your tasks be relating to safety and health? It depends upon the organization. No two organizations approach safety and health in the same manner. Your tasks might fall into these categories:

Traditional Tasks	Nontraditional Tasks
Inspect/Hazard recognition	Lead and demonstrate actively caring
Mitigate hazards and exposures	Give positive feedback
Conduct safety meetings/briefings	Ensure employee engagement
Safety contacts/One-on-one conversations	Evaluate safety and health performance of direct reports/Hold employees accountable
Incident response/Root-cause analysis	Conduct force-field analyses/Look at the big picture
Perform job safety analyses	Assess climate and perceptions
Conduct observations	Perform crisis/conflict intervention
Compliance/Enforce internal and external rules and regulations	Assess employee workload capacity, fatigue, stress levels, and overall well-being
Report/Document leading and lagging performance indicators	Adopt "smart" safety technology in consult with your safety and health department

In addition, you are responsible for certain day-to-day safety and health actions not easily spelled out or measured. Safety and health issues, concerns, and incidents (including near misses) often occur spontaneously. All supervisors must ask themselves these questions:

1. How well do I understand my safety and health responsibilities?
2. Do I know what is expected of me?
3. Do I know the reach of my power/authority?

Many supervisors feel as though they are disempowered go-betweens. We'll discuss later how supervisors leverage micro-power (Kras, Portillo, and Taxman 2017, 215–236). It's important to reach agreement on how your safety and health performance will be measured—preferably not solely on the basis of past injury and illness rates, which can be matters of random luck.

Above all, regarding safety and health, your role as supervisor is to engage regularly (daily) in predefined tasks. What are those tasks? That's up to you, your safety and health department, your senior leadership, and the culture of your organization. This book suggests what the essential, potentially life-saving safety and health tasks might be.

This book is also directed at those who influence the performance of supervisors.

SENIOR LEADERS

If supervisors are not achieving desired results specific to safety and health, you, as a senior leader, are partially responsible. Most supervisors try their best to accomplish what is asked of them by their manager. Some common reasons for failure to achieve desired results include:

- The supervisor may not know what it is you want accomplished.
- There may be conflicting signals coming from you. ("Safety first"—but get the rush orders out today!)
- The supervisor may judge what you want by how you reward performance, instead of by what you say.
- There may not be enough hours in the day to do all of the things that you say you want done.
- It could be that your systems have loaded the supervisor with so much recordkeeping and report writing that it's impossible to do what you want.
- It could be that your "rightsizing" or "flattening" of the organization has spread the ranks of your supervisors so thin that they simply cannot supervise.
- It could be that, in transitioning to teams, you've gotten rid of supervisors and not replaced them and not thought out team roles, team functions, team responsibilities, or team accountabilities.
- It could be you expect your people to do things beyond their capabilities.

These are a few examples of conditions that exist in many organizations. Flattening managerial layers (or whatever name you call it), reengineering, and a raft of other methods used to transform and realign organizations often take place without clear role definitions for those affected. Without adequate training for those in new settings, new jobs, new titles, etc., the result is often chaos.

In Kyle's consulting, he has found that following the introduction of new approaches from the executive level, these new methods of conducting business are often not clearly perceived at the very next level, are quite fuzzy at the second level down, are not only very fuzzy below that, but can be resented at the supervisory level—usually because supervisors simply may not fully understand the executive intent.

What is the impact on the workforce when corporate change occurs? At the front line, employees know whether doing the job safely is important to their supervisor and to the organization. Frequently, at this level, there is no impact from executive-planned changes; the change never quite gets to the front-line level. On the front lines (where the work is done), whether employees have a supervisor, a team leader, a facilitator, or whatever else he or she is called, is frankly often immaterial. On the front line they just do their work (thank God), and get the job done. The culture ("what goes on around here every day") is what signals whether safety is a "core value" of the organization or simply lip service. The concept of safety culture is often used to illustrate that there are social processes in organizations that help or hinder behaviors or outcomes regarding occupational health and safety (Nordlöf et al. 2017, 92–103).

Executives don't have to be irrelevant to those on the front line—as they often are. Executives can have a powerful impact not only by saying things but, more importantly, by making things happen.

This book spells out a number of things a supervisor (or whatever title you use) can do that will yield desired results in safety and health. At the senior level, your job is to decide which accountability style fits you: SCRAPE (the System of Counting and Rating Accident Prevention Effort—tight accounting for safety and health tasks), SBO (Safety by Objectives), or MENU (weekly reporting)—as described in chapter 5. Implement the style you feel most comfortable with.

This, of course, assumes that (a) you are not satisfied with your current safety and health performance and (b) you are willing to take an active role to make changes to achieve desired results. It will take you, the senior leader, to champion the change needed.

MID-LEVEL MANAGERS

If supervisors are really going to spend their time, effort, etc., on safety and health to get the results your executives want, they will only do so if you make it happen. The old textbooks said the supervisor was the key person to achieve desired safety results. That was not true. We know a supervisor reacts to what is important to his or her boss, you—the supervisor's direct report. What is of crucial importance to mid-level managers is of crucial importance to supervisors who report to them. Supervisors react to your goals, desires, wishes, and measures.

The roles in safety and health are simple and clear-cut:

1. Front-line supervisors execute agreed-upon safety and health-related tasks to an acceptable level of performance.
2. Middle and upper managers are accountable for:
   a. safety and health performance at the front line
   b. the quality and consistency of that performance
   c. personally engaging in agreed-upon safety and health-related tasks.
3. Executives visibly demonstrate their priority of safety and health.

Obviously, your role as a mid-level manager is key. You oversee supervisory performance that ensures safe behaviors, safe procedures, and working conditions exhibited by those working on the front line.

SAFETY AND HEALTH STAFF

The responsibility of the safety and health staff is to advise and facilitate the safety and health roles of supervisors. This is accomplished through one-to-one interactions: safety and health staff to supervisors, supervisors to managers, supervisors to front-line employees, and managers to front-line employees. These interactions must be happening every day. Safety and health staff meetings with supervisors must take place on a regular basis. Safety is about people looking out for each other each and every day. It includes safety and health staff looking out for supervisors as well as front-line employees and managers. This is how workplace safety is achieved—not by writing down audit protocols. Pieces of paper don't save lives (Petersen 2003).

Companies can be improved through interpersonal relationships. Supervisors should concentrate more on relationships than on physical conditions and standards.

The only way your supervisors can do this—the only way you can do this as a safety and health professional—is to tap the intelligence of the front-line employee. If front-line employees are not a part of what supervisors are doing, not part of what you're doing, you're missing out. Everyone must feel part of the team, all working for a common objective. Safety and health pros can help supervisors facilitate processes of safety improvement teams and process safety ad hoc teams and can influence employee behavior. There are any number of ways to use people's brains to make things better (Petersen 2003). Both you as a professional and your front-line supervisors must tap into people's talents.

Positive Organizational Scholarship (POS) is another factor (Robson et al. 2016). POS focuses on positive outcomes, processes, and attributes of organizations. Positive outcomes, such as organizational coordination, organizational performance, and organization energy, are derived from identifying positive deviance in a population of individuals, understanding the basis of the positive deviance, and applying the gained knowledge to others in the employee population for their benefit.

EMPLOYEES/TEAM MEMBERS

Your "safety role" is simple—work in such a manner that you and your fellow workers won't get hurt. You must get involved in your organization's safety and health activities. And, if you are in a high-performance organization with no supervisor, then your role is much larger. You and your peers must take over—do all of the things that must be done to ensure safety and health. These might be inspecting, investigation, coaching, motivating—all of the things discussed in the remainder of this book.

No matter your organization structure, as a team member it is up to you to make it happen: to create a culture that actively demonstrates safety to be a key value in this organization.

WHERE ARE YOU NOW?

Before continuing, perhaps you ought to determine where you currently stand as a supervisor in terms of safety and health. You'll get a better idea by studying the 16 questions that follow and analyzing your responses. For each question, choose the answer that best describes your current situation.

1. Do I have a *job description* that indicates precisely what I am to do in regard to safety and health?
   (a) No
   (b) I have a job description, but it doesn't mention safety and health.
   (c) Yes
2. Do I know exactly how much *power/authority* I have in safety and health?
   (a) No
   (b) Yes
   (c) I've discussed it with my boss, and we've come to some agreements.
3. Do I know exactly how I'm going to be *measured* in safety and health?
   (a) No
   (b) Yes
   (c) I've discussed it with my boss, and we've come to some agreements.
4. Do I know exactly what I am *expected to do* in safety and health?
   (a) No
   (b) All that counts are outcomes—no injuries or illnesses.
   (c) Yes
5. Do I know what is considered *acceptable performance* in safety and health?
   (a) No
   (b) No injuries or illnesses, I guess.
   (c) Yes
6. How much *time* do I spend on safety and health?
   (a) No time
   (b) It is a constant job.
   (c) A few hours a week
7. Am I familiar with *regulatory standards*?
   (a) What's that?
   (b) Yes
   (c) Those sections that apply to me
8. Have I made a list and corrected all *violations* of the law in my area?
   (a) No
   (b) Once
   (c) Regularly

9. Have I set up a *system of priorities*?
   (a) No
   (b) Yes
   (c) Yes. It's in operation.
10. Have I *kept my boss aware* of my status on enforcing compliance and encouraging best practices?
    (a) Heaven forbid
    (b) Once I did.
    (c) Regularly
11. Have I *documented* everything I've done in safety and health and compliance?
    (a) No
    (b) In part
    (c) Yes
12. Do I know what *engages my people*?
    (a) Who cares?
    (b) Everything, I think.
    (c) Yes, I know.
13. Do I know what *alienates my people*?
    (a) Who cares?
    (b) Nothing
    (c) Yes, I know.
14. Do I know when to use *corrective action*?
    (a) Always
    (b) Never
    (c) Yes, I know.
15. Do I know how to work with *people who won't follow basic safety rules*?
    (a) The same way as with anyone else
    (b) No, I don't.
    (c) Yes, I do.
16. Do I know how to influence *behaviors* of those that work for me to ensure work is done in a safe manner?
    (a) No
    (b) I don't know what "safe behaviors" look like.
    (c) Yes, I lead by example—always exhibiting safe behavior.

There are obviously many other questions that could be asked, but these will give you an idea of your current status relating to your safety and health activities.

Score yourself three points for any (c) answer, two points for a (b) answer, and one point for an (a) answer. If you scored 45 or more, you have no worries—and probably no injuries or illnesses. If you scored between 35 and 44, you still need to work at it. If you scored 25 to 34, you're not quite there. If you scored under 24, maybe you ought to see the boss about a transfer—or read on.

This book is written for you, the supervisor, the person in the organization who makes it happen, whether it is safety, quality, production, or anything else that management wants done.

However, we've learned through the years that in many (probably most) organizations, safety and health doesn't get accomplished by supervisors (or by anyone else). Far too often it is talked about but not acted on; it is only addressed when you're not busy; and it quickly disappears in your rush periods. This is easy to understand when we look at management theory and research about why supervisors do what they do—and why they don't do what management "says" it wants done.

THE JOB IS NOT GETTING DONE

It has been a fundamental belief since the beginning of occupational safety and health endeavors that, if anything is to be accomplished, it will be accomplished by the front-line supervisor. Safety and health professionals believe this—so do managers at all levels. Unfortunately, possessing this core belief has not gotten the job done.

Through the years, there has been substantial progress making physical conditions safer and healthier, but most of the real progress occurred during the early years of the effort. In recent years, progress has slowed in some cases, has reached a plateau in others, and serious injuries and fatalities have continued to plague many organizations.

One of the causes of safety performance leveling off is our inability to transform our fundamental belief about supervisory responsibility into supervisory action. Many supervisors are not effective in managing safety and health. If they were, actions would lead to continued performance improvements. The principal reasons for supervisors falling short are:

- Management is seldom sufficiently clear about what it wants done in safety and health. The prevailing attitude is: "It's your responsibility, now go do something about it."
- Management almost never follows up to see if the supervisor has in fact done anything in safety and health. At most, someone may look at an injury and illness record.
- Management almost always measures the supervisor in areas other than safety and health when evaluating performance standards.

Given this type of leadership, why should a supervisor spend any time and effort on safety and health? This book aims to answer this question by first clarifying and simplifying what a supervisor should do in order to achieve agreed-upon safety and health results. There is no mystery to it—as long as certain tasks are done regularly and routinely, results should follow. And secondly, this text will show how management can clearly, simply, and effectively measure supervisory performance in safety and health.

This book is not intended to be a comprehensive safety and health reference for supervisors. It will not answer specific questions about what is hazardous to health and well-being and what is safe. In the Internet age, hundreds of references are available. The National Safety Council's annual "Injury Facts" is one example. The OSHA website's A–Z topic index is another. Google "industrial safety hazards," and you'll get more than 3.4 million results.

REFERENCES

Colombo, Simon. 2019. "The Holistic Risk Analysis and Modelling (HoRAM) Method." *Safety Science* 112, no. 2 (February): 18–37.

Flon, Jean-Marc. 2016. DSNA Paris-CDG, "Ground Safety Nets: The use of ground safety nets as part of a global SMS strategy." PowerPoint presentation, Fourth Safety Forum, Brussels, Belgium, June 2016. https://skybrary.aero/bookshelf/books/3493.pptx.

Geller, E. Scott. 1991. "If only more would actively care." *Applied Behavior Analysis* 24: 607–612.

Kras, Kimberly, Shannon Portillo, and Faye Taxman. 2017. "Managing from the Middle: Frontline Supervisors and Perceptions of their Organizational Power." *Law & Policy* 39, no. 3 (July): 215–236. https://doi.org/10.1111/lapo.12079.

Nordlöf, Hasse, Birgitta Wiitavaara, Hans Högberg et al. 2017. "A cross-sectional study of factors influencing occupational health and safety management practices in companies." *Safety Science* 95 (June): 92–103.

Petersen, Dan. 2003. "Charting Your Course." Interview by Dave Johnson. *Industrial Safety & Hygiene News*, Sept. 2003.

Spencley, Rodney. 2015. "Safety, Quality and Productivity: A Holistic Approach." DPR Construction online post, May 28, 2015. https://www.dpr.com/media/blog/safety-quality-productivity-holistic-approach-construction-injury-free.

PART I

Defining Supervision

CHAPTER 1

The Supervisor's Job

A lot has been written about the job of the supervisor. What characteristics separate a good supervisor from a not so good one?

DIMENSIONS OF TALENT

What dimensions of talent are needed for good supervision? We have no idea. Many of the articles dealing with leadership include lists of the characteristics essential to leadership. Tom Peters (best known as the coauthor of *In Search of Excellence*) enumerates 48 "things that matter" (Peters 2009). Gallup lists five (Adkins 2015). The *Harvard Business Review* scores 16 (Zenger and Folkman 2014). The Institute for Corporate Productivity settles on four (Fontana 2017). The most frequently listed traits focus on being a motivator, building relationships, modeling behavior, assuming accountability, solving problems, and driving results.

When human resource managers discuss with other executives the kind of person who can fill a supervisory capacity, certain characteristics crop up with monotonous regularity: technical competence; leadership maturity; coaching ability; conflict management skills; humility; honesty; being straightforward, trustworthy, communicative, and empathetic; and caring about your people.

Most researchers studying leadership have pretty well rejected the personality-trait approach. In general, results appear to support the notion that while certain personality characteristics are present in all leaders, these traits are also distributed among everyone else in the world.

HOW SUPERVISORS ARE CHOSEN

Another factor to consider in looking at the profile of supervisors is how a person is actually promoted into supervision. In past decades, promotion decisions could be routinely different from official policy, as described in the 1950s by Professor Melville Dalton, a sociologist at UCLA, in an analysis of managerial promotion in a firm with a total workforce of about 8000 (Dalton 1959). The company's official policy emphasized ability, honesty, cooperation, and work rate as advancement criteria. Additional factors included age, employment background and service, formal education, and relevant training.

Dalton, though, found none of these factors were really permanently used. Instead, Dalton found unofficial requirements were routinely at play in promotions at three other companies he studied. At the time of this early research, the conclusion was that there seemed to be no identifiable ideal traits for a supervisor. And even if there were, according to Dalton's work, it was doubtful if supervisors would actually be selected by these traits.

Today, there are still basically two tracks that endure as leading to supervisory roles. One track involves formal education, such as a college degree, with variations on the theme that often in the past focused on engineering, especially in large manufacturing organizations. In this education-focused track, upon landing his or her first job, the graduate becomes a sort of front-line first lieutenant. Some organizations call this instant supervisor a "shake and bake" supervisor (Kello 2017), quickly processed to become the boss of employees twice his or her age.

The second track produces supervisors who have come up through the ranks. Sometimes they are promoted on merit and experience and technical knowledge. In other instances, it is less a matter completely based upon merit but rather is a mix of who you know and whether you're a team player, are compliant, and fit in.

Even today, it isn't just character or personality—or even smarts—that get a person promoted into supervision. Education and a college degree on the one hand, and a show of tenacious effort coming up through the ranks, seem to be the major factors.

KEY ELEMENTS OF SUPERVISION

One well-known management consultant, Edward C. Schleh, lists eight basic elements of supervision (Schleh 1966):

1. *Goal setting.* The first responsibility of any supervisor is to set goals for his people and to spell out exactly what he expects from them. The definition of objectives should be in terms of results, not just actions. This seems obvious but is very rarely done consistently.
2. *Training.* Second, a supervisor should be responsible for training his people. This is particularly important at the first-line supervisory level. There is a strong tendency to refer a new worker to an experienced worker for training. The results are often poor, because the older person is not held accountable for the instruction. The new hire often develops bad work habits, which are later hard to change.
3. *Follow-up.* While no supervisor should look over the shoulders of his people all the time—micro-manage—he or she must make sure goals are being met according to plan and schedule. For example, a sales

manager must follow up to make sure a salesman has understood and is practicing the right sales approach. An accounting department head must follow up to be sure that all the legal requirements of posting are understood. A manufacturing supervisor must follow up to make sure that his people or team understand corporate policies and values.

4. *Conflict management.* Fourth, a supervisor must intervene when necessary to take corrective actions. This task, of course, is usually thought of as a nasty one, and nobody really likes to exercise discipline, but it is and must be part of a supervisor's job at any level in the organization.
5. *Motivation.* A fifth duty of supervision is to encourage your people. Everyone drags from time to time, and a supervisor works to help others regain their enthusiasm. A new supervisor sometimes thinks his job stops with delivering orders coming down the chain of command. If he operates in this way, he just does not get as much out of his people as he could.
6. *New processes.* Another responsibility is the installation of new work processes. Only the supervisor can integrate new processes into operations.
7. *Talent development.* Seventh, a company must rely on a supervisor to develop the skills and knowledge of his people for future promotion. The foremen must develop their people, the superintendent must develop his foremen, the plant manager must develop his superintendents, and so on down the line. This is a basic responsibility of every managerial job.
8. *Fixing accountability.* Finally, it is the responsibility of any supervisor to call his people to account. Employees must be straightened out if necessary or complimented for an accomplishment. Feedback is critical. Just as the supervisor must hold his people accountable for outcomes and for certain procedures, he or she also is held accountable for outcomes and for following the chain of command. In later chapters this will be discussed in detail, for the real key to the success of any safety and health process (or any other activity) is how well you perform. This depends on how strictly your boss holds you accountable.

Your Responsibilities as a Supervisor

We're going to ask you now to think about your job as a supervisor—what you do—what your tasks and responsibilities are in your organization.

Important research has been conducted in this area. In one study of 75 front-line supervisors, most viewed themselves as disempowered go-betweens who feel deprived of the power/authority of the organization and in their role as leaders. This results from a lack of decision-making power regarding daily issues, and also a lack of policy influence.

Front-line supervisors contend that they are caught in a vise trying to adhere to directives from above, reconcile their own beliefs about policy, present policy to employees, and follow up with superiors to share employee concerns (Kras, Portillo, and Taxman 2017).

Front-line supervisors disagree among themselves about how much authority and decision-making power they actually possess. In terms of discipline, many supervisors feel unsupported by upper management in initiating disciplinary action. Many feel they have no power to regulate and assess the performance of those they supervise. Often there is a lack of clarity in the organization regarding disciplinary procedures and protocol. As a result, supervisors tend to pass information about infractions or violations up the chain of command without being involved in the decision of appropriate disciplinary action or how to manage a problem employee. The study found some supervisors felt uncertain about pursuing discipline for fear of being disciplined themselves as a result of the problem employee. Too many times documented disciplinary issues go unresolved (Kras, Portillo, and Taxman 2017).

Finally, a primary contributor to front-line supervisors' feelings of disempowerment is the practice of bypassing the chain of command. Employees will seek out assistance or advice from mid-level managers or even from those higher in the organization, rather than from their immediate supervisor.

Supervisors describe this as "answer hopping." If an employee doesn't like the answer given by a supervisor, or doesn't feel the supervisor can solve a problem, the employee goes around or over the supervisor to higher-ups. This leads to supervisors feeling disrespected and that their power is illegitimate (Kras, Portillo, and Taxman 2017).

In the first exercise in this chapter, you will find a list of *duties and responsibilities* that are typical for supervisors. As a supervisor in your organization, you may or may not be responsible for these—only you know. There are no right and wrong answers; the purpose of the exercise is to clarify your thinking.

Next, we'll ask you to look again at the list to assess whether you have the *power/authority* to accomplish what you need to in each of your areas of responsibility.

Then we'll ask you to look at the list a third time to determine whether you are held *accountable* for results in your areas of responsibility. If so, how are you being measured?

From your answers to these questions, we can determine fairly accurately how important specific supervisory tasks are to your organization. The tighter the measurement, the more important it is in management's eyes, and the more effort you'll put into it.

When you have finished the first exercise, take it to the person you report to and see how he or she views your responses. Discuss differences of opinion on items you marked "Don't know." This conversation in itself should improve your supervision. Not only will you have a clearer idea of what your responsibilities are, you and your boss will be in agreement on what they are.

Supervisory Tasks and Responsibilities

Listed below are 48 sample tasks and responsibilities. (Some of them may not be a part of your job, and this is certainly *not* a comprehensive list.) Put a check mark in the column under the heading that best indicates your responsibility for the tasks listed at the left ("Yes," "No," "Don't know").

Usually you will have responses in all three columns. This is normal. Do not be dismayed to find you have a number of check marks in the third column ("I don't know"). Everyone does.

	Yes	No	I Don't Know
New Employees			
1. Hire			
2. Accept or reject applicants			
3. Report on probationary employees			
Training Employees			
4. Orient new employees			
5. Explain safe operations/rules			
6. Hold regular production meetings			
7. Hold regular safety meetings			
8. Hold prejob/preshift safety briefings			
9. Coach employees on the job			
Production			
10. Control quantity			
11. Control quality			
12. Stop a job in progress			
13. Authorize changes in setup			
14. Requisition supplies			
15. Control scrap/waste			
16. Establish and monitor housekeeping standards			
Safety			
17. Remove unsafe tools from production			
18. Investigate incidents and noninjury incidents			
19. Conduct root cause analyses of accidents/incidents			
20. Establish hazard inspection teams			
21. Inspect/audit your own department			
22. Correct/mitigate unsafe conditions			
23. Hold one-on-one safety contacts/talks with your employees			
24. Recognize/reward positive safe acts by employees			
25. Correct unsafe acts			
26. Ensure regulatory compliance			

	Yes	No	I Don't Know
Discipline			
27. Recommend promotions or demotions			
28. Transfer employees out of your department			
29. Transfer an employee to a less desirable job			
30. Grant pay raises			
31. Issue warnings			
32. Suspend			
33. Terminate/discharge			
Assigning Work			
34. Prepare work schedules			
35. Assign specific work			
36. Delegate authority to employees			
37. Authorize overtime			
Coordination			
38. Authorize maintenance and repairs			
39. Make suggestions to superiors for improvements			
40. Discuss problems/employee concerns with management			
41. Recommend changes in policy			
42. Improve work processes/methods			
Cost Control			
43. Reduce waste/scrap/spoilage			
44. Maintain production records			
45. Develop a budget for your department			
46. Approve expenditures			
47. Reduce employee turnover			
48. Communicate cost-control issues to your employees			

WHAT AUTHORITY DO YOU HAVE?

We hope this first exercise has generated some confusion in your mind about your responsibilities as a supervisor. And we hope your uncertainties are resolved with your boss so you can have a clearer perception of your job and what you are responsible for. Shortly, you'll go through a similar process to see if you have any confusion about your power/authority—that is, how much clout do you have to get things done?

Formal Aspects of Authority

Let's start with some definitions to clarify an important yet fuzzy concept. Sometimes when we talk of power/authority, we think about something formal, something granted automatically by rank. Power/authority can be defined by one's military rank, for example. The captain may not know exactly how much authority he has or even what it is, but he knows he has more than the lieutenant and less than the major.

We can also define power/authority by calling it a kind of muscle or leverage. It is an institutional mechanism that aims to define which of two members in a relationship will be the superior. Authority is potential extra power given by an organization to some of its members in order to guarantee a hierarchy of power controls.

Sometimes the power delegated has nothing to do with hierarchical relationships. For example, the organization may assign someone the power to spend some of its money for supplies. But very often authority also includes power over other people, power to restrict or punish, and power to reward.

Degrees of Power/Authority

So far we have discussed power and authority as a black and white sort of thing—either we have it or we don't. But it doesn't work that way. Seldom, for instance, do we lack any power or authority in a situation. We can always extend some influence. On the other hand, we rarely have complete authority over people or priorities. Authority is usually limited in terms of dollars we can spend, man-hours we can commit, and other similar job-related constraints.

To clarify how much authority you have on your job, consider these five degrees of authority we've defined.

1. *Almost complete authority.* You can make any decision related to an area of responsibility, and you can implement that decision without having to check with anybody. You don't even have to inform anyone else.
2. *Decide and implement but keep superiors informed.* You can make a decision, and you can implement your decision, but you must tell your boss what you've done.
3. *Decide, but check.* The decision is yours, but you cannot implement your decision until you've cleared it with the boss.
4. *Let the boss decide.* You can gather the facts but are required to have the boss make the decision.
5. *Influence only.* You have no authority except your personal influence.

These are not the only ways organizations classify power. Often organizations define degrees of authority in more concrete terms, such as the amount of dollars an individual can spend without approval.

Research has shown that the management of safety can be grouped into three categories relating to power and authority: (1) managing information, (2) making decisions, and (3) influencing others. All three are shaped by day-to-day contexts or social interactions. Access to safety-related information is power. Proactive participation in decision-making to improve safety performance confirms the power of being an "agent of change." Influencing—explaining the implications of safety risks, the broader safety picture, potential consequences (safety time, resources, impact on customers, etc.) in clear, simple, and pragmatic language—is a powerful means to get employees to understand underlying reasons for decisions and policies and the safety vision of the internal culture (Callari, Bieder, and Kirwan 2019).

Advantages and Disadvantages in Using Power/Authority

Organizational structures seem to be designed with power and authority in mind. Traditionally, we build organizations in the shape of pyramids because that shape makes exercising authority easier. Pyramids create differences in rank and status, and the people in higher ranks can use their authority to influence lower ranks.

So-called flat organizations, also known as horizontal organizations, have a structure with fewer levels of authority, few or no levels of middle-management relationships sandwiched between staff and executives. In the "flattest" organizations, there are no titles, seniority, managers, or executives.

Zappos, an online shoe company, has a structure called "holacracy," in which the company is structured around the work that needs to be done rather than the people who do it (Wohlsen 2014). Everyone is equal. This structure works best in small to mid-size organizations and is rare in its truest form.

Large organizations may start out flat but install hierarchical structures as they grow (such as Facebook and other tech start-ups). Superiors in organizations almost naturally turn to authority whenever change challenges subordinates. The very idea of using power and authority rests on this assumption: authority empowers people who possess more of it to change the behavior of those who have less of it. In fact, we usually define the superior in a relationship as the person with more authority.

From the manager's viewpoint, the advantages of power are substantial. For example, it can be used immediately for an immediate result, without justification. You don't have to know much about any particular employee to be fairly certain that firing him or cutting his pay or demoting him will strike at some important personal needs that keep him compliant. But you might have to know a good deal about the same employee to find out how to make work more interesting for him, or to positively engage him in his work, or to change his attitude about his job.

Another advantage is power's directness. Power does not require much subtlety or understanding of people's motives. It is, for example, simpler to reprimand children when they misbehave than to distract them or provide substitute satisfactions or explain why what they did was wrong. Given a hundred children, it's easier to keep them in line by disciplining a few than teaching them all to feel responsible for their own behavior.

Also, exerting power is often personally gratifying to the superior and attractive. Power often fits neatly into our need to blow off stress. When you reprimand a child, you not only change behavior, but you also provide yourself with an outlet for the tensions that have built up inside you as a result of problems and conflicts. This same release of tension can apply to relationships with your boss, your spouse, or anyone else.

Power is sometimes seen as a way for a superior to guarantee superiority. If subordinates know that superiors can and will deliver negative reinforcement readily, they are likely to behave respectfully and submissively, at least in the presence of the supervisor.

Using power has another advantage: speed. A do-it-now-or-else order usually gets a job done without having to waste time and energy on an explanation. Many day-to-day decisions must be made quickly, without the "pollution" or interference of bureaucratic pressures or considerations that are too "political" or time-consuming. Said one manager: "I had sound reasons to believe that there was a risk." Taking action, making a decision on this basis, is a form of power (Callari, Bider, and Kirwan 2019).

But using formal power or authority also produces negative by-products. When a supervisor interferes with an employee's efforts to satisfy the supervisor's own important goals or needs, the employee may not tolerate micro-management for very long. Resentment or resistance often causes a manager to discover he has changed behavior he had not intended to change as well as (or instead of) behavior he did intend to change. Children who are scolded every time their hand goes into the cookie jar may learn to keep their hand out, or they may learn to go to the jar only when you're not looking. They may also learn that you are out to keep them from getting what they want, and what they think they need.

Employees who are chewed out whenever they are caught loafing may learn to act busy when you're looking. You have become an enemy, and they are provided with a challenging game to play against you: Who can think up the best ways of loafing without getting caught? This is a game they feel justified to play because of your actions. It also is a game they can invariably win. It is also fun to play.

Another difficulty with using your authority is that it may be irreversible. It is not as effective to pat a subordinate's head after lecturing him as it is to lecture him after patting, for human beings have memories and will recall positive and negative exchanges. Using power that is perceived by the individual as "negative" tends to reduce feedback rather than build it. A series of bad experiences for an employee may well destroy the possibility of further communication and cooperation between him and you, the supervisor. And once you've lost him, you're in trouble. It will be extremely difficult to reestablish positive contact and engagement.

All in all, the advantages and disadvantages of using power suggest restrictive methods may be effective only in situations that meet certain conditions. Such conditions might be (1) when you are trying to bring about a change in a specific behavior, rather than in a generalized action or in an attitude; (2) when restrictions are not seen by an employee as depriving or belittling; and (3) when speed or safety or uniformity are critical to your task.

Keep in mind that we are talking about formal authority, the kind of power that has been officially assigned. Power to influence behavior also comes from other sources besides technical competence, such as nontechnical skills, gaining credibility, becoming trustworthy (through experience, role, position, personal influence), and negotiating (Callari, Bider, and Kirwan 2019).

The next exercise in this chapter is designed to help you assess whether you have formal authority in certain situations. It looks at the same areas as those in the previous exercise and asks you to assess the degree of power you believe you have in each area. When you have finished, take the exercise to your boss and discuss your responses.

YOUR AUTHORITY AS A SUPERVISOR

Listed below are the same tasks and responsibilities presented in the exercise earlier in this chapter. (Again, some of them may not be a part of your job, and this is certainly *not* a comprehensive list.) For each responsibility, you may have some degree of power to get things done, whether over people, over expenditures, or both. Put a check mark in the column under the heading that best describes the degree of power you have over the situations listed at the left.

Again, you will usually have responses in all columns, and you may have difficulty in deciding. If so, enter a question mark under the column that seems right.

	Complete Authority	Decide and Implement but Inform	Decide but Check	Boss Decides	Influence Only
New Employees					
1. Hire					
2. Accept or reject applicants					
3. Report on probationary employees					
Training Employees					
4. Orient new employees					
5. Explain safe operations/rules					
6. Hold regular production meetings					
7. Hold regular safety meetings					
8. Hold prejob/preshift safety briefings					
9. Coach employees on the job					
Production					
10. Control quantity					
11. Control quality					
12. Stop a job in progress					
13. Authorize changes in setup					
14. Requisition supplies					
15. Control scrap/waste					
16. Establish and monitor housekeeping standards					

	Complete Authority	Decide and Implement but Inform	Decide but Check	Boss Decides	Influence Only
Safety					
17. Remove unsafe tools from production					
18. Investigate incidents and noninjury incidents					
19. Conduct root cause analyses of accidents/incidents					
20. Establish hazard inspection teams					
21. Inspect/audit your own department					
22. Correct/mitigate unsafe conditions					
23. Hold one-on-one safety talks with your employees					
24. Recognize/reward positive safe acts by employees					
25. Correct unsafe acts					
26. Ensure regulatory compliance					
Discipline					
27. Recommend promotions or demotions					
28. Transfer employees out of your department					
29. Transfer an employee to a less desirable job					
30. Grant pay raises					
31. Issue warnings					
32. Suspend					
33. Terminate/discharge					
Assigning Work					
34. Prepare work schedules					
35. Assign specific work					
36. Delegate authority to employees					
37. Authorize overtime					
Coordination					
38. Authorize maintenance and repairs					
39. Make suggestions to superiors for improvements					
40. Discuss problems/employee concerns with management					

	Complete Authority	Decide and Implement but Inform	Decide but Check	Boss Decides	Influence Only
Coordination					
41. Recommend changes in policy					
42. Improve work processes/methods					
Cost Control					
43. Reduce waste/scrap/spoilage					
44. Maintain production records					
45. Develop a budget for your department					
46. Approve expenditures					
47. Reduce employee turnover					
48. Communicate cost-control issues to your employees					

HOW ARE YOU MEASURED?

We have one more process to go through to round out, we hope, your picture of your job. This has to do with how you are held accountable for the various aspects of your job.

Let's define accountability as active measurement by management to ensure compliance with its will. In other words, accountability pins down the question of whether—and how—the boss is measuring you to ensure you are carrying out the tasks he told you to do.

Types of Measurement

How does management measure your performance? Usually it's done with some kind of numbers game. In production, your department's performance is probably measured either by how many widgets it produces or by whether it meets a quota (or by a percentage of a quota). These are numerical measurements, used mostly in production, in quality control, and in cost control, where it is easy to develop them.

However, it is not easy to use a numerical measurement for many areas of your job, such as new employee orientation, training, discipline, engagement, leadership, or building teamwork. Management must devise other measures, such as a spot-check method or a report from you that states whether you did the required task.

Tasks that are not easily measured with numbers are usually not measured frequently or effectively by management. This means your boss has a much better handle on your production results than he does on your leadership effectiveness or management of safety. Because of this, you probably spend considerably more time and effort on things that improve production than you do on things related to leadership and safety. You know you can show results in production by concentrating on it. You can literally ignore training, safety, coaching, team building, and other aspects of leadership for months and management will never know the difference.

How you are measured dictates where you spend your time. The tighter the measure, the more you will pay attention to the area.

Results versus Activity Measures

There are two other methods management uses to measure your performance in a single area. It can measure the end results, the outcomes of your effort, or it can measure whether you are carrying out your defined tasks. An example is in safety. Results measurement simply asks how many injuries have happened to your crew, how many lost workdays resulted, and what was the financial impact to the company. On the other hand, activity metrics ask how many times you have talked to your people about safety, or how many times you've audited your department.

Activity metrics tend to be tighter, more restrictive. Results metrics tend to give you more leeway and allow you to be more discretionary—to do whatever you want as long as you get results. Management often uses activities measures while you're learning a task. Once you are highly competent, it measures results.

Degrees of Accountability

No one escapes being measured in some way on the job. How you are assessed depends on what your tasks are and how much authority you have. Just as there are degrees of power, there are degrees of accountability. For instance, one company describes three levels of accountability.

1. *Strong accountability.* Must accept heavy responsibility for contributing to the achievement and effectiveness of end results; requires active participation and the initiation of action.
2. *Medium accountability.* Must accept a secondary responsibility to contribute to the achievement and effectiveness of end results, perhaps through an interrelated function or perhaps heavy in one facet of a many-faceted accountability. Also requires active participation and the initiation of action within the area of the persons concerned.
3. *Light accountability.* Must accept accountability for contributing to a goal, but not for initiating any action.

Your Job's Accountabilities

Look again at the 48 tasks and responsibilities listed in the previous two exercises. For each task, you will be asked to determine: (1) if the boss is holding you accountable—actually measuring your performance on a regular basis; (2) how the boss measures you in that area; and (3) whether the measurement is based on your results or on your activities. The purpose again is to clarify your job.

If you are confused about any of the answers, meet with your boss and get the point clarified. It is crucial to your success to know how you are measured.

YOUR ACCOUNTABILITY AS A SUPERVISOR

For each task that is part of your job, identify whether your boss is, in fact, measuring your performance (yes or no). (Again, some tasks may not be a part of your job, and this is certainly *not* a comprehensive list.) Briefly state how she measures it (numerical or other—state specifically the measure she uses), then indicate whether the measure is a results (R) or an activities (A) measure. Finally, check what degree of accountability is used: strong (S), medium (M), or light (L).

	Measured		Type of Measure		Degree of Measurement		
	Yes	No	R	A	S	M	L
New Employees							
1. Hire							
2. Accept or reject applicants							
3. Report on probationary employees							
Training Employees							
4. Orient new employees							
5. Explain safe operations/rules							
6. Hold regular production meetings							
7. Hold regular safety meetings							
8. Hold prejob/preshift safety briefings							
9. Coach employees on the job							
Production							
10. Control quantity							
11. Control quality							
12. Stop a job in progress							
13. Authorize changes in setup							
14. Requisition supplies							
15. Control scrap/waste							
16. Establish and monitor housekeeping standards							

	Measured		Type of Measure		Degree of Measurement		
	Yes	No	R	A	S	M	L
Safety							
17. Remove unsafe tools from production							
18. Investigate incidents and noninjury incidents							
19. Conduct root cause analyses of accidents/incidents							
20. Establish hazard inspection teams							
21. Inspect/audit your own department							
22. Correct/mitigate unsafe conditions							
23. Hold one-on-one safety talks with your employees							
24. Recognize/reward positive safe acts by employees							
25. Correct unsafe acts							
26. Ensure regulatory compliance							
Discipline							
27. Recommend promotions or demotions							
28. Transfer employees out of your department							
29. Transfer an employee to a less desirable job							
30. Grant pay raises							
31. Issue warnings							
32. Suspend							
33. Terminate/discharge							
Assigning Work							
34. Prepare work schedules							
35. Assign specific work							
36. Delegate authority to employees							
37. Authorize overtime							
Coordination							
38. Authorize maintenance and repairs							
39. Make suggestions to superiors for improvements							
40. Discuss problems/employee concerns with management							
41. Recommend changes in policy							
42. Improve work processes/methods							

	Measured		Type of Measure		Degree of Measurement		
	Yes	No	R	A	S	M	L
Cost Control							
43. Reduce waste/scrap/spoilage							
44. Maintain production records							
45. Develop a budget for your department							
46. Approve expenditures							
47. Reduce employee turnover							
48. Communicate cost-control issues to your employees							

WHERE DOES SAFETY FIT INTO YOUR JOB?

We hope these three exercises have helped you discover some aspects of your job that you didn't realize before. Supervisors going through this process usually learn things they were previously not aware of. But what does all of this have to do with safety and health?

Quite a bit, we think. First of all, one of the categories you looked at was safety and health. Under that category we listed ten specific tasks.

The Function of Safety

Before we look at your specific responsibilities and tasks in safety and health in chapter 4, let's look at the field itself. What is safety and health, and where does it fit into your job?

For many years the slogan "safety first" was widely popular, and it's still proclaimed today in some quarters. Safety and health professionals believed and preached this for a long time. Today we realize that we really do not want "safety first" any more than we want "safety last." Either exhortation means safety is considered as something separate from the other aspects of production. Obviously, we want effective production first (without it, no one would have a job), but it should be accomplished in such a manner that no one is hurt or made ill and human losses are minimized.

Previously, safety and health professionals designed and implemented "safety programs" for their companies. The aim was to superimpose a safety program on the organization. Today, professionals realize that what is really needed is organic safety, or "integrated" safety, and not some artificially inserted program. Safety must be an integral part of a company's procedures. We do not want production *and* a safety program, or production and safety in different silos, or production *with* safety. Rather, we want safe production. Perhaps an effective moniker summarizing the interaction between safety and other responsibilities of your job might be "Safety is the job; the job is safety."

The goal of management in general is efficient production—production that maximizes profit. To achieve this goal the organization has two basic resources: (1) employees and (2) facilities, equipment, technology, and materials. Management brings many influences to bear upon both of these resources. The company's workforce is affected by training, selection and placement processes, employee health programs, and employee relations. Facilities, equipment, technology, and materials are influenced by maintenance, research, and engineering. These influences and basic resources are brought together through various procedures.

The function of a safety and health process ("program" is a restrictive term; programs have beginnings and endings; a "process" keeps rolling along in a continuous improvement cycle) is to build safety and well-being into procedures and continually audit the execution of these procedures to ensure the controls are adequate. These tasks are accomplished by continually asking why certain acts and conditions are allowed and whether certain known controls exist. Figure 1.1 depicts the relationship of these forces graphically.

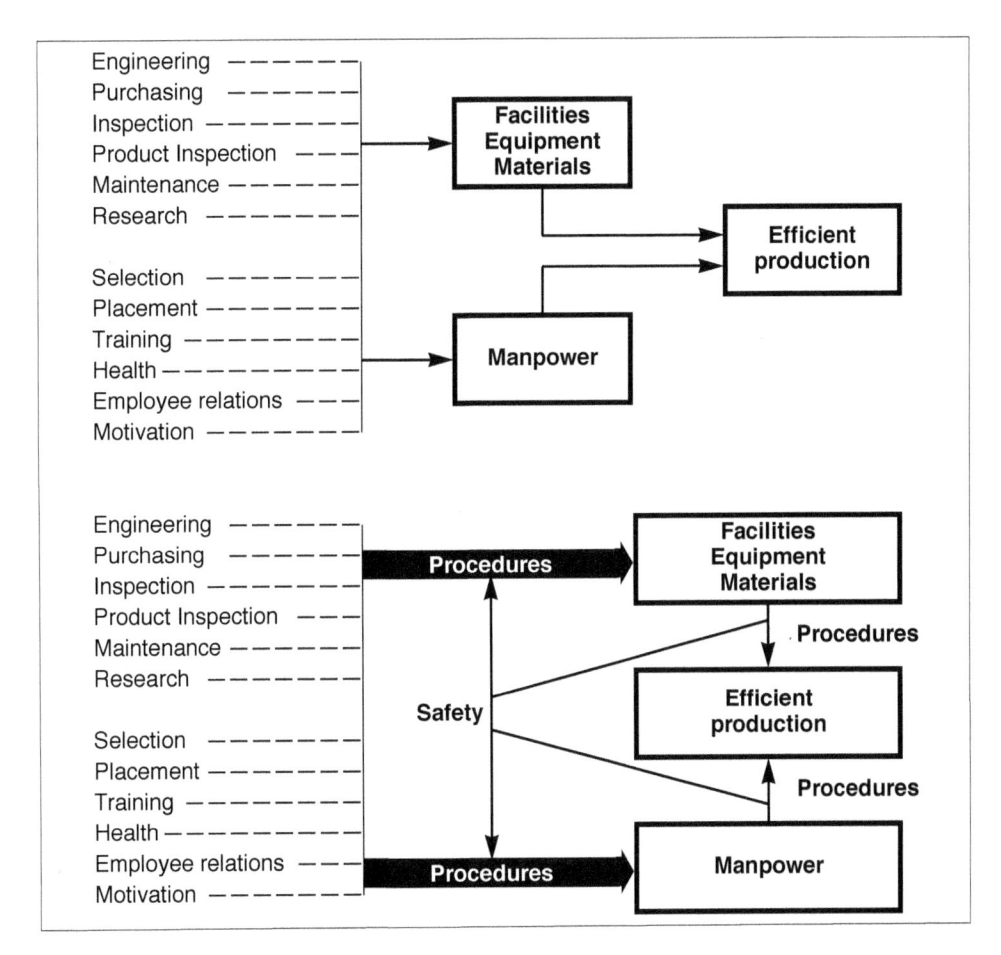

Figure 1.1 Graphic representation of integrated safety. From *Techniques of Safety Management* by Dan Petersen. Copyright © 1989 by Dan Petersen.

Safety and health is not just a resource, an influence, or a procedure, and, as stated, it certainly is more than a "program" manual. Safety and health is a state of mind, the atmosphere of an organization, a cultural value that must become an integral part of each and every procedure the company has, and a personal value instilled within each and every employee. This is what we mean by "built-in" or "integrated" safety and health. It is the only brand of safety and health that is permanently effective.

Research supports these constituents of integrated safety and health: embedded commitment of managers and workers; the ambition that all incidents are preventable; constant and updated communication; effective supervisor communication; decentralized, discretionary safety activities; safety empowerment; safety justice; safety learning; an "open" atmosphere for speaking up; a dialog on incidents; and a focus on things that go right (Zwetsloot et al. 2017).

Relating the concept of "integrated" or "built-in" safety and health aspects of your job merely means that you include them among your many considerations in anything performed in your department. When you plan, schedule, issue work orders, train, communicate, or do anything else, one of the facets of your job that you consider is safety and health. This is a frame of mind more than it is just another duty. Or stated better, if it is a frame of mind, it is not just another duty for you—it defines you as a leader.

Priorities

Many supervisors start out and carry on with the concept of safety and health being separate from production. Such a belief makes it difficult to build safety and health into regular work systems and activities. If such a distinction is made, it immediately places a supervisor in an either/or "choice" situation. Daily, perhaps hourly, he or she must choose between safety and health versus production. He then must give priority to one or the other—production or safety and health.

Obviously, if a decision must be made, safety and health cannot win. Why? Profit, defined as production, is the name of the game, the bottom line, the reason the manager exists; it is the job. We then have placed safety and health in an either/or situation. By "building in" safety as the way we do business, by integrating and embedding it, we do not force ourselves to make a choice—we strive for safe production.

REFERENCES

Adkins, Amy. 2015. "Only One in 10 People Possess the Talent to Manage." Posted on Gallup News, April 13, 2015. http://news.gallup.com/businessjournal/182378/one-people-possess-talent-manage.aspx.

Callari, Tiziana C., Corinne Bieder, and Barry Kirwan. 2019. "What is it like for a middle manager to take safety into account? Practices and challenges." *Safety Science* 113 (March): 19–29. https://doi.org/10.1016/j.ssci.2018.10.025.

Dalton, Melville. 1959. *Men Who Manage*. New York: Wiley.

Fontana, Francesca. 2017. "Key Traits for Best Team Leaders." *The Wall Street Journal*, September 19, 2017. https://www.wsj.com/articles/key-traits-for-best-team-leaders-1505818803.

Kello, John. 2017. Interview by Dave Johnson. *Industrial Safety & Hygiene News*, October 2, 2017.

Kras, Kimberly, Shannon Portillo, and Faye Taxman. 2017. "Managing from the Middle: Frontline Supervisors and Perceptions of their Organizational Power." *Law & Policy* 39, no. 3 (July): 215–236. https://doi.org/10.1111/lapo.12079.

Peters, Tom. 2009. "The Heart of Business Strategy: 48 Things That Matter." tompeters! (blog). February 2009. http://tompeters.com/2009/02/the-heart-of-business-strategy48-things-that-matter/.

Petersen, Dan. 1989. *Techniques of Safety Management: A Systems Approach*, 2nd ed. Goshen, NY: Aloray.

Schleh, Edward C., 1966. "The Dangerous Supervisory Gap." *Dun's Review and Modern Industry*, LXXXVII, No 2 (February).

Wohlsen, Marcus. 2014. "The Next Big Thing You Missed: Companies That Work Better Without Bosses." *Wired Magazine*, January 7, 2014. https://www.wired.com/2014/01/holacracy-at-zappos/.

Zenger, Jack, and Joseph Folkman. 2014. "The Skills Leaders Need at Every Level." *Harvard Business Review*, July 30, 2014. https://hbr.org/2014/07/the-skills-leaders-need-at-every-level.

Zwetsloot, Gerard I.J.M., Pete Kines, Linda Drupsteen et al. 2017. "The importance of commitment, communication, culture and learning for the implementation of the Zero Accident Vision in 27 companies in Europe." *Safety Science* 96 (July): 22–32.

CHAPTER 2

The Dynamics of Supervision

One might infer (improperly) that as supervisors we can "motivate" our people. This is really not true—you cannot actually "motivate" anyone. Motivation comes entirely from within—employees motivate themselves. Our definition of motivation is the "desire by employees to want to do what you want them to." An employee who wants the same goal you want is the key, for then you have no obstacles in getting them to act in the manner and direction you both prefer.

UNDERSTANDING WORKERS

You can influence your employees' decisions by creating an atmosphere that allows individuals to comfortably choose to go in the direction you want them to go. The only way you can effectively do this is by truly understanding each person—each one's needs, wants, and way of thinking.

To be sure, behavioral scientists have a different perspective than most. Behavioral science holds that consequences (such as recognition or corrective actions or feedback based on observations) motivate behavior and related attitudes. "People do what they do because of what happens to them when they do it," writes psychologist Dr. E. Scott Geller (Geller 1996).

In the book, *Nudge*, Richard Thaler and Cass Sunstein talk of influencing behavior by being a "choice architect" (Thaler and Sunstein 2008). As fallible humans, we often make poor choices and bad decisions that can put us in harm's way (due to cognitive biases, such as being overly optimistic and overconfident, conformity, herd thinking, and taking the path of least resistance). Supervisors can be "choice architects" by nudging their people to make safe and healthful choices. "The best way to help humans improve their performance is to provide feedback," write the authors.

THE SINS OF SUPERVISION

Knowing and understanding those who report to you is important, but it is also important to know yourself and how you handle your job. Poor supervisory practices can produce negative outcomes just as poor attitudes and lack of awareness can. Do you recognize any of your tactics in the following summary of what turns off employees? (Valentine 1965)

Using micro-management tactics. Through lack of confidence in his own staff, a supervisor may install expensive, time-consuming systems, hoping they will make an operation foolproof. Instead, all the constricting regulations, restraints, records, and checks interfere with both work performance and the exercise of judgment by employees. Employees have to spend too much of their time checking and double-checking petty details. Their initiative is bound to be stifled in the dense undergrowth of rules.

Being a poor communicator. Giving vague directions and instructions frequently causes costly misunderstandings—misunderstandings that could have been avoided if the employees had been told clearly what they were supposed to do.

Being inconsistent. Frequent arbitrary changes in work rules and department policies can be murder on employee morale. An employee should be able to feel that the standards for judging his work won't change from day to day.

Ignoring employee talent. The supervisor who is too busy to show any interest in developing the skills and knowledge of subordinates won't make much headway in achieving his own goals.

Playing favorites. A supervisor can't treat all of his subordinates alike, but must be impersonal in the supervisory approach.

Opposing new ideas. Wearing blinders to ward off new ideas is one way to alienate a progressive, dynamic department or team. Some supervisors get nervous when a subordinate suggests a fresh way of doing things—they know the old way works, so why take chances on an untried method? Once this reluctance to consider new ideas becomes known throughout the team, the supervisor can relax—new ideas won't be offered anymore. Who wants to make the boss unhappy?

Abusing status privileges. Supervisors have a special status of which they can be justly proud. Certain privileges perhaps have been earned by the promotion to managerial ranks. Misusing these privileges betrays the responsibilities of supervision and loses the trust of employees.

INCONGRUENCE THEORY

Let's examine some of the reasons behind a few of our safety and health challenges and other management problems as explained by Chris Argyris (Argyris 1957). Argyris suggested that the problems of worker apathy and lack of effort are not simply a matter of individual laziness. Rather, they are often healthy reactions by normal people to an unhealthy environment created by common management policies. More specifically, Argyris stated that most adults are motivated to be responsible, self-reliant, and independent. But the typical business organization confines most of its employees to roles that provide little opportunity for them to act in this manner.

Argyris proposed and tested a theory (called the Incongruence Theory), which provides supervisors some insights into the reasons why humans commit errors. First, he looked at our development from an infant into an adult. As a child we are passive and dependent on our parents. We exhibit few behaviors; our interests are shallow and short term. At all times, we are a subordinate in our relationships with our parents and are relatively lacking in self-awareness. As we mature this changes.

The mature adult is active and is an independent creature. We exhibit many behaviors, and our interests are deep and long term in nature. We view ourselves as an equal in most relationships, not as a subordinate, and we are self-aware. This evolution is what maturation is all about.

Argyris then looked at the characteristics of organizations. In his view, all organizations, whether industrial, governmental, mercantile, religious, or educational, are structured according to certain principles.

Chain of command—this creates superior–subordinate relationships. It creates dependency on the boss, passivity on the part of the worker, and shorter and shallower interests on the part of the worker.

Short span of control—this creates dependency and reduces the freedom and independence of the worker.

Unity of command—there is only one boss, which again creates dependency and heightens the subordinate role of the worker.

Specialization—the work is broken down into small, simple tasks, and each task is assigned to a separate worker. This creates shorter, shallower interests; a lack of self-fulfillment and self-importance; fewer behaviors; dependency; and passivity.

A basic conflict exists between the characteristics of the mature worker and the characteristics of the organization. They pull at cross-purposes. Yet this seems to be inevitable.

Argyris suggested this conflict causes people to quit (turnover); to quit mentally (apathy); to disengage (presenteeism—showing up for work but not caring); to lose motivation and interest in the company and its goals and values; to coalesce around informal groups; to cling to intimate group norms instead of company-established norms; and to evolve a psychological mindset against the organization, believing the organization is wrong in most things it attempts to do. These factors also cause safety incidents because of inattention, disregard of rules or procedures, and a poor "attitude" toward the organization and safety and health.

Typical management reaction to these symptoms is more control, more specialization, more pressure. Management believes even more strongly that "they" (the workers) must be controlled (treated like children). The problem becomes circular. If workers are treated as if they are children, they begin to act like immature people.

What can we do about it? Since we cannot feasibly change mature people into immature ones (nor would we want to), the only option is to look at the organization and see how its characteristics can be changed. This leads us to organizations (and safety and health processes) with less control, less specialization, and less superior–subordinate relations and moves us on to thoughts about participative leadership and job enrichment—the subject of our next discussion.

WHAT MOTIVATES PEOPLE

After considering how to turn off employees, let's look at how to motivate them.

A wealth of research has been conducted on what effective supervisors do that is different from what ineffective supervisors do. One researcher, Dr. Rensis Likert, found that supervisors with the best performance focus their primary attention on the human aspects of their subordinates' problems and on building effective work groups with high-performance goals. These supervisors are referred to as employee-centered leaders. (Job-centered managers are concerned more with completing tasks than with how the work routine affects the employees.) Figure 2.1 presents the findings from this study (Likert 1961). It indicates that employee-centered supervisors (with strong people skills) tend to have better productivity records than job-centered supervisors.

Dr. Likert's studies also found a marked inverse relationship between the amount of unreasonable pressure the workers feel and the productivity of the department (see figure 2.2). Feeling a high degree of pressure is associated with low performance. General, rather than close supervision, is associated with high productivity. This relationship is shown in figure 2.3. Supervisors in charge of low-producing units tend to spend more time with their subordinates than do the high-producing supervisors, but the time is broken into many short periods in which they give specific instructions: "Do this, do that, do it this way."

Genuine interest on the part of a superior in the success and well-being of subordinates has a marked effect on their performance, according to Dr. Likert. Figure 2.4 shows that high-producing supervisors tend either to ignore the mistakes their subordinates make, knowing that they have learned from the experience, or to use these situations as educational experiences by showing how to do the job correctly.

The supervisors of the low-producing units, on the other hand, tend to be critical and punitive when their subordinates make mistakes. Thus, one way to motivate employees is to be supportive, to set high goals, to avoid micro-managing or "bugging" employees with close supervision, and to limit criticism of performance.

It should be noted that what motivates employees includes factors outside of the supervisor's responsibility: company size, company turnover, company financial performance, safety culture, senior leadership commitment, senior leadership knowledge, existence of formalized routines, and how performance is measured and evaluated (Nordlöf et al. 2017).

Positive Organizational Scholarship (POS) is another factor (Robson et al. 2016). POS focuses on positive outcomes, processes, and attributes of organizations. Positive outcomes, such as organizational coordination, organizational performance, and organization energy, are derived from identifying positive deviance in a population of individuals, understanding the basis of the positive deviance, and applying the gained knowledge to others in the employee population for their benefit.

	Job-Centered	Employee Centered
High-producing sections	1	6
Low-producing sections	7	3

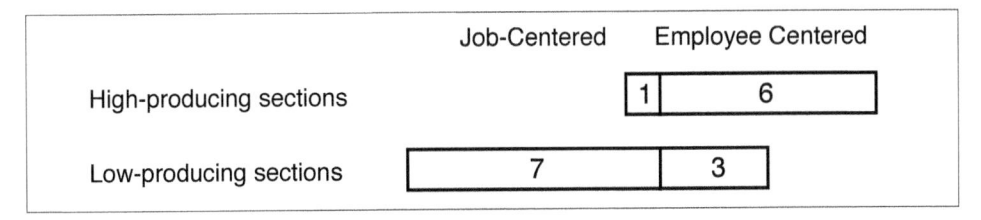

Figure 2.1 Productivity of employee-centered supervisors vs. job-centered supervisors

	Department Productivity	
	Below Average	Above Average
The ten departments which feel the least pressure	1	9
The middle eleven departments	6	5
The ten departments which feel the most pressure	9	1

Figure 2.2 Relationship between pressure felt by employees and their production

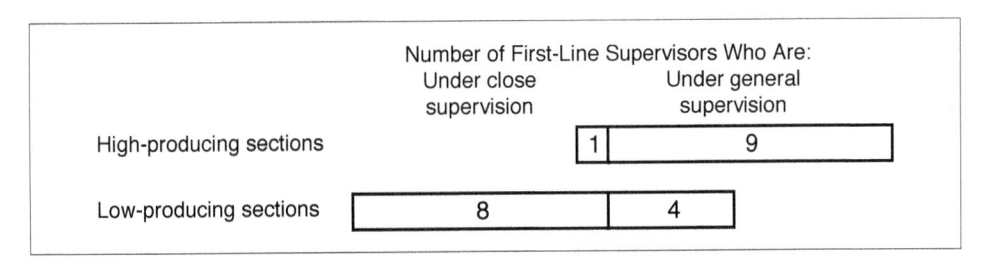

	Number of First-Line Supervisors Who Are:	
	Under close supervision	Under general supervision
High-producing sections	1	9
Low-producing sections	8	4

Figure 2.3 Relationship between closeness of supervision and production

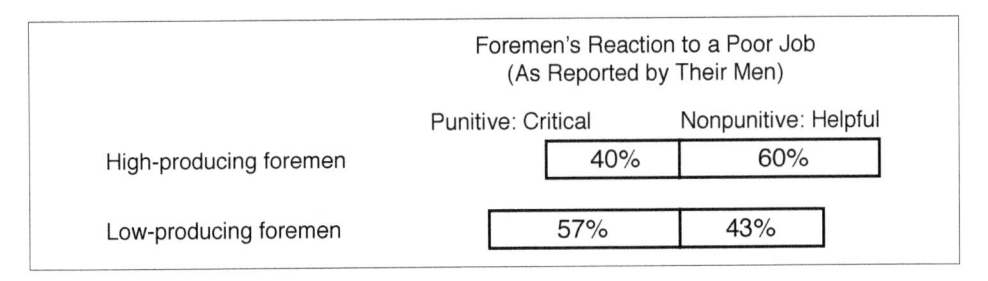

	Foremen's Reaction to a Poor Job (As Reported by Their Men)	
	Punitive: Critical	Nonpunitive: Helpful
High-producing foremen	40%	60%
Low-producing foremen	57%	43%

Figure 2.4 Relationship between supervisor's reaction to a poor job and production

Theory X versus Theory Y versus Theory Z

Different authors use different terms, different classifications, and different labels for various types of supervisors. Douglas McGregor used as his basis of classification some basic assumptions the supervisor makes about the nature of human beings (McGregor 1960). On the one hand, according to McGregor, is the Theory X supervisor who holds the basic assumption that people do not like to work and must be forced or coerced into it. In contrast, the Theory Y supervisor believes that people innately like to work and achieve. Obviously, the management styles of supervisor X and supervisor Y will be quite different because of these assumptions.

Theory Z was developed by William Ouchi in his book, *Theory Z: How American Management Can Meet the Japanese Challenge* (Ouchi 1981).

Theory Z has often been characterized as the "Japanese" management style. Theory Z essentially advocates a combination of all that's best about theory Y and modern Japanese management. It places a large amount of freedom and trust with workers and assumes that workers have a strong loyalty and interest in team working and the organization.

Theory Z also places more reliance on the attitudes and responsibilities of the workers, Theory X and Theory Y are mainly focused on management and motivation from the manager's and organization's perspective.

Developed more than 50 years ago, Theory X and Theory Y continue to be embraced by many organizations, Theory Z less so, perhaps due to American culture's emphasis on individualism and Japanese culture's emphasis on consensus.

So let's focus on X and Y. Supervisor X will check and double-check employees to make sure first, that they are actually on the job and second, that they are working. This supervisor will build in many controls to ensure that the jobs he has responsibility for are being performed properly.

Supervisor Y will spend time removing barriers between employees and their work. These obstacles could be production delays, foul-ups, or company policies and rules with which he does not agree. The supervisor will try to do whatever is necessary for employees so they can concentrate on the work tasks at hand. Once this is done, employees will achieve as they want to, one would believe, and the job the supervisor is responsible for will get done. Management thinking today is that the Theory Y supervisor is more successful at achieving results and engaging the workforce.

DUAL FACTOR THEORY

Chris Argyris and other behavioral scientists conclude that *job enrichment* is a necessity. In 1968, Frederick Herzberg first coined the term and expressed the principle (Herzberg 1966). Herzberg's interest in job enrichment grew out of his discovery of what might be called the dual factor theory of job satisfaction and motivation.

```
TRADITIONAL
|—————————————————————————|
Dissatisfaction                                    Motivation

MOTIVATION-HYGIENE
|—————————————————————————|
Dissatisfaction                                    No
                                                   satisfaction
|—————————————————————————|
```

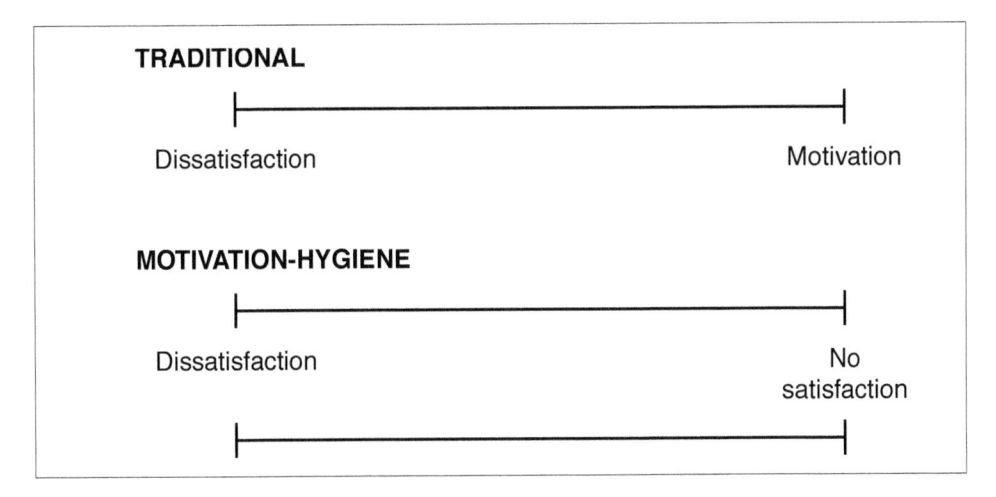

Figure 2.5 The dual factor theory

The essence of Herzberg's theory can be illustrated by the traditional way of viewing dissatisfaction and motivation as simple opposites on a single line. Herzberg, by comparison, placed motivation on a separate and distinct line from dissatisfaction (see figure 2.5). The classical approach to motivation has concerned itself only with the environment in which the employee works; that is, the circumstances that surround a worker during work and things that are given in exchange for work. Herzberg considered this concern with the environment a never-ending necessity for management, but said it is not sufficient in itself for effective motivation. That requires consideration of another set of factors, namely, experiences inherent in the work itself.

Herzberg asserted that work itself can be a motivator. Traditionally, work has been regarded as an unpleasant necessity rather than a motivation. He suggested that these qualities are motivators (in this order): achievement, recognition, work itself, responsibility, and growth. Qualities deemed as agents of dissatisfaction are: company policies and administration, supervision, working conditions, interpersonal relations, money, status, and security.

In other words, the factors in the work situation that motivate employees to be engaged are different from the factors that dissatisfy employees and cause them to disengage. Motivation stems from the challenge of the job while dissatisfactions more often spring from factors peripheral to the job.

Job enlargement is another motivational tool. Job enlargement means taking responsibility for more duties and tasks that are not defined in the job description. Job enrichment gives more control and managerial access to perform tasks and responsibilities. Job enlargement is horizontal; job enrichment is vertical expansion (Management Study Guide n.d.).

Getting Engagement

After reading about various theories of management, you probably have a good idea of what engages those you supervise. Let us summarize a few of the kinds of practices that motivate your employees to have the same goals you want (Kras, Portillo, and Taxman 2017):

1. Being employee-centered (a person who is supportive, sets high goals, does not "bug" workers, and is not overly critical)
2. Using Theory Y assumptions and Theory Y leadership styles
3. Providing a job that has purpose and meaning
4. Exerting power in micro-level ways (such as setting standards of work, scheduling meetings, working better with fewer resources, having knowledge of employees' workloads, modeling consistent behavior, and setting individual standards for work performance)

ATTITUDES

We are concerned in safety and health work with job behavior; job behavior is governed by a person's attitude. Our attitudes are the result of our own personal experiences, and their emotional content often is more important than the facts involved.

Attitudes have three main components: *cognitive* (our beliefs), *affective* (our feelings), and *behavioral* (how we act toward the attitude object). Using attitude to change behavior is difficult because it is time-consuming work and because we intellectualize, rationalize, make excuses—anything rather than accept the logic. Affecting changes in behavior often leads to changes in attitude. Why? Behavioral observation and feedback is more direct and less time-consuming. "If people act in a certain way on the 'outside,' they will adjust their 'inside'—including perceptions, beliefs and attitudes—to be consistent with their behaviors" (Geller 1996).

Attitude and Safety

In his book, *Supervisor's Guide to Human Relations*, Dr. Earle Hannaford defines *attitude* as the potential for action and *safety attitude* as "a readiness to respond effectively and safely, particularly in tension-producing situations." He suggests there are four steps in building attitudes (Hannaford 1967) (see figure 2.6).

Dr. Hannaford's work with attitudes has shown the relationship between attitudes and results in the area of safety (see figure 2.7). As is readily evident in figure 2.7(A), the poorer the safety attitude of the employee, the greater the number of lost-time injuries during the five-year period studied.

FOUR STEPS IN ATTITUDE FORMATION	TYPICAL SAFETY ACTIVITIES TO USE
Step I Laying the Foundation for the Attitude	**Mass Media** Safety slogans, safety posters, safety talks. Motion pictures and sound strip films of general safety nature. Training classes and demonstrations for groups on job methods and theory. Company safety policies. Safety contests and competitions of a group or company nature.
Step II Personalizing the attitude for the individual	**Learned Responses and Habit Formation** On-the-job training in correct safe work methods. Good supervision—immediate correction of violations of safe working practices to build safe habits. Individual participation in safety meetings, safety planning and safety inspections. Motion pictures and sound strip films dealing with job methods and sequences. Recognition of personal contributions by boss and higher authority figures. Individual safety awards.
Step III Fixation of the Attitude Emotional Set	**Emotional Set** Discussion of actual job-related accidents with individual participation. Role playing—permits identification with and projection of self by individual. Motion pictures with high emotional content relating to safety in general and to job performance. Actual demonstration of their personal interest in safety by the boss and higher management—making it the No. 1 item—catching the attitude from authority figures.
Step IV Keeping the attitude alive.	**Attention, Memory and Emotional Set** Checkup on attitude status of individuals and groups using industrial safety attitude scales for employees and supervisors to see where emphasis is needed. Attitude surveys.

NOTE: Plan safety program to offset "safety program fatigue" by using some of the items designed to provide for Steps I, II, and III since employees may be in any one of these steps or may have regressed from III to II, or II to I.

From *Supervisor's Guide to Human Relations* by Earle Hannaford. Copyright ©1967 National Safety Council. Used with permission.

Figure 2.6 Using practical safety program activities to build good safety attitudes

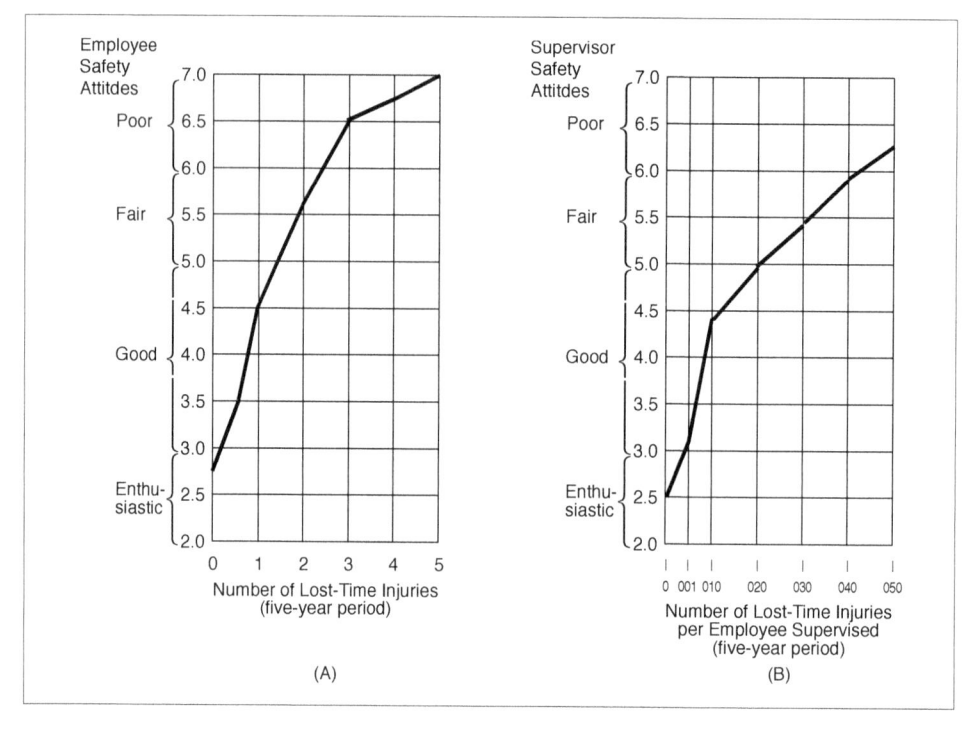

Figure 2.7 Relationship between employees' and supervisor's safety attitudes

The 769 male employees studied came from 47 companies representing a cross-section of various industries—companies with excellent, average, and poor safety records. Figure 2.7(B) shows that as the supervisor's safety attitude test score worsens the number of lost-time injuries per employee under him increases. Obviously, the main conclusion to be drawn from this study is that a positive attitude toward safety fosters safe working practices.

Attitude Development

Robert Mager's book, *Developing an Attitude Toward Learning*, gives us an insight into attitude development that can be directly applied to developing safety attitudes (Mager 1968). He reports the findings of a study he made to determine students' attitudes toward different academic subjects and what formed the attitudes. According to Mager's study, a subject area tends to be favored because the person seems to do well at it; because the subject was associated with liked or admired friends, relatives, or instructors; and because the person was relatively comfortable when dealing with the subject.

Conversely, a least-favored subject seems to become that way because of a low aptitude for it, because it is associated with disliked individuals, and because the subject matter is associated with unpleasant conditions.

Thus, the main factors that help mold an attitude toward a subject are: the conditions that surround it, the consequences of coming into contact with it, and the way that others react toward it (modeling).

Positive and Negative Conditions

When a person receives instruction in significant subject matter (safety, for instance), he should be in the presence of as many positive and as few negative conditions as possible. Recall the outcomes of Positive Organizational Scholarship. If a subject that initially has no special significance is presented to someone on several occasions while that person is undergoing unpleasant experiences, that subject may become a signal to escape, to get away from the unpleasantness. On the other hand, if a person is introduced to a subject while in the presence of pleasant conditions, that subject may become a signal to stick around because the person likes the association.

Mager illustrates this concept by describing the reaction of most people when a doctor moves a hypodermic needle toward them. They tend to back away or turn their heads to avoid seeing this signal of forthcoming pain. There is nothing bad about the sight of the hypodermic needle the first time we see one. But after experiencing pain while in the presence of the needle, the sight of it becomes a signal of coming pain. It is as though the mere sight of the needle becomes a condition to be avoided.

How can this concept be used with those you supervise?

First of all, if supervisors don't already know what employees consider good and bad conditions, they ought to find out immediately. Any form of punishment is obviously bad to them. Most forms of social interaction are good, or fun, for them. Competitions and game-type situations are good for most. Participation is good for almost everyone, being told what to do is bad, and so on.

Use what you learn about your employees' ideas of what are good and bad working conditions to determine when and how to present safety and health instruction under the most favorable circumstances possible. If this is done, employees should become more receptive to learning and accepting your safety and health procedures.

Consequences

How a supervisor reacts to a person's efforts to learn about and follow safe procedures is another important factor in determining the success or failure of a safety and health process. If you want to increase the probability that someone's response will be repeated, follow it immediately with a positive consequence.

"Commitment develops from recognizing the positive consequences gained and the negative consequences avoided when applying one's skills," Professor E. Scott Geller explains. "When workers perform tasks for certain and positive consequences, they avoid impulsive behavior and work toward long-term goals" (Geller 2018).

For example, if an employee always puts flammable waste material into the proper receptacle, commend that person for it. Further, if an employee questions you about a safety regulation, answer as clearly, thoroughly, and respectfully as you can, even if it is from your viewpoint an irrelevant question. Brushing aside the question or belittling the individual might keep that person from talking with you about a much more important issue later. As Susan Scott writes in her book *Fierce Conversations*, "a universal talent is the ability to avoid conversations about attitude, behavior, or poor performance" (Scott 2002).

If you want to reduce the probability that the behavior will occur again, follow it immediately with an unpleasant (aversive) consequence. In other words, criticize those who do not follow good safety procedures.

This all seems obvious, but perhaps one point is a little confusing. In one case, we seem to say corrective actions are bad, in the next breath, we say they are good. Which is it?

In the first case, we were talking about work conditions. Here corrective action is not recommended. A safety process built on a punitive environment will not succeed. It is aversive. Seeing the other guy get nailed creates an aversive atmosphere for you. Also, a punitive orientation means you must have safety rules tightly set to make corrective actions fair. This is aversive, because it is "telling them what to do."

On the other hand, corrective action following an unsafe act might work for the individual alone. But here the problem is whether we can be sure he will no longer perform the act or he will merely make sure you don't catch him at it next time.

Aversives and Positives

What in a work situation is an aversive and what is a positive? Although it isn't always possible to know whether an event is positive or aversive for a given individual, some conditions and consequences are universal enough to provide us some direction.

First, let's discuss aversives. Mager suggests that we define an aversive as any condition or consequence that causes a person to feel smaller or makes his or her work seem inconsequential. Here are some common *aversives* adapted from Mager that might apply to safety and health and safety and health training.

Pain—not too applicable to training, but applicable to safety and health
- An injury is aversive.

Fear and anxiety—things that threaten various forms of unpleasantness, such as
- telling the worker by word or deed that nothing he can do will help him to succeed
- telling the worker, "You won't understand this, but . . ."
- telling the worker, "It ought to be perfectly obvious that . . ."
- threatening the exposure of ignorance by forcing the worker to do something in front of his group that embarrasses him
- being unpredictable about the standard of acceptable performance

Frustration creators
- presenting information in larger units or at a faster pace than the worker can handle (The more motivated the worker is, the greater the frustration when his efforts are blocked.)
- speaking too softly to be heard easily (blocking the worker's effort to come into contact with the subject)
- keeping secret the intent of the instruction or the way in which performance will be evaluated
- teaching one set of skills and then testing for another
- testing for skills other than those stated in announced objectives
- refusing to answer questions

Humiliation and embarrassment
- publicly comparing an employee unfavorably with others
- laughing at an employee's efforts
- spotlighting an employee's weaknesses by bringing them to the attention of the group
- belittling an employee's attempt to approach the subject by such replies to his questions as, "Stop trying to show off" or "You wouldn't understand the answer to that question"
- repeated failure
- special classes for accident repeaters

Boredom caused by
- presenting information in a monotone
- presenting "canned" or generic information
- insisting the employee sit through instruction covering something the person already knows
- providing information in steps so small that they provide no challenge or require no effort
- using only a single mode of presentation (no variety)

Physical discomfort
- allowing excessive noise or other distractions
- insisting the worker be physically passive for longer periods of time than he can tolerate

Positives create an environment more conducive for everyone—the supervisor and those he supervises. There is less tension and distress and a greater willingness to engage in new ideas. Here are some positive conditions or consequences:
- acknowledging responses, whether correct or incorrect, as attempts to learn and following them with accepting rather than rejecting or labeling comments ("No, you'll have to try again" rather than "How could you make such a stupid error!")
- reinforcing or rewarding employees for trying and succeeding

- providing instruction in steps that will allow success most of the time
- receiving learning responses in private rather than in public
- providing enough signposts so that employees always know where they are and where they are expected to go
- providing an employee with statements of your instructional objectives that are comprehended when first encountered
- detecting what an employee already knows and dropping that from training (thus not being boring or disengaging by teaching what is already known)
- providing feedback that is immediate and specific to the response
- giving the employee some choice in selecting and sequencing subject matter, thus making positive involvement possible
- providing some control over the length of the instructional session
- relating new information to old information within the experience of the employee
- treating the employee as a person rather than as a number
- making sure the employee can perform with ease—not just barely—so that confidence can be developed
- expressing genuine delight at seeing the worker succeed

Modeling

Another way behavior is strongly influenced and attitudes are formed is through modeling (learning by imitation). The research on modeling tells us that, if we want to teach our employees behaviors, we must exhibit those behaviors ourselves. We must behave the way we want our employees to behave. When we teach one thing and model something else, the teaching is less effective than if we practice what we preach. If you want your team to wear personal protective equipment (PPE), for instance, you should wear PPE yourself at all times.

Attitude Development

To summarize what is known about developing attitudes generally and adapting that knowledge to safety and health, we can say that attitude and behavior toward a subject may be influenced by the work conditions and stimuli associated with the subject matter, by the consequences of how an employee connects to the subject matter, and by modeling. Approach and avoidance behaviors also are influenced by the things you do and say. But simply preaching about a procedure used regularly for safety and health purposes has seldom been very successful in influencing behavior.

THE GROUP

Each employee decides for himself whether to work, how hard to work, and how safely to work. Each employee decides this based on self-beliefs and values, the environment, the boss, the company, and/or the entire situation. Each employee also decides based on individual knowledge, skills, and the group's norms—beliefs and values—toward an issue. All you can do is to create influences—nudges—to help each individual decide, to extend some influence over what you cannot fully control, and to recognize and understand those influences over which you have no control.

Perhaps this sounds weak, as if you have little real power. In fact, according to research, many supervisors indeed believe they have little real power. They feel they have responsibility but little authority. In a word, they feel disempowered.

This is not true. Even though you can only *influence*, some of those influences you can bring to bear are powerful indeed. It is true that in the final second of decision-making before the incident (or nonincident) you have no power. But if you have used your influence well (say as a choice architect), you have done a great deal to determine whether the incident will occur.

Group Influence

Have you thought about the influence of peers on the individual? A group of co-workers makes numerous daily choices that can result in injury. How does "group think" toward safety and health affect an individual's attitude? If it is "sissy stuff" to his peer group, how will he look at safety? If the team has decided hard hats are not to be worn, will he wear his?

Each employee is obviously important as an individual contributor, but each is also an integral part or a member of a group or team. Each supervisor must manage a crew as separate individuals, but also collectively. Just as chemical elements combine to make other substances with entirely different properties, individuals interact to produce a collective effort that has entirely different properties than what an individual might do on his or her own. We have to recognize the group's properties as well as the individual's properties. A group or team or work cell has a distinct personality of its own. Each makes its own decisions. Each sets its own work goals. These may be identical with management's goals, or they may be different. Peers will also set their own safety and standards and live by their standards regardless of what management's standards are.

What Is a Group? What Is a Team?

A group or team is a collection of people who interact or communicate regularly and who see themselves as a distinct unit. Also, members of a group, or teammates, are bound to one another in a state of mutual dependence. In other words, there is something at stake (work goals, relationships, feelings of belongingness, respect, trust), and so-called "tribal" members share in those stakes. Consider fanatical fans of a sports team as members of the same tribe. This interdependence may have nothing to do with the work task that the group performs, but it is a part of the group identity itself or relationships within the group—the tribe. Thus, in a group or team, each member may depend on the others for the satisfaction of needs for affection, affiliation, or security.

The formation and development of groups and teams depend on two factors. One is a collection of individuals with needs and desires; the second is a task. Most important is the social need to belong. Studies have shown that those who work alone or with only one or two people are not as happy as those who work within a group. What behavioral scientists call "belongingness" matters.

Related to the social need for affiliation is the need to give and to receive affection. The affiliation need causes people to want to be with other people. The need for affection, the desire to be liked, causes them to conduct themselves in a way that will please those with whom they interact regularly. An additional characteristic of individuals who enter into groups or teams is the desire to further their self-interest. The individual feels that his self-interest will be best served if he is acting with, or is at least associated with, other people. The idea is sometimes strictly a case of strength from unity, but it is more often a case of the individual feeling that if several people want and work for what he wants, his chances of success are better than if he goes it alone.

Whatever the situation, the formation of a group requires both a collection of individuals with certain needs and desires but also with a purpose. Neither is sufficient by itself. A collection of individuals without a common goal is still a collection of individuals without bonds.

Group Norms

A factor that often influences the safety and well-being of a person, but is not always understood, is the existence of what sociologists call group norms. Group norms are the informal, and at times unspoken, laws that govern the way people in a group should behave and should not behave. Very often, when members of a group are asked what their norms are, they can't identify them, yet unconsciously their behavior is strongly influenced by the norms.

Group norms are the accepted attitudes about various things in the group situation. These include attitudes about how workers behave toward their boss, how they react to safety and health regulations, and how they react to production quotas. Norms "codify" into recognized, accepted, and enforced patterns of employee behaviors and attitudes about the company, about choices and decisions, and about merit systems. If a member of a group takes on a pattern of behavior or expresses an attitude in violation of what is commonly accepted by the group, there are ways of punishing that individual and reeling that person back into line.

In an organization, if the norms developed within the work group are favorable to safety and health, the group itself will encourage and even enforce safe and healthful practices much better than if there is the threat of punitive measures, corrective actions, and adverse consequences. However, group norms often develop that are contrary to accepted safety and health rules. A group might have an attitude that safety is for sissies or that safety is inconvenient, time-consuming, and cumbersome (as in wearing PPE). We don't really know why this thinking becomes entrenched, but we know it does.

Often management's first response is to issue a mandate that will force the person to violate the norms of his peers and tow the party line. If group bonds are tight, with a high degree of group identity cohesiveness, the member will violate management's direction rather than run the risk of being alienated from his work group. We ought to understand this phenomenon, and our objective should be to find some way to change the group norm and get this phenomenon working positively for safety and health rather than against it.

Peer Pressure and Conformity

The power of peer pressure and conformity has been shown many times in controlled experiments. Figure 2.8 illustrates a test with high school graduates, all men, with good eyesight. They were to tell whether two lines were the same length or not. Most of the pairs of lines were noticeably different in length.

When these men were alone, they were almost 100% correct in judging which line was longer. But then they became the unsuspecting victims of group think. Each sat in with a group, and all judged the lines. All the other people in the group were conspirators who had been told to call out wrong answers (Asch 1952).

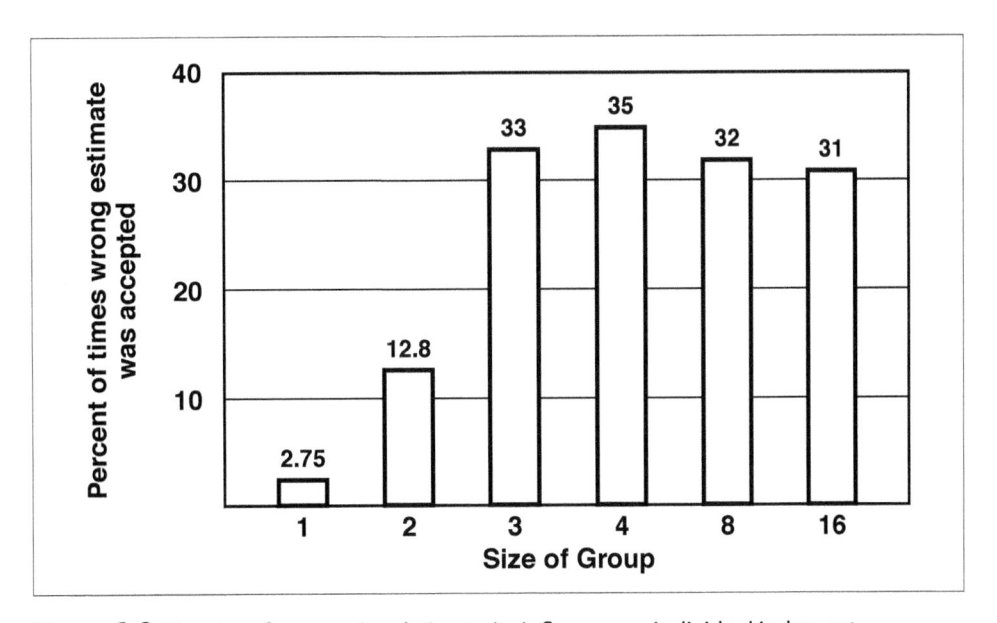

Figure 2.8 The size of a group in relation to its influence on individual judgment

The first two columns on the left in figure 2.8 show that the victims were only slightly misled when one or two others preceded them with the wrong answer. But when three or more others gave wrong answers before them, one-third of the victims gave in. They took the group's word rather than what their eyes told them—the majority effect. It is significant that a group of three others was as powerful as a group of 16 for misleading the victims.

Some of the victims said later, after being told of the practical joke played on them, that the line lengths honestly seemed to change as they heard each of the others in the group call out the wrong answer. A few of the victims deliberately gave answers they felt were wrong; they did not want the group to think them weird. But most of the victims felt the group must be right because it was unanimous.

Somewhat similar results occurred in tests that involved judging the size of a rectangle. Those being tested tended to change their estimates to be more like the one they were told a group of 20 to 30 people had made.

A change in one's group affiliations may cause shifts in attitudes and behaviors. This was demonstrated in an analysis of 2500 blue-collar workers in a factory in the Midwest. The psychologists had records of the attitude of each of these employees toward the union and toward the management. A year later the employees who had been promoted to foremen or elected stewards were followed up.

The ones elected stewards had been no more pro-union than the rest, and the ones promoted to foremen had not been any more pro-management than the others. However, within a short time after the promotion, or election, the employees' attitudes had shifted. The newly elected stewards became much more pro-union than they had been formerly. The new foremen became much more pro-management than they had been a few months previously. (These shifts in attitude were larger, and more widespread, among the new foremen than they were among the new stewards.) (Kelly 1969)

A group's culture puts more pressure on workers than do the standard procedures written in company manuals. In safety and health work, peer pressures, the urge to conform, and group norms are perhaps the most important determinants of worker behavior. The group sets its own safety and health rules for behavior, and their choices and decisions are governed by their rules, not management's.

Safety and health processes must not only speak to the individual but also attempt to understand the group's norms and to influence those norms to be safety and health-oriented. As a supervisor, your department's safety and health processes must help build strong work groups with goals that align with your goals in order to achieve desired safety and health results.

Building Teamwork

We can determine the strength of teams by observing some characteristic symptoms of strong and weak teams. In a *strong team*, the members voluntarily

- try to seek respect, trust, and praise from the rest of the team
- seek recognition from the team leaders (not management); exert pressure on weak team members
- put special efforts into achieving team goals

The key to identifying strong teams seems to lie in the word "voluntarily." In a strong team, the members seem to want to achieve all the above. It is important to them as individuals wanting to conform to the goals and norms of the team.

Here are some characteristic symptoms of a *weak team*. In such teams, the members
- form cliques or subteams
- seek little cooperation, respect, and trust
- are unfriendly
- take no initiative
- avoid responsibility
- have little respect for company policies

Each supervisor might do well to stand back and observe teams in action. If one can observe any of the above identifying characteristics, perhaps that supervisor needs to try to build a stronger team. To be sure, supervisors must be aware of their own biases or filters when observing their teams. "To be able to identify underlying misalignments on your team, you have to reduce the biases that distort your judgment and cause you to miss important cues. Without this observer's mindset, you will have a hard time diagnosing team problems" (Moussa, Boyer, and Newberry 2016). You will be vulnerable to being blinded to critical information.

There are four elements essential to a strong team:

1. *Individual competence*—Each member of the team must have the ability to pull his own weight.
2. *Individual maturity*—Each member must be mature. This means the team dislikes the "prima donna" who can, but will not, do her share. They dislike the "yes man" who exerts more effort pleasing the boss than the team. They dislike the "let George do it," pass-the-buck type.
3. *Individual strength*—Each member must have not only the ability and the maturity to do his job, each individual must also have the strength to earn team respect. This means no "weak links," no "alienated loners."
4. *Common objectives*—Each team must have goals the members support.

In the above listing, you can see that the first three deal with qualities or characteristics of individuals that we cannot readily change. You can extend some influences of course, but basically the strength of the team depends on the individuals you initially place in the team.

You might ask yourself several questions before assigning individuals to teams. How did you initially select your employees?

Are you looking at the competence, maturity, and strength of each person before placing them in a work team? This does not mean you cannot hire and use the loner or the prima donna. It does mean you should place the person in a work situation in which they cannot destroy a strong team and not place them in a situation in which a strong team is essential to meet defined goals.

What about shuffling certain individuals into other teams? At times, transfer of only a few individuals makes the difference in the strength of a team.

Your influence can be greatly felt in developing common objectives, the fourth essential for a strong team. By doing a better job of goal-setting, motivating, and communicating in regard to safety and health, you can make sure your goals become the chosen team goals.

Steps to Building Stronger Teams

In a classic demonstration of what forces build team cohesiveness, a team that lacked cohesiveness was transformed into a highly cooperative team within a few days. This quick building of cohesiveness was not done by asking for teamwork. No exhortations about cooperation or slogans or posters picturing the one weak link in the chain were used. The scientists just touched off the natural forces that are available when people are in teams.

The demonstration was carried out with 12-year-old boys in a secluded camp provided by the Yale University Department of Psychology. The boys did not realize they were part of an experiment. The person they thought was the caretaker of the camp was Dr. Muzafer Sherif, a psychologist. Here is an outline of the procedures by which random collections of boys were transformed into highly cohesive teams within a very short time (Sherif 1956).

Physical Proximity

The boys were strangers to each other at the start. After they had been in camp a few days, they were divided into two teams. Each team was housed in separate living quarters. This is similar to most business situations in which strangers are put together in spaces separated from other work teams. Being thrown together physically presents a chance for interactions to occur that would not otherwise take place, thus providing an entering wedge for building team spirit, at least on a micro level.

Sharing Common Goals

These separated teams of boys proceeded to set goals for their respective teams. They decided on decorations for and arrangement of their quarters and on other activities that appealed to their own group. Each team worked for high production on these goals and ways of reaching them. The members participated fully in deciding their shared activities. Sharing in making decisions and then working together to reach these shared goals are prime factors in building cohesiveness.

Setting Up an Organization and Accepting Leadership

These boys had not worked together for more than a few hours before they began to pool their efforts. They spontaneously organized duties within the teams.

They noticed that some members were adept at special activities, so they used these experts. They quickly divided the work and defined the responsibilities of different members. Each member soon understood what role he was expected to play. These teams also quickly came to look to a few members to play *higher roles* in coordinating the others. Captains and lieutenants emerged. These accepted leaders were from within the team, not from outside it. In a business, however, the person the company designates as boss may not be the one the team would have designated. Management usually has its appointed leaders, and the team has its informal leaders.

Developing Team Symbols

The boys had scarcely agreed upon their accepted leaders before the members were clamoring for symbols to identify themselves as distinct teams. They invented nicknames and some jargon for their activities. Business teams do this if they are cohesive, and the vocabulary of one department may sound like Greek to the department down the line. The boys also developed some secrets—as offices do through the grapevines, and as families do in family jokes.

The boys' teams bought caps and T-shirts in the colors they decided on as distinctive symbols. Adults seem to have much of this same kid stuff in them. Railroaders favor a certain style of work clothes that are a trademark of their team. A house painter feels disloyal to his occupational team unless he works in painter's whites. Work clothes are part of the role that team members are expected to play. Many organizations that have achieved OSHA's Voluntary Protection Program status display team unity and identity in caps, T-shirts, logos, and slogans.

When teams want such distinctive symbols, it is evidence of cohesiveness. But it does not necessarily follow that wearing a work uniform designed by the company will build cohesiveness.

Competing with Natural Enemies

The situation with boys in the experiment was such that each team quickly looked upon the other as a natural enemy. Teams tend to hold together more firmly when threatened by some adversary, or when some stress makes the members realize they are dependent on each other for security or perhaps for survival. Friction and stress situations are not rare within a business. One department often looks upon another as a competitor. One clique considers the other clique a rival. Each clique then holds together more strongly than before, cooperates less, and feuds more with the rival clique. You can call these feuds and in-fighting turf wars. In case you, the appointed leader, are dogmatic and self-centered, the workers may become more cohesive, but the binding force is the goal of frustrating you rather than cooperating with you.

In the case of the boys in the experimental teams, natural rivalry was exploited by egging the two teams into competitive contests. Little encouragement was needed; each team was itching to prove its superiority.

To intensify this rivalry, the experimenters rigged some of the contests. This made the losers furious at their opponents. Each team held closer together than ever and engaged in open as well as secret warfare. There were pitched battles in which the boy who had previously been the crybaby became the overnight hero of his team but a despised villain to the other team. To protect life and limb, it became necessary for the experimenters to order the hostilities be stopped. Merely giving the order and policing the groups was not even adequate at this point.

Liking the People in the Team

Many social psychologists put likeability near the top of the list in building cohesiveness. You've got to like (or is it respect and trust?) the people to become a part of the team in order for the team to literally work. There is, however, a reciprocal relationship here. Cohesiveness seems to be built easiest when the people are mutually attractive to begin with. But as cohesiveness develops, people who have not previously seemed attractive become so if they are in our team. The people in *our team* usually seem to us to be a little more capable, as well as more attractive, than their counterparts in competing teams.

Research and experimentation then suggest some ways to build stronger work teams. You can utilize the following methods:
- Place people in physical proximity. If workspace does not automatically allow this (as in a shipping department), you can bring people together periodically for meetings and to participate as a team in the decision-making process.
- Allow the team to set its own goals in safety and health.
- Allow the team to organize itself in safety and health. Let members select their own enforcers, inspectors, talk-givers, committee representatives, departmental monthly safety and health director, and so on.
- Permit the team to develop its own symbols for itself and for safety and health.
- Set up competitions with rival departments to see who can have the best safety and health record, inspection results, or observation results, for instance.

DISCIPLINE

Senior leaders, through their definition of policy, make the decision that they want safe and healthy performance from their people. Senior leaders, however, do not seem to be able to force safe and healthy performance even with the most sophisticated technologies now coming on the scene, such as using mobile devices and apps to allow employees to conduct their own inspections and report on hazards and near misses. This notion of enforcement brings us to consider the effective use of discipline.

It must be stated, though, according to recent research (Johnson 2017), organizations (69%) want their supervisors to be safety leaders, not just enforcers. Still, the same research shows almost two-thirds of organizations (64%) expect supervisors to discipline employees for at-risk behavior and safety rule violations.

Unfortunately, the word discipline too often strikes a negative note in the minds of supervisors as well as employees. To employees, it means rules must be obeyed or penalties will be levied. To supervisors, it means a generally unpleasant, confrontational task, the results of which almost always lead to antagonism, alienation, and disengagement. Research indicates such confrontations are a challenge to about one-third (32%) of supervisors.

Yet discipline need not always be negative; it can and should be a positive process from the standpoint of both parties.

Guidelines in Using Discipline

A good supervisor tries to create a climate in which employees willingly abide by company rules. But even the best supervisor cannot expect perfection; rules will still be broken. What a supervisor does about these violations not only influences the future behavior and attitude of the employee involved, it can also have serious effects on the morale of the team, group, or department. Here are some guidelines (Baer 1966) to help use discipline more effectively.

Know the rules and make sure your employees know them.

You can't maintain discipline unless you know what is allowable and what is not.

Don't ignore violations.

A supervisor doesn't have to issue a formal reprimand or initiate disciplinary steps every time a rule is broken. What a supervisor does will depend upon the nature and the circumstances of the violation and the employee's past performance. The important point is that a supervisor must do something.

Get all the facts.

Most arbitrated disputes are over the facts of a discipline case. As soon as a supervisor believes there has been a violation, he or she should document exactly what happened.

Choose the most appropriate disciplinary action.
Perhaps nothing puts a supervisor's judgment to the test more sharply than determining what discipline to give an employee who has violated a rule. The supervisor must draw the fine line between punishment that is too severe to be just and punishment that is too mild to be corrective.

Administer the discipline properly.
Telling employees they are being penalized for breaking a rule isn't any more pleasant for the supervisor than for the employees. This is the critical time for the supervisor to remember that the purpose of the discipline is corrective, not punitive. It is also the time for what author Susan Scott calls "fierce conversations"—discussions that are robust, intense, strong, powerful, passionate, unbridled, uncurbed, and untamed (Scott 2002). You need to be passionate about protecting your people but keep your emotions in check. Conversations are laden with potential emotional explosions that will do no one any good.

Walter Baer, in a seminal article, "Discipline: When an Employee Breaks the Rules" (Baer 1966), developed the following checklist to use when you are faced with a situation in which you must take disciplinary action.

1. Do I have the necessary facts?
    (a) Did the employee have an opportunity to tell his side of the story fully?
    (b) Did I check with the employee's immediate supervisor?
    (c) Did I investigate all other sources of information?
    (d) Did I hold my interviews privately to avoid embarrassing the employee?
    (e) Did I exert every possible effort to verify the information?
    (f) Have I shown any discrimination toward an individual or group?
    (g) Have I let personalities affect my decision?
2. Have I administered the corrective measure in the proper manner?
    (a) Did I consider whether it should be done individually or collectively?
    (b) Am I prepared to explain to the employee why the action is necessary? For instance—
        (1) Because of the effect of the violation on the employer, fellow employees, and himself.
        (2) To help him improve his efficiency and that of the department.
    (c) Am I prepared to tell him how he can prevent a similar offense in the future?
    (d) Am I prepared to deal with any resentment he might show?
    (e) Have I filled out a memo or written a letter for his personnel file describing the incident, to be signed by the employee? A copy of this memo or letter should be given to the employee, and he should be told that he may respond in writing—for the record.

(f) In determining the specific penalty, have I considered the seriousness of the employee's conduct in relation to his particular job and his employment record?
(g) Have I decided on the disciplinary action as a corrective measure—not a reprisal for an offense?
3. Have I done the necessary follow-up?
(a) Has the measure had the desired effect on the employee?
(b) Have I done everything possible to overcome any resentment?
(c) Have I complimented him on his good work?
(d) Has the action had the desired effect on other employees in the department?

To this list, Susan Scott adds these common errors made while disciplining (Scott 2002):

Blaming—"You really screwed up this time."
Labeling—"You're an apathetic worker."
Using sarcasm or black humor—"Apparently you take shortcuts believing you're Superman."
Attaching global weight to the infraction—"This ruins our safety record for the year."
Threatening or intimidating—"You try that shortcut again, and you'll never see your kids again."
Exaggerating—"You break more safety rules than anyone in the company."
Saying "If I were you"—A loaded phrase implying you should have done it my way. It's like saying, "Why can't you be more like me?"
Asking "Why did you do that?" instead of "What were you trying to do?" "Why" questions usually trigger a defensive response.
Making a blatantly negative facial expression. How you really feel, regardless of what you say, is written all over your face.
Being unresponsive, refusing to speak. The message: You don't care about safety; you don't care about the person.

Punishment and Safety

Norman Maier in his text, *Psychology in Industry*, describes a study that shows the relationship between punishment and safety results (Maier 1965).

Disciplinary action is often associated with safety incidents or safety violations so that, regardless of how a superior feels about punishment, he may be involved in administering penalties. What does a supervisor do when he finds an employee breaking a company regulation for which disciplinary action is specified?

Many supervisors have reported to the author the dilemmas they face when a good worker commits a violation. They know that suspending an employee often creates hardships, destroys friendly relations, and lowers morale. Sometimes grievances are filed and, when this occurs, their decisions are frequently reversed.

They also know that they can get into trouble if they ignore violations because all guilty persons are supposed to receive the same penalty. It is not uncommon for higher supervisors to demand strict enforcement of company regulations. Some companies go so far as to have the safety and health department police the job because supervisors are too lax. When they take this action, they remove safety from the supervisor's duties. Campaigns and training programs are then instituted to make supervisors more safety conscious. Supervisors disillusioned by such experiences resolve the dilemma by not "seeing" the violations.

Disempowered supervisors can actually fear taking disciplinary actions, feeling the threat of being disciplined themselves because of having a problem employee in their group. "We're just worker bees," said one supervisor. "We don't have control over our situation. We just make it comfortable and palatable" (Kraus, Portillo, and Taxman 2017).

Let us take a specific situation in which a supervisor thinks he has found a lineman working on top of a utility pole without his fall protection harness. Should he attempt to determine whether a violation has occurred? If he does, he motivates the lineman to lie or to defend himself, which leads to unpleasant relations and poor cooperation. If he ignores the incident, he shirks his duty, possibly allows harm to the employee, and may bring on trouble for himself with his superiors. Yet he is expected to build morale and carry out company regulations.

An experiment using 154 pairs of real supervisors in a simulated situation was performed to determine what supervisors do when confronted with this problem. One member of each pair acted as the supervisor, the other acted as a lineman who had neglected to follow a safety regulation but engaged his harness when he saw the supervisor approaching. The supervisor suspected a violation.

The results are shown in figure 2.9. At point A, the supervisor decides whether to discuss the violation. If he decides to discuss it, he reaches point B. Denial of a violation will settle the matter since he cannot prove a violation. However, if the man admits the violation, the supervisor moves to decision point C where he must decide whether to suspend the worker. The outcomes with regard to the objective of future safety are shown with each of the decisions in the box at the right side of the diagram.

Interestingly, 25% of the supervisors did not discuss the violation, but instead talked generally about the company safety drive. The rest brought up the question of the violation. In these pairs, 40% of the linemen denied the violation and were not suspended, while 60% admitted it. Admission required the supervisor to make a further decision. Of these, 85% decided not to suspend the worker as required by the company regulation, while 15% suspended him. From this, it is very evident that various supervisors in the same company see their obligations quite differently when confronted with the same situation.

Even the failure to suspend the guilty worker can get the supervisor into trouble because this represents discriminatory treatment, which a union will use in cases of suspensions made by other supervisors. Nevertheless, most of the supervisors did not comply with the regulation in this specific situation. Although a simulated situation may not be representative of real life, the supervisors regarded the results as realistic. (Simulated situations are needed to obtain statistical data on the same situation. Unfortunately, real-life instances do not lend themselves to repetitions of the same situation.)

After the supervisors had completed their talks with the linemen, the linemen were asked what effect this conversation would have on their use of fall protection equipment in the future. The percentages of times that compliance was later accomplished as a result of the various decisions (did not discuss, denial and no suspension, deciding against suspension, deciding for suspension) was very much the same (67% to 74%) for three of the decisions, but in the case of suspension, it dropped to 50%. Thus, as far as safety is concerned, the decision not to discuss the specific violation was the simplest way to obtain satisfactory results.

This experiment has been repeated many times. Punishment invariably produces the lowest future compliant response. In addition, the linemen report that their production will suffer and that they will try to avoid being caught in the future. Subsequent use of this case indicates that supervisors are less punitive than higher management personnel and that staff employees (including safety professionals) are the most punitive. It is one thing to have the task of administering punishment and facing the punished worker, but quite a different thing to have the impersonal task of setting up the regulations. Punishment takes on a different meaning in a general context or abstract sense than when applied to a particular individual.

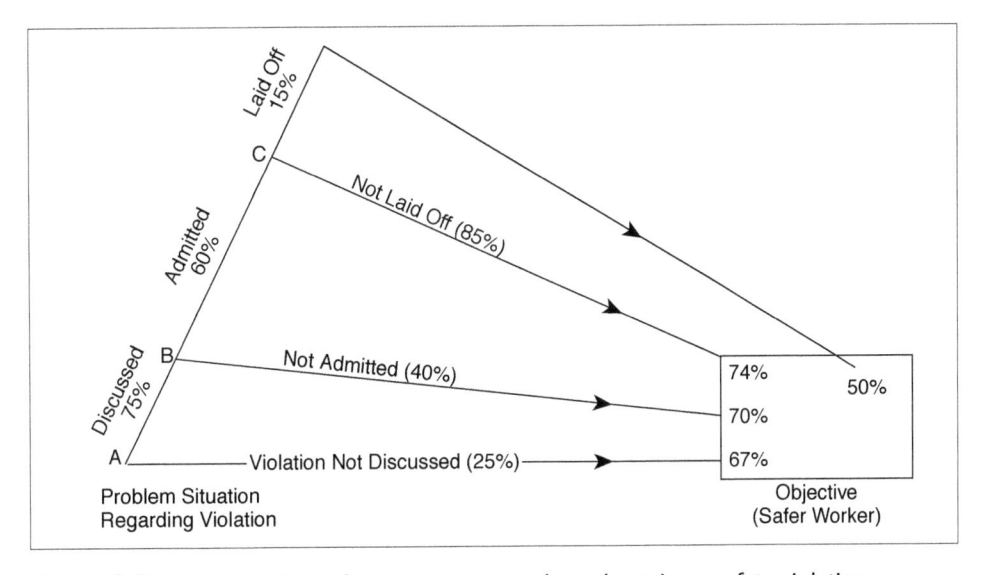

Figure 2.9 Decision points a foreperson meets when observing a safety violation

Decision	Frequency Percent	Result Grievance, Percent
Full three-day layoff	34.9	45
Reduced layoff	4.6	
Warning	22.7	
Forgiven	7.5	2
Consult higher management	8.7	
Consult workers	3.5	
Other	4.6	
No decision	13.4	43

Figure 2.10 Decision regarding punishment for violations challenged by a union steward (From L.E. Danielson and N.R.F. Maier, "An Evaluation of Two Approaches to Discipline in Industry," *Journal of Applied Psychology*, 40 (1956): 319–329.

Also, supervisors may be less likely to nail a violator than a higher-up because supervisors are more in touch with what Scott calls "ground truth"—what is actually happening on the ground versus official policy (Scott 2002).

In the foregoing experiment, the violation was in doubt. The supervisors used this doubt as an excuse for not suspending the worker. They also said that the punishment (3-week layoff) was too strict.

In another simulated experiment dealing with a violation of a no-smoking regulation, the violation was made clearcut, the penalty was only a 3-day suspension, and the supervisor already had suspended the employee. What would he do when a union steward attempted to get him to change his decision?

The results are shown in figure 2.10. Only 34.9% of the supervisors failed to alter their decision, with another 13.4% unable to settle the matter in the allotted time. Both outcomes resulted in a good percentage of grievances. Supervisors who take a less rigid stand and do some problem-solving retain labor's good will. In these instances, grievances are rare.

Scott gives an example of a less rigid stance (Scott 2002). Identify your contribution to the problem. What role if any did you play in creating the problem? Ask the following questions. "Did you not communicate clearly? Did you not clarify safety priorities? Did you not model safe behavior?"

The legalistic stance of determining guilt and involving punishment, even if accepted by the company philosophy, is not supported by supervisors in general. They are inclined to recognize the feelings of the crew and to think in terms of future safety and the effects on morale.

Supervisors should be trained in the merits of positive motivation. Obviously, people do not want to have incidents or injuries, so attempts to make incidents less attractive by punishment miss the point. If people behave in unsafe ways, it is due to the presence of conflicting goals. Punishment is frequently seen as the price for getting caught and, therefore, often motivates employees to find ways to avoid detection or to reduce the pain of the penalty. The Federal Aviation Agency, which can ground pilots for violating safety regulations, discovered that the pilots' union pays the grounded pilot salary during the layoff, thus neutralizing the punishment.

One cannot conclude that all forms of punishment can or should be abolished. Instead, the need is to find better ways to accomplish objectives by studying the motivational alternatives.

THE PROBLEM WORKER

Motivation, positive team attitudes, and disciplinary action can combine to produce an effective safety and health process. But another factor may be present that can spoil even the best record and safety management system. This factor is the problem worker—the active resistor—the person who is likely to have an incident because of physical or psychological reasons.

Can We Predict?

Reducing safety incidents by selection and placement assumes we can foretell who will have such events. It is fairly predictable that certain situations or precursors (such as nonroutine work, work with contractors, and other factors) will be likely to produce serious injuries or fatalities. However, knowing who will be injured or have an incident is quite a different thing; this assumes that those who have negative events are in some identifiable way different from those who do not. We can examine what might be identifiable by looking briefly at the various incident causation theories and at some research findings on the relationship between incident and personal measurable factors.

We will start by looking at the terms we are using. First, there is a difference between an accident repeater and a person who is accident-prone. An accident repeater is an individual who has more than one accident of the same type within a short period of time.

A person who is accident-prone has significantly more accidents than others.

Research indicates that there is no such thing as one type of accident-prone person. Rather each individual behaves in safe and unsafe ways, depending on many variables, including the environmental hazards to which he is exposed.

Conventional wisdom in the United States is that accident proneness does exist in some people for short periods of time, and in others for relatively long periods of time. In both instances, it is predictable if properly measured at the right time. If an individual has one or more accidents, it does not mean he is accident-prone.

Accident proneness refers to relatively consistent characteristics that make the person more susceptible to accidents. There are such people, but their number is small and their contribution to the total accident rate is slight.

Studies have tended to deemphasize the concept of accident proneness as a major cause of accidents. A survey of 27,000 industrial and 8000 nonindustrial accidents indicated that the accident repeater contributed only 0.5% of them, whereas 75% resulted from relatively infrequent experiences of a large number of persons.

Through an analysis of this survey, Dr. Morris Schulzinger came to these conclusions about accidents (Schulzinger, 1956):

> The tendency to have accidents is a phenomenon that passes with age, decreasing steadily after reaching a peak at the age of 21. The accident rate at the age of 20 to 24, in both industrial and non-industrial areas, is two and a half times higher than at the age of 40 to 44, four times higher than at the age of 50 to 54, and nine times higher than at the age of 60 to 65.
>
> Most accidents involve young people. Seventy percent of the non-industrial accidents happen to people under the age of 35 and nearly 50 percent to those under the age of 24.
>
> Men are significantly more likely to have accidents than women. The ratio of male-to-female accidents is two to one in the non-industrial setting and, apparently, even higher in the industrial setting.
>
> Most accidents (74 percent) are relatively infrequent, solitary, experiences for large numbers of individuals (86 percent of those studied). These figures were identical in the industrial and non-industrial setting, and remained constant nearly every year for a 20-year period.
>
> Those who suffer injuries each year, over a period of three years (3 to 5 percent of the group surveyed), account for a relatively small percentage of all the accidents (0.5 percent).
>
> Irresponsible and maladjusted individuals are significantly more apt to have accidents than responsible and normally adjusted individuals.

Schulzinger's studies indicated that, when the period of observation is sufficiently long, most accidents happen to individuals with a low degree of proneness. The relatively small percentage of the population that contributes a disproportionate number of accidents is essentially a shifting group, with new persons falling in and out of the group.

His experience suggests that in the course of a life span almost any normal individual under emotional life strain or conflict may become temporarily accident-prone and suffer a series of accidents in fairly rapid succession. Most persons, however, find solutions to their problems, develop defenses against their emotional conflicts, and drop out of the highly accident-prone group after a few hours, days, weeks, or months.

However, some persons do remain highly accident-prone throughout life, with or without lapses of years of freedom from the accident habit. The latter are the only truly accident-prone individuals. Again, they contribute to only a relatively small percentage of all accidents.

Thus, the concept of accident proneness, which at first glance would seem to lead us to an improved safety performance through employee selection, upon close examination seems to pose some real difficulties. We could, perhaps, screen out the tiny percent of irresponsible and maladjusted individuals who are truly accident-prone, but the cost would undoubtedly be not worth it. We could hire only older workers or only females, but these approaches are, obviously, not feasible either. Or, having successfully identified this year's crop of accident repeaters, we'd find that they are not next year's crop.

Physical or Mental Problems

Both physical and mental problems are often causal factors in accidents and injuries. You should know how to handle these kinds of situations. Although you are not a physician or a psychiatrist, there are a few steps you can take.

- Become aware of any existing problems in your people. You can do this by merely observing them. Any distinct behavior change is usually a tip-off to a problem.
- Ask questions. Ask at least enough so that you know what's going on. The information will be helpful in case of a sudden serious problem and will assist medical personnel. Also, it demonstrates to the worker that you care.
- Seek professional medical help. Don't get in over your head—don't attempt to diagnose potential mental health issues.

Obviously, in some situations you'll have to adjust tasks, schedules, and other aspects of the work in order to assign your people in the light of their physical and mental capabilities. In fact, the Americans with Disabilities Act mandates you do this in certain circumstances. If you identify or suspect a disability, physical or mental, and if that disability affects a person's work, you may have to probe further and get help. Your normal observations as you supervise as well as the special techniques of inspection, observation, and interviewing will all be valuable aids in spotting potential problems.

Substance Abuse Problems

A study from Quest Diagnostics revealed that 4.2% of the US workforce tested positive for illicit drugs in 2016, the highest rate since 2004. The surge in failed drug tests was driven by increases in marijuana, cocaine, and methamphetamine use. It represents 420,000 possibly impaired workers out of the database of 10 million workforce drug-test results. Seven out of ten drug tests were for preemployment screening. Experts suggest looking for these symptoms in workers (Quest Diagnostics n.d.):

- odor of burned grass on the clothing or stained fingers (from smoking marijuana)
- watery eyes

- musty odor, excessive use of candy and soft drinks, no appetite, upset stomach often (from using heroin)
- long medical records
- frequent unexplained absences
- frequent late arrivals and early departures
- often short of money
- poor quality of work (many mistakes and errors)
- increased accidents
- sudden riches (from pushing drugs)
- frequent rest breaks to rest areas (for a fix)
- possession of suspicious paraphernalia
- sleeves rolled down in hot weather
- dark glasses worn constantly

A few words about workers and the country's opioid epidemic are relevant. While economists have paid more attention to the opioid epidemic's role in keeping people out of work, about two-thirds of those who report misusing pain relievers are on the payroll. Castlight Health, a benefits platform, estimates that opioid abusers cost employers nearly twice as much in healthcare expenses as their clean co-workers—an extra $8,600 a year.

In 2017, 57% of employers said they performed drug tests, according to the National Safety Council. Out of those, more than 40% did not screen for synthetic opioids like oxycodone. The National Safety Council survey found that 29% of employers reported impaired job performance due to prescription painkiller use, while 15% cited an injury or near miss that they attributed to the drugs. As many as 70% said their workforce had been affected in some way (Saraiva, Laya, and Smialek 2017).

Your early recognition of a drug problem is the key to a successful prevention and rehabilitation program at your company. If your observation indicates a possible problem, begin to look closely at the worker's performance. Poor job performance is a reason for taking helpful action. The kinds of actions you might take are:

- Document the unsatisfactory performance—tardiness, absenteeism, errors, accidents.
- Discuss these deficiencies with the employee but discuss only the performance deficiencies on the job.
- Discuss the situation with your boss if you do not get improvement as a result of your discussions with the employee.
- Suggest the employee get medical help if you get no progress from your discussions and you are convinced it is in fact a medical problem. Do not accuse him of anything. (Obviously, if the person is incapacitated on the job, escort him to medical help.)

- Suggest that disciplinary action will be in order if improvement does not come and if the employee does not get help. If the worker's or anyone else's safety is in jeopardy, don't wait to make needed changes.

Alcohol Problems

According to a study by the Substance Abuse and Mental Health Services Administration (SAMHSA), an annual average of 8.7% of full-time workers aged 18 to 64 used alcohol heavily in the past month (Bush and Lipari 2014).

According to the "Dietary Guidelines for Americans 2015–2020," US Department of Health and Human Services and US Department of Agriculture, moderate drinking is up to 1 drink per day for women and up to 2 drinks per day for men (US Department of Health and Human Services 2015).

SAMHSA defines binge drinking as 5 or more alcoholic drinks for males or 4 or more alcoholic drinks for females on the same occasion. SAMHSA defines heavy alcohol use as binge drinking on 5 or more days in the past month (National Institute on Alcohol Abuse and Alcoholism 2019).

Many of the symptoms of an alcoholic substance-abuse disorder are similar to those that indicate drug usage. If you note these problems, the worker may be in need of your help. Here again, you, the supervisor, are the key to detecting or suspecting a problem. You are in the best position to know what's going on—the truth on the ground.

The kinds of actions you might take with an alcohol problem are basically the same as with a drug problem. Document, discuss with the worker, discuss with your boss, suggest medical help if you don't get performance improvement, and suggest that disciplinary action might be forthcoming if improvement does not occur. Again, involve yourself only in matters relating to the employee's lack of performance on the job.

Temporary Problems

As we indicated earlier in discussing accident proneness, everybody is prone to have accidents at some time or other. There is much research now on theories that will shed some light on this. One theory states that a person is much more likely to incur an injury if the person has experienced a difficult change in his life recently. Researchers have quantified the kinds of changes that might happen to a person and come up with a "danger range." If, for instance, a person has recently experienced a divorce, the death of a loved one, or a job change, the individual is much more likely to have a safety incident in the near future than someone who has not undergone such an experience.

Other theories suggest that, with proper observation, you can identify when an employee is in a personal crisis. During this period, a person is much more likely to have an incident. Crises intervention techniques, employee assistance programs (EAPs), and occupational medical and health services are used in some companies to help workers through difficult periods.

Your company may be utilizing some of these approaches. If not, you can do much the same thing by being aware of your people's situations. Keep looking for abrupt behavior changes. These invariably mean that something is wrong somewhere.

Stress

Just as body parts wear out when subjected to overuse, people also can become ill when subjected to daily stress on or off the job. Psychological stress causes physical illness of all kinds (ulcers, hypertension, epilepsy, hives, and many others). These stress-caused illnesses can increase your organization's healthcare expenditures.

You can tremendously assist your people by paying attention to them and putting your focus on stressors they are facing either on or off the job. You can also assist them by staying alert to whether they are exhibiting any of the telltale warning signs that show they are heading toward stress-related illnesses.

REFERENCES

Argyris, Chris. 1957. *Personality and Organization*. New York: Harper & Row.

Asch, Solomon E. 1952. *Social Psychology*. Englewood Cliffs, N.J.: Prentice-Hall.

Baer, Walter E. 1966. "Discipline: When an Employee Breaks the Rules." *Supervisory Management* (February): 20–23.

Bush, Donna M., and Rachel Lipari. 2015. "Substance Use and Substance Use Disorder by Industry." *The CBHSQ Report*. Substance Abuse and Mental Health Services Administration (SAMHSA). April 16, 2015. https://www.samhsa.gov/data/sites/default/files/report_1959/ShortReport-1959.html.

Danielson, L.E., and N.R.F. Maier. 1956. "An Evaluation of Two Approaches to Discipline in Industry." *Journal of Applied Psychology* 40: 319–329.

Geller, E. Scott. 1996. *The Psychology of Safety*. Philadelphia: Chilton Books.

Geller, E. Scott. 2018. "The Communication Dynamic for OSH." *Professional Safety*, September 2018.

Hannaford, Earle. 1967. *Supervisor's Guide to Human Relations*. Chicago: National Safety Council.

Herzberg, Frederick. 1966. *Work and the Nature of Man*. Cleveland, OH: World.

Johnson, Dave. 2017. "State of the EHS Nation 2017." Reader Survey. *Industrial Safety & Hygiene News*, October 2017.

Kelly, Joe. 1969. *Organizational Behavior*. Homewood, IL: Richard D. Irwin, Inc.

Kras, Kimberly, Shannon Portillo, and Faye Taxman. 2017. "Managing from the Middle: Frontline Supervisors and Perceptions of their Organizational

Power." *Law & Policy* 39, no. 3 (July): 215–236. https://doi.org/10.1111/lapo.12079.

Likert, Rensis. 1961. *New Patterns of Management*. New York: McGraw-Hill.

Mager, Robert. 1968. *Developing an Attitude Toward Learning*. Belmont, CA: Fearon Publishers.

Maier, Norman R.F. 1965. *Psychology in Industry*, 3rd ed. Boston: Houghton Mifflin Company.

Management Study Guide. n.d. "Job Enlargement—Meaning and its Benefits to the Organization." Accessed December 3, 2019. http://www.managementstudyguide.com/job-enlargement.htm.

McGregor, Douglas. 1960. *The Human Side of Enterprise*. New York: McGraw-Hill.

Moussa, Mario, Madeline Boyer, and Derek Newberry. 2016. *Committed Teams: Three Steps to Inspiring Passion*. Hoboken, NJ: Wiley.

National Institute on Alcohol Abuse and Alcoholism. US Department of Health and Human Services and US Department of Agriculture. 2019. "Dietary Guidelines for Americans 2015–2020." Accessed March 25, 2019. https://www.niaaa.nih.gov/alcohol-health/overview-alcohol-consumption/moderate-binge-drinking.

Nordlöf, Hasse, Birgitta Wiitavaara, Hans Högberg et al. 2017. "A cross-sectional study of factors influencing occupational health and safety management practices in companies." *Safety Science* 95 (June): 92–103.

Ouchi, William. 1981. *Theory Z: How American Management Can Meet the Japanese Challenge*. New York: Avon Books.

Quest Diagnostics. n.d. Quest Diagnostics Drug Testing Index. Accessed January 3, 2020. https://www.questdiagnostics.com/home/physicians/health-trends/drug-testing.

Robson, Lynda S., Benjamin C. Amick III, Cindy Moser et al. 2016. "Important factors in common among organizations making large improvement in OHS performance: Results of an exploratory multiple case study." *Safety Science* 86 (July): 211–227.

Saraiva, Catarina, Patricia Laya, and Jenna Smialek. 2017. "Opioids on the Job Are Overwhelming American Employers." *Bloomberg*, September 17, 2017. https://www.bloomberg.com/news/articles/2017-09-20/overdosing-on-the-job-opioid-crisis-spills-into-the-workplace.

Schulzinger, Morris. 1956. *Accident Syndrome*. Springfield, IL: Charles C. Thomas.

Scott, Susan. 2002. *Fierce Conversations: Achieving Success at Work & Life, One Conversation at a Time*. New York: Viking.

Sherif, Muzafer. 1956. "Experiments in Group Conflict and Cooperation." *Scientific American* (November): 54–58.

Thaler, Richard H., and Cass R. Sunstein. 2008. *Nudge*. New Haven, CT: Yale University Press.

US Department of Health and Human Services and US Department of Agriculture. *2015–2020 Dietary Guidelines for Americans*, 8th ed. December 2015. Accessed January 10, 2020. Available at https://health.gov/dietaryguidelines/2015/guidelines/.

Valentine, Raymond F. 1965. "Problem Solving Doesn't Have to Be a Problem." *Supervisory Management* (March): 23–26.

PART II

Navigating the World of Safety and Health

Chapter 3

The Safety and Health Job

Good safety and health performance does not just happen—it is the result of a number of people doing a number of activities well. Taken as a whole, these initiatives are today best described as a safety and health system.

Traditionally, this collection of recommended procedures and actions was called a *safety program*. But, in the past 50 years, health hazards have emerged as a significant challenge to be confronted, expanding the job of many professionals. Think of skin diseases or disorders; respiratory conditions; poisonings; hearing loss; heat stress disorders; bloodborne pathogens; occupational tuberculosis; and musculoskeletal disorders of the muscles, nerves, tendons, joints, cartilage, and spinal discs.

Consider, too, that today many professionals prefer the term "system" to "program;" programs have beginnings and endpoints and carry the baggage of "another flavor of the month" program that can be easily dismissed by employees.

HOW SAFETY AND HEALTH GETS ACCOMPLISHED

Typical components of safety and health processes include:

Management's statement of policy
Safety and health rules/Exposure limits
Definitions of responsibility
Screening of employees
Placement of employees
Training of employees (orientation)
Ongoing training
Supervisory training
Motivational activities
Inspections/Risk assessments
Incident reporting/Investigations
Recordkeeping
Record analyses/Analytics
First-aid/Emergency preparedness
Medical treatment (on or off site)
Hazard identification/mitigation

Who Performs Safety and Health Activities?

A number of people are involved.

Top management: Those who decide what they want done and then set direction or policy. Top leaders do more than decide, they model what they want done.

They get involved. They offer support. They attend safety meetings, participate in audits, and ask employees where the next safety incident is going to happen and why.

Middle management: The layer in an organization located between policymakers and first-line supervisors. Middle managers have recurrent safety-related actions, or repetitive patterns of action. Three major middle-management actions are (1) managing safety-related information, (2) making safety-related decisions, and (3) influencing others in terms of safety practices.

The middle-management mindset toward safety is shaped by fundamental values and beliefs, background and experience, perceived role, and one's personal approach to safety (Callari, Bieder, and Kirwan 2019).

Staff personnel: These are the various specialists who have a function of assisting the top in setting policy, of working with the middle in often ill-defined ways, and of influencing the first-line supervisors in a number of ways to get them to want to do what the specialty staffs and management want done.

The supervisor: In the eyes of most safety and health professionals, the first-line or front-line supervisor executes the most critical functions. The second most critical functions are those of top management.

A National Safety Council survey brought out a number of interesting points (Planik, Driesen, and Valardo 1967). The purpose of the survey was to determine the factors deemed most important to a comprehensive industrial safety program, as it was called at the time.

The major areas and the top-rated activities in each organizational layer are:

1. Supervisory Participation (SP)
   - enforcing safe job procedures
   - setting an example by safe behavior
   - training new or transferred employees in safe job procedures
2. Middle-Management Participation (MP)
   - setting an example by behavior in accord with safety regulations
   - restating management's position on safety
   - using safety as a measure of management capability
3. Top-Management Participation (TP)
   - setting an example by behavior in accordance with safety regulations
   - assigning someone, or a staff, to coordinate safety and health on a full- or part-time basis
   - publishing a policy expressing management's attitude on, and value for, safety and health
4. Engineering, Inspection, Maintenance (EIM)
   - specifying guards on machinery before it is purchased
   - setting up a formal lockout-tagout procedure
   - establishing a system of preventive maintenance for tools, machinery, plant, and other items and areas
   - inspecting tools and equipment periodically

5. Screening and Training Employees (ST)
   - making safety and health a part of every new employee's orientation
   - including safety and health in supervisory training courses
   - including safety and health requirements in job procedures based on job safety analyses
6. Coordination by Safety Personnel (CSP)
   - advising management in the formulation of safety and health policy
   - analyzing safety and health activities to determine their effectiveness
   - assisting and advising other departments on various safety and health-related matters
7. Forming a Recordkeeping System (R)
   - requiring the department supervisor to conduct investigations of disabling injuries
   - using a standardized injury investigation form
   - including recommendations in injury statistics reports
8. Motivational and Educational Techniques (ME)
   - providing employees a list of general safety and health rules
   - establishing a procedure for disciplining violators of safety and health rules
   - holding workplace safety and health meetings

The rank order of the major areas is as follows:
- supervisory participation
- top-management participation
- engineering, inspection, maintenance
- middle-management participation
- screening and training employees
- records
- coordination by safety and health personnel
- motivational and educational techniques

The first five areas represent what might be considered the basics, the rest are somewhat peripheral. The ten subitems from the major areas considered to be most important are:
- enforcing safe job procedures (SP)
- setting an example by safe behavior (SP)
- middle management setting an example by behavior in accord with safety requirements (MP)
- training new or transferred employees in safe job procedures (SP)
- making safety and health a part of every new employee's orientation (ST)
- top management setting an example by behavior in accordance with safety regulations (TP)

- top management assigning someone to coordinate safety and health on a full- or part-time basis (TP)
- including safety and health in supervisory training courses (SP)
- top management publishing a policy expressing management's attitude on, and value for, safety and health (TP)
- advising management in the formulation of safety and health policy (CSP)

Supervisory and top-management participation is the emphasis of the survey results. This indicates that most people saw the supervisor as the crucial link directly affecting employee behavior and overall safe performance. Top management must provide the initial thrust and impetus; the supervisor must maintain program momentum daily; and middle management must participate to create the chain of communication and command.

Naturally, safety and health work has evolved since the National Safety Council (NSC) survey in 1967, which was replicated in 1992. In a 2016 survey by *Industrial Safety & Hygiene News* magazine (Johnson 2016), readers ranked these priorities in order of importance:

- build and/or maintain a safety culture
- reduce serious injuries and fatalities
- lower OSHA recordable incident rate
- lower workers' compensation costs
- get senior leadership safety and health buy-in
- develop and track safety and health performance indicators
- develop personal leadership skills
- implement/maintain a behavior-based safety program
- select, purchase, and use effective and updated PPE
- develop/maintain a formal safety and health management system
- develop/maintain an employee wellness program

Major challenges identified in the survey, again ranked in order, are:

- get consistent employee behavior reliability/consistent safe behaviors
- put safety and health on equal footing with production
- safety training of employees
- getting senior leadership buy-in for safety and health
- OSHA compliance

In 2016, OSHA issued "Recommended Practices for Safety and Health Programs." The voluntary guidelines listed ten activities to build a sustainable safety and health structure (OSHA 2016):

1. Set safety and health as a top priority.
2. Lead by example, practice safe behaviors, make safety and health part of your daily conversations.
3. Implement a reporting system for incidents, hazards, and concerns.

4. Provide training.
5. Conduct inspections.
6. Ask workers for their ideas regarding hazard controls.
7. Assign workers the task of implementing hazard controls.
8. Identify foreseeable emergency scenarios and develop contingency plans.
9. Consult with workers before implementing changes in work organization, equipment, or materials.
10. Set aside regular times to discuss ways to improve safety and health performance.

According to OSHA's recommended practices, the most important activities, in order of significance, are:
1. Management leadership
2. Worker engagement
3. Hazard identification and assessment
4. Hazard prevention and control
5. Education and training
6. Program evaluation and improvement
7. Communication and coordination for host employers, contractors, and staffing agencies

Top Management

Other than the first-line supervisor, the person considered most important to any safety and health effort is the big boss. His role is to:
- issue and sign safety and health policy
- receive information regularly as to who is and who is not doing what is required in safety and health as determined by some set criteria of performance
- initiate positive and/or negative rewards for that performance
- model safe behaviors
- participate in safety and health activities
- set safety and health performance expectations and hold subordinates accountable for performance

Systems for getting information to the boss regularly usually come from the supervisor's regular reports.

Middle Management

The NSC survey was first completed in 1967. The survey was replicated in 1992. The results were almost identical. The main difference was that employee involvement and participation (engagement) had become the fourth most important category, following top-management visibility, supervisory action, and middle-management participation. Today, engagement has taken on an even more vital role, as there are fewer middle managers and supervisors in general.

The survey spelled out what the role of the middle manager might be: it is his or her role to restate policy, to participate in safety and health meetings, to review employee safety and health performance, to establish checks to ensure adherence to safety and health goals, to set an example, to utilize safety and health performance as a measure of management capability, and to serve on investigating committees.

It should be noted that in the 25+ years since the 1992 survey many organizations have become leaner, with fewer middle-management ranks. Responsibilities formerly attributed to middle management now either flow up to senior leaders or below to line-employee ownership (Gratton 2011).

The Safety and Health Professional

What a safety and health professional does is crucial to successful performance in any organization. First, the professional should structure systems of measurement so that accountability can be fixed and rewards can be properly applied to the right people at the right time to reinforce desired behavior. Some of these systems might incorporate on-the-job observations by peers and supervisors, audits, and leading and lagging performance metrics.

Second, the professional must be a facilitator with the ability to influence: someone who orchestrates aspects of the safety and health management system that are not completely under their control. This includes ensuring safety and health is included in orientation; safety and health training is provided where needed; safety and health is a part of supervisory development; various processes are initiated and completed to help keep the organization's attention on safety and health; and safety and health is included in employee selection, in medical surveillance and treatment, and in other areas.

Third, the professional must be a technical resource and a subject matter expert, knowing how to investigate in depth, where to access technical data, what standards are applicable, and how to analyze new products, equipment, technologies, operational processes, and any problems that arise.

Fourth, the professional must fill the role of systems analyst, or data analyst, searching for reasons and sifting through data (analytics) to learn why accidents and near accidents happen and whether proper controls are in effect.

Fifth, the professional must build a system that goes in the direction management wants the organization to go. If it's a team approach, the professional, with input from management, must decide how to hold teams accountable for safety and health. If management wants to go down the road of employee involvement and engagement, the professional must develop methods of communication, information-sharing, and employee safety decision-making.

We need safety people spending less time on computers and their smart phones and more time on the floor. How can you manage people without knowing what motivates or demotivates them?

The Supervisor

The major role in a safety and health management system belongs to the first-line supervisor. Everything that everybody else does has minimal impact if the supervisor fails to do his or her job. What the job entails differs from company to company. Still, there are seven universal tasks that belong to the supervisor.

1. Investigate all safety incidents and close calls to determine underlying causes.
2. Inspect routinely and regularly to uncover hazards and exposures.
3. Coach people so they know how to work safely.
4. Lead and inspire people so they want to work safely.
5. Set department-specific safety and health-related activities designed to reduce incidents.
6. Track safety and health activities and hold employees accountable.
7. Lead the safety and health effort by actively caring for employees, and lead by example.

Remember, safety is about one-to-one interactions and relationships: supervisors to managers, supervisors to workers. Safety is about these interactions occurring every day. It is people every day looking out for each other.

Traditionally, managers and supervisors have had nicely documented, carefully defined, and compartmentalized roles. This tradition is characterized by organization charts and by such terms as "delegation," "line," and "staff." But studies show clearly that successful managers in modern organizations operate in a manner very different from the traditional view.

Leonard Sayles, in *Managerial Behavior* (Sayles 1964), discusses some "common sense tales" of management theory and shows how each is not valid in practice.

A manager should take orders from only one person—his or her boss. Most managers, in fact, work for or respond to many people (stakeholders, customers, or those in a position to make demands upon them).

The manager does no work; managers get things done only through the activities of subordinates. Actually, the manager must carry on many relationships with others and participates in activities of all sorts to get things done.

Most of a manager's time and energy is devoted to supervising subordinates. In reality, the manager is *not* in contact with subordinates a significant portion of the time.

A good manager manages by looking at outcomes. Actually, methods of continuous feedback are required.

To be effective, a manager must have power and authority equal to his responsibility. In fact, a manager almost never has power equal to his responsibility. A manager must depend on the actions of many people over whom he has not the slightest control.

The facts of organizational behavior make it perfectly plain that the modern manager operates in a continually changing context where things are not as simple as the "principles of management" might suggest.

Today, these points are more obvious than ever. Organizations have fewer managers due to corporate "rightsizing," cost containment, greater worker empowerment, and the flattening of organizational layers. Fewer supervisors exist, and their span of control is invariably greater. Supervisors in some organizations have been relabeled "team leaders," "facilitators," or "change agents." There are often fewer one-on-one conversations with employees as there "just isn't time anymore." There is more paperwork (CYA stuff) and computer/smart-phone time. There is often a push to focus on upstream decisions, conditions, and measures to ensure "continuous process improvement," and so on.

All of this changes the role of the supervisor—it may even shift the supervisory role to work teams. This will be discussed later in this chapter.

THE SUPERVISOR'S ROLE IN SAFETY

A fundamental principle has always been that the first-line supervisor is the lynchpin in any safety and health system. Whether you accept this key role, though, is not always guaranteed. It depends on many variables.

The attitude of most supervisors lies along a broad spectrum, ranging from total acceptance to flat rejection of safety and health and their role in safety and health processes. Most typical is the organization in which supervisors do not shrink from this responsibility, but at the same time do not really embrace it either. Nor do they treat it as they would any of their other defined production duties and tasks. Usually their *safety hat* is worn less frequently than their *cost-control hat*, or their *production hat*, or their *quality-control hat*. In most organizations, safety and health is not considered to be as important to the supervisor as many, if not most, of the other duties that he or she is required to perform.

Too often, safety and health is still considered largely a periodic policing function, a matter of rules enforcement and regulatory compliance only.

Your attitude toward safety and health and your performance in these areas depends on three things:

1. Whether you are able to perform. Can you do it? Albert Bandura calls this self-efficacy.
2. Whether you believe performing in safety and health is a part of your supervisory job. Will it work? Will it achieve positive outcomes? Is it a personal value? Bandura calls this response-efficacy.

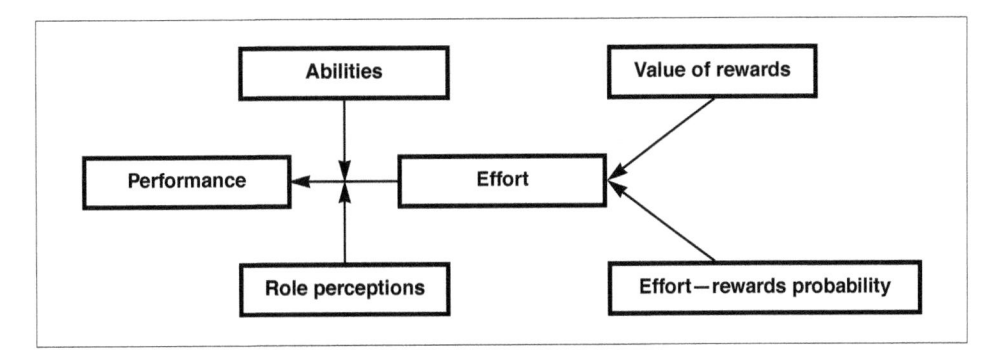

Figure 3.1 Factors affecting performance

3. Whether you try. Is it worth it? Are the consequences worth the effort? (See figure 3.1.)

In most cases today, the answer to all three questions is "yes." You are the pivotal lynchpin between management and employee safety and health actions and communications, and your management knows your value. Management, because of this knowledge, will measure your safety and health performance in well-defined areas, which will undoubtedly include at least these:
- whether all incidents are investigated and investigated to the point that root causes are found and removed; many organizations today include near-incident investigations (close calls, near misses)
- whether routine, regular inspections/audits are made to find and fix hazards
- whether new employees as well as experienced ones are regularly and routinely coached to improve their performance
- whether all employees are motivated to want to work safely (leadership)
- whether you encourage and provide time and resources for your employees to engage in department-specific health and safety activities designed to reduce the potential for injuries

SAFETY WHERE THERE IS NO SUPERVISOR

To improve corporate performance, one trend has been to decide there are levels of the traditional management hierarchy that we can do without. In some organizations this has meant the flattening of the organizations—reducing the number of middle managers and the number of layers of the hierarchy. This approach—from a vertical to horizontal structure—makes sense in the age of digital data dissemination and widespread automation. In flattening the structure, thanks to technology, we have become more efficient, more productive.

In other organizations, a decision has been made to go to team management, eliminating front-line supervisors. This decision has great historical underpinnings—

we have known since the old Hawthorne studies of the 1920s that the most productive work units are those where there is no formal supervision. It might be remembered, however, that in those early studies team leadership was only an experiment and, as a result, people responded very positively (the Hawthorne Effect as it was later called).

As we go from supervisor control to team control, how do we ensure an incident/illness-free operation? The team approach requires us to reassess how safety and health can be accomplished in any organization and come to a new understanding.

THE TOTAL INVOLVEMENT CONCEPT

First, the *high-performance team concept* needs to be defined. This is something different from worker participation, engagement, or empowerment. The team concept suggests that decisions will be made and problems will be solved by work teams, not by individuals. Empowerment, participation, and engagement can all happen in a hierarchical structure, when management simply asks workers to help them in managing the organization, or one function of it, such as safety and health.

In a traditional, but worker-centric organization, little is changed when it comes to safety and health. We still have clear accountability within the management structure for proactive, daily performance of activities that prevent incidents, although workers may perform many of them. But accountability remains clear—it remains in line management, from CEO to first-line supervisor.

The Team Concept

The team concept changes the traditional game. First, there is no line supervisor to hold accountable through the management tool of measurement coupled with rewards. When it comes to safety and health, there are other factors to consider.

Here are key safety and health principles in a team environment:
- The supervisor is the key person (Heinrich 1931); today, there may not be a supervisor.
- The Three E's of Safety (adapted from Heinrich 1931)—Engineering, Education, and Enforcement—are used; two of these (education and enforcement) were traditionally the supervisor's responsibility.
- Safety and health should be managed (Petersen 1970).
- The key is accountability (Petersen 1970); how do we measure and reward a team?
- Management starts with a clear definition of roles—what is the role of the team?
- Who will do the traditional supervisory tasks of inspecting, investigating, motivating, training, conducting one-on-ones, behavior observations, etc.?

Our Attempts to Date

As we launch into high-performance models, we seem to have opted for one of several default positions based on these assumptions:

1. We assume that teams will automatically take care of safety and health along with everything else.
2. In many cases, we also assume that, by merely removing a person (the supervisor), teams are ready for self-directed (team) management.
3. Management assumes it should treat the team like a supervisor, saying, "You are responsible for your own safety, now do something about it."
4. We assume that, with employees now in charge of safety and health, management is "off the hook" and no longer has a role to play—it has abdicated responsibility. This development led in recent years to changes in behavior-based safety processes to ensure that *employee-driven processes* do not exclude or exempt senior leaders from important safety and health responsibilities.
5. We assume that all people are ready to take over. Some are not prepared. Or willing. Some are happy to just do their thing.
6. We assume that all employees want a piece of the action. Some do not. We have created a three-tiered organization: (1) management, (2) involved employees, and (3) uninvolved employees. This creates friction and tension in some organizations.
7. We sometimes assume that, if the team approach doesn't work, we can always take back authority. However, when senior leaders do this, it results in considerable chaos (a mild description). Occasionally we find it works brilliantly, resulting in unheard-of success.

We've identified some of the pitfalls; now, here are some ideas on how to achieve success with team approaches.

Successful Teams

Many organizations have been successful in utilizing the team approach. Small units have made the transformation with remarkable results. Talk with team members in successful companies in a variety of industries (food processing, oil and gas extraction, railroads, steel and automotive manufacturing companies) and you will never see such excitement from hourly employees as those experiencing team participation and true engagement. And, without fail, the resultant safety and health records have been superb.

However, the opposite is also true—organizations where going to team approaches has produced problems, discontent, reduced morale, increased friction, and occasionally utter chaos.

So what are the differences?

Probably a number of things: organizational preparedness for team participation, the planning that goes into the change, the amount of input employees have in the change decision and process, and other factors.

In organizations that have achieved desired results, some actions management has taken—things that your organization might well consider—are:

1. Define within management exactly where you are willing to go by defining what you mean by "participation." Is it to get better input so management can make better decisions? Is it to share decision-making? Is it to turn decision-making over to the teams? And which decisions will management retain?
2. As best you can, check the maturity level of everyone who will be involved both in management and in production. Find out if you are "ready." This can be done through interviews or perception surveys. Also, before going to teams, look at the degree you've allowed self-management in the past.
3. Check the amount of confidence and trust that exists between management and the employees. Culture surveys can help in the assessment.
4. Clearly define the ground rules—the guidelines, defining what is allowable in decision-making and what is not (complying with regulations, adhering to core corporate values, etc.).
5. Allow great flexibility within your guidelines. For instance, "You must have a system for your team for recording and evaluating behavioral observations. How you do it is up to you."
6. Require each location/team to have an annual (or periodic) review of their safety and health plan. Have an annual (or periodic) check of each unit to see whether they are carrying out the plan.
7. Conduct periodic gap analyses to determine where your plans are coming up short and missing expectations.
8. Hold each location/team accountable for what they have agreed to do.
9. Determine what core elements should be dealt with in each plan but allow great flexibility in what each location/team can do to achieve the expected results within those core elements.
10. Require intermediate self-checks in shorter intervals, making frequent adjustments as needed.
11. Ensure that rewards/positive reinforcement from management are based on measurements associated with the completion of safety and health activities not outcomes (i.e., injury rates).

An Example

In the 1990s, the Procter & Gamble Company was pioneering team approaches and high employee involvement and experienced excellent results. While turning over many of the safety efforts to employee teams, they set the ground rules for locations/units/teams by identifying *key elements* that teams must deal with (Earnest 1994).

Gene Earnest, former Senior Manager, Corporate Safety for Procter & Gamble, and a pioneer in implementing behavior-based safety techniques in workplaces, explained:

> The P&G corporate safety group developed what is known as the Key Elements of Industrial Hygiene & Safety. In effect, these are the "what counts" activities for IH&S and are the basis for site surveys. It was believed that if these activities were effectively implemented, injuries and illness would be reduced, and conversely, if they were done poorly, injuries and illness would increase. Because line management was involved in the development of this list, there was "buy-in."
>
> I cannot stress enough the importance of having a clearly identified IH&S program against which goals can be established at all levels of the organization and people held accountable for before-the-fact measures of injury and illness prevention. I recognize that certain areas of safety are "soft" and do not readily lend themselves to measurement; however, injury- and illness-producing events will invariably be linked to behavior (of management and/or non-management) that is observable and measurable. What is being measured will vary depending upon the role of the individual.
>
> The Key Elements of IH&S referred to previously are divided into four major categories and nine subcategories (as shown in figure 3.2).
>
> Each key element is rated by the surveyor utilizing a scale of zero to ten where 0 means "nothing has been done" and 10 means the key element

Element	Profile Rating	Priority
I. ORGANIZATIONAL PLANNING AND SUPPORT		
A. EXPECTATIONS AND INVOLVEMENT		
B. GOAL SETTING/ACTION PLANNING		
II. STANDARDS AND PRACTICES		
A. STANDARD IMPLEMENTATION		
B. SAFE PRACTICES		
C. PLANNING FOR SAFE CONDITIONS		
III. TRAINING		
A. SITE TRAINING SYSTEMS		
IV. ACCOUNTABILITY AND PERFORMANCE FEEDBACK		
A. BEHAVIOR OBSERVATION SYSTEM/SAFETY SAMPLING		
B. BEHAVIOR FEEDBACK		
C. PERFORMANCE TRACKING		

Figure 3.2 Industrial hygiene and safety key elements

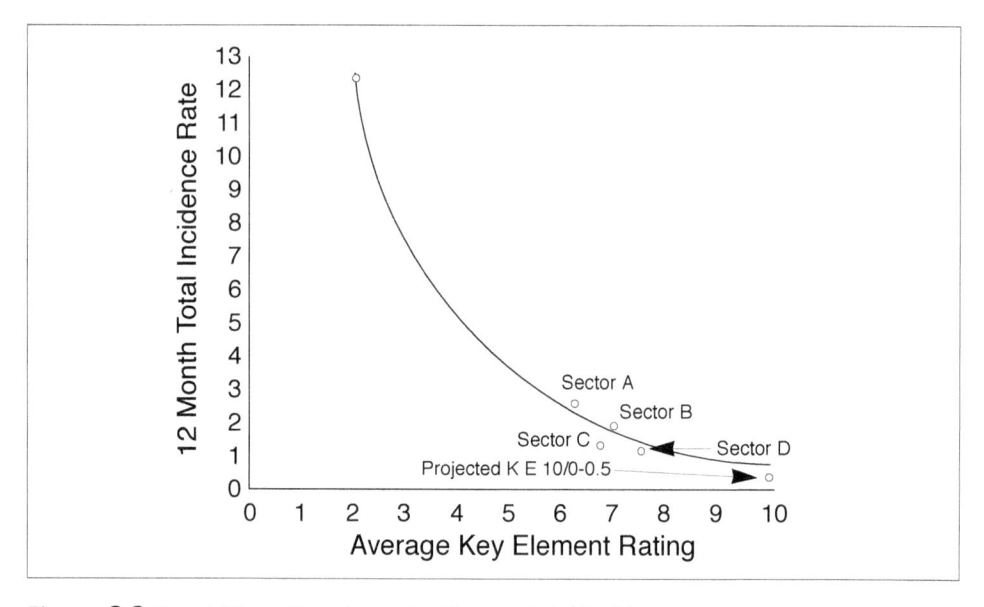

Figure 3.3 Acquisitions: Key element ratings vs. total incident rate

is "fully implemented and effective." Calibration to ensure that assigned ratings on surveys do not vary plus or minus one point is accomplished by corporate liaison accompanying the business sector surveyor on select surveys worldwide. Training and qualification programs for site health and safety resources also include exercises to ensure that people entering the role fully understand the industrial hygiene and safety key elements and how the ratings are assigned and calibrated.

The validity of this approach is evident from the graph (figure 3.3) that illustrates the correlation between key element ratings and total incidence rates.

New acquisitions have typically had total incidence rates (TIRs) of 12 and above, and they have had Key Element ratings on the initial survey of 2–3 (out of 10). Established business sectors (A through D) have considerably higher Key Element ratings and correspondingly lower TIRs. The process of phasing in acquisitions typically requires several years. The projected TIR for a facility having a Key Element rating of 10 is 0–0.5.

Procter & Gamble teams dealt with the key areas in ways appropriate to, and compatible with, the culture of the team, but they would be dealt with.

Then some criteria were established for each. For instance, under the key element "Expectations and Involvement," a number of criteria were provided to measure the teams' accomplishments against this key element, such as:
- Health and safety responsibilities and expectations are established for roles/individuals within each level of the organization.
- A performance feedback system exists and is utilized to hold each person accountable for meeting his/her responsibilities/expectations.

- Job performance in the area of health and safety is perceived to have an effect (good or bad) on a person's career (pay, selection, promotion) the same as cost, quality, etc.

Under the key element "Behavior Observation System/Safety Sampling," a number of criteria were provided, such as:

1. Program structure
   — Each unit has a formal Behavior Observation System (BOS) with a "system owner" identified.
   — All employees have been trained in the purpose, structure, and management of the BOS.
   — All employees at all levels of the organization make observations.
   — Observations focus on behaviors. Behaviors listed on the observation form are focused on:
     - monitoring critical behaviors, and this is periodically updated
     - reducing target injuries/illnesses or monitoring potential injury/illness sources
     - monitoring new policies and procedures
   — Behaviors listed are clearly safe/unsafe (no gray areas).
   — Each person makes observations on a regular, frequent, and planned schedule at random times.
   — People are trained in the observation cycle and observation techniques.
   — Observations are made at random times—at least one BOS survey/shift (recommended).
   — The percent of safe behavior correlates with injury and illness results.

After unit expectations were clearly established, it was up to the unit to perform. New acquisitions were given a defined period to come up to established expectations in the key-element areas.

Units were measured in several ways. Total Company Incidence Rate was one way. Another was how well the unit achieved progress in the key elements. A Key Element Rating (KER) was assessed on each unit periodically (see figure 3.4). Goals were set for both types of ratings. A corporatewide goal was to achieve an 8+ KER/1.5 TIR at all sites.

As a result of concentrating on key elements and requiring them at each location, the corporation continued the decline in its TIR, reaching the lowest in its history.

Other Best Practices

Frito-Lay achieved excellence from the standpoint of distilling what kinds of behavior are important and necessary, then being held accountable for them. Results

	Rating	Priority
TE/DEPARTMENT _____ DATE _____		
I. ORGANIZATIONAL PLANNING AND SUPPORT		
A. EXPECTATIONS AND INVOLVEMENT		
B. GOAL SETTING/ACTION PLANNING		
II. STANDARDS AND PRACTICES		
A. STANDARD IMPLEMENTATION		
• Handling Chemicals: Key Ingredients, Hazardous Sys., Chemical Mgmt. • Life Threatening/Major Business Interruptions • Potentially Serious		
B. SAFE PRACTICES		
C. PLANNING FOR SAFE CONDITIONS		
III. TRAINING		
A. SITE TRAINING SYSTEMS		
IV. ACCOUNTABILITY AND PERFORMANCE FEEDBACK		
A. BEHAVIOR OBSERVATION SYSTEM/SAFETY SAMPLING		
B. BEHAVIOR FEEDBACK		
C. PERFORMANCE TRACKING		
OVERALL RATING		

OVERALL RATING
0   2   4   6   7   8   9   10

Figure 3.4 Rating corporate key elements

are sustainable. Supervisors and middle managers engage in certain actions on a regular basis—it's their job. Accountability isn't about whether you've had safety incidents. Being accountable has to do with the actions you take—carrying out the activities you have been hired to do, trained to do (Williamsen 2007).

Another approach to safety and health best practices was articulated by Ann R. Klee, VP for Environment, Health and Safety, General Electric (GE), speaking at the opening session of the 30th annual meeting of the Voluntary Protection Program Participants' Association (VPPPA) in National Harbor, Maryland, in 2014. "GE has embraced and implemented human and organizational performance (HOP)," said Klee. HOP is an operating philosophy focused on protecting people, products, and property from human error. It starts by recognizing that human error is part of the human condition. Performance improvement is pursued through identifying hidden weaknesses and traps associated with the operating systems that GE workers must navigate to do their jobs.

Industrial Safety and Hygiene News published Klee's presentation (Johnson 2014).

> The GE corporate EHS team oversees and supports HOP goals with training, tools and cross-business forums. The team also oversees long-term plans for HOP integration developed by individual GE businesses using risk-based prioritization. Participation by operational leaders and employees has been critical to achieving early successes and discovering new synergies with disciplines outside of EHS such as quality and LEAN manufacturing.

One EHS consultant calls HOP the anti-behavior-based safety approach. The emphasis is not on observing and correcting (or praising) individual behaviors but on operational systems.

HOP also calls into question the goal of many safety professionals of achieving and sustaining zero injuries. The HOP philosophy accepts human error as inevitable and works around human foibles by reducing weaknesses and traps—risks—in work processes through stringent auditing and risk assessment and mitigation controls based on the severity and probability of risk.

REFERENCES

Callari, Tiziana C., Corrine Bieder, and Barry Kirwan. 2019. "What is it like for a middle manager to take safety into account? Practices and challenges." *Safety Science* 113 (March): 19–29. https://doi.org/10.1016/j.ssci.2018.10.025.

Earnest, Eugene R. 1994. "What Counts in Safety." *Insights Into Management* 6 (Second Quarter): 2–6.

Occupational Safety and Health Administration (OSHA). 2016. "Recommended Practices for Safety and Health Programs." October 2016. https://www.osha.gov/shpguidelines/.

Gratton, Lynda. 2011. "The End of the Middle Manager." *Harvard Business Review*, January–February 2011.

Johnson, Dave. 2014. "GE Embraces Human and Organizational Performance." *Industrial Safety & Hygiene News*, September 2014.

Johnson, Dave. 2016. "EHS State of the Nation Survey." *Industrial Safety & Hygiene News*, January 2016.

Planik, T., G. Driesen, and F. Valardo. 1967. "Industrial Safety Study." *National Safety News*, August 1967.

Sayles, Leonard. 1964. *Managerial Behavior*. New York: McGraw-Hill.

Williamsen, Mike. 2007. "The Culture of Safety: An Interview with Safety Pioneer Dan Petersen." *Professional Safety*, March 2007.

CHAPTER 4

Key Safety and Health Tasks

In this chapter, we will be talking about specific tasks you, as a supervisor, must perform if safety and health processes are to work. They are:
- communicating regularly with your workers and encouraging their participation
- hazard identification and assessment
- hazard prevention and control
- investigating safety incidents (and near misses) to identify causes and bring closure to findings

Two critical tasks—leadership skills to inspire your people to work safely and coaching your people to perform safely—are covered in chapters 6 and 7.

Communication, identifying and assessing hazards, preventing and controlling hazards, and investigating safety incidents and near incidents are four core competencies—musts—for safety and health systems to be effective.

There are others that you should carry out and perform effectively, such as education and training; evaluation and improvement of processes; communicating and coordinating for host employers, contractors, and staffing agencies; behavioral observations; safety and health meetings (preshift, postshift, weekly, monthly, etc.); reporting audit findings, incident and exposure causes, and employee concerns to upper management; integrating new safety technologies (such as smart PPE and remote monitoring) into operations; rules enforcement and discipline, when necessary; and assessing your people for signs of fatigue, distress, overexertion, substance abuse, and potentially violent/abusive behavior.

COMMUNICATIONS AND WORKER ENGAGEMENT

The first core supervisory responsibility is to communicate daily with your workers, encouraging their input.
- Give employees the necessary time and resources to participate in safety and health systems.
- Recognize and provide positive feedback to those who engage in activities.

- Be accessible and visible and invite employees to talk to you about safety and health and to make suggestions.
- Establish a system that encourages employees to report injuries, illnesses, close calls/near misses, hazards, and other concerns, and respond promptly. Allow anonymous reporting to reduce fear of reprisal (Petersen 2003).
- Follow up and report back to employees frequently about action taken in response to their concerns and suggestions.
- With the buy-in of your senior leaders, permit employees to initiate or request a temporary suspension or shutdown of any work activity or operation they believe to be unsafe.
- Converse with employees about finding solutions to reported issues. Listen. Probe. This is called "positive social dynamics" and "supportive internal support"—important factors found in organizations making larger improvements in occupational safety and health performance (Robson et al. 2016).
- Give employees information they need to understand safety and health hazards and control measures in the workplace. Some OSHA standards require employers to make specific types of information available to workers, such as Safety Data Sheets (SDS), injury and illness data (may need to be redacted and aggregated to eliminate personal identifiers), and results of environmental exposure monitoring conducted in the workplace (prevent disclosure of sensitive and personal information as required).

Other useful information for employees to review can include:
- chemical and equipment manufacturer safety recommendations
- workplace inspection reports
- incident investigation reports (prevent disclosure of sensitive and personal information as required)
- workplace job hazard analyses

Provide opportunities for employees to participate in all aspects of the program, including but not limited to, helping them:
- develop safety and health processes and set goals
- report hazards and develop solutions that improve safety and health
- analyze hazards in each step of routine and nonroutine jobs, tasks, and processes
- define and document safe work practices
- conduct site inspections
- develop and revise safety and health procedures
- participate in incident and close-call/near-miss investigations
- train current co-workers and new hires

- develop, implement, and evaluate training programs
- evaluate performance of processes and identify ways to improve them
- take part in exposure monitoring and medical surveillance associated with health hazards

To further employee engagement in your safety and health activities:
- Ensure all your employees can participate regardless of their skill level, education, or language.
- Provide frequent and regular feedback to show your employees that their safety and health concerns are being heard and addressed.
- Allow sufficient time and resources to facilitate employee participation.

HAZARD IDENTIFICATION AND ASSESSMENT

The second core responsibility of a supervisor in a safety and health system is inspecting for hazards and potentially dangerous exposures to harm. Inspection is one of the primary tools of safety and health. At one time, it was virtually the only tool, and it still is the one most used.

According to the National Safety Council (Krieger and Montgomery 1997): "The primary purpose of inspection is to detect potential hazards so they can be corrected before an incident occurs. Inspection can determine conditions that need to be corrected or improved to bring operations up to acceptable standards, both from safety and operational standpoints. Secondary purposes are to improve operations and thus to increase efficiency, effectiveness and profitability."

Many articles have been written about safety and health inspections, and many have asked the question: "Why inspect?" Some typical answers have been:
- Check the results against the plan.
- Reawaken interest in safety and health.
- Reevaluate safety and health standards (both internal and external standards).
- Teach safety and health by example.
- Display the supervisor's sincerity/authenticity about safety and health.
- Detect and reactivate unfinished business.
- Collect data for meetings.
- Note and act upon both safe and unsafe behavior trends.
- Reach first-hand agreement with parties (managers and nonmanagers) on working-condition deficiencies and other system flaws responsible for unsafe behaviors.
- Improve safety and health standards (both internal and external standards).
- Check new facilities.
- Spot unsafe conditions.
- Improve housekeeping.
- Check safety signage and communication displays.

Systematic inspection is the basic tool for maintaining safe conditions and checking unsafe practices. Each company, plant, or department should develop its own checklist. Sample checklists, stressing work areas or work practices or both, are shown in figures 4.1 through 4.5.

The format of figure 4.1 is typical of many companies' approach.

Figure 4.2 is similar to figure 4.1, but is more detailed.

FOREMAN'S INSPECTION FORM

Name _____ Date _____

Item	Good	Poor	Disposition
Housekeeping			
Aisles			
Piling			
Floor surfaces			
Tools			
Condition			
Grounding			
Guards			
Personal protection			
Miscellaneous			
Ladders			
Slings			

Figure 4.1 Typical inspection form

Figures 4.3 and 4.4 concentrate on unsafe practices, while figure 4.5 is designed for the concept of multiple causation and symptomatic safety.

SAFETY INSPECTION CHECKLIST

Plant or Department _____ Date _____

This list is intended only as a reminder. Look for other unsafe acts and conditions, and then report them so that corrective action can be taken. Note particularly whether unsafe acts or conditions that have caused accidents have been corrected. Note also whether potential accident causes, marked "X" on previous inspection, have been corrected.

(✓) indicates **Satisfactory**   (X) indicates **Unsatisfactory**

1. FIRE PROTECTION
   Extinguishing equipment ❏
   Standpipes, hoses, sprinkler heads
     and valves ❏
   Exits, stairs, and signs ❏
   Storage of flammable material ❏

2. HOUSEKEEPING
   Aisles, stairs, and floors ❏
   Storage and piling of material ❏
   Wash and locker rooms ❏
   Light and ventilation ❏
   Disposal of waste ❏
   Yards and parking lots ❏

3. TOOLS
   Power tools, wiring ❏
   Hand tools ❏
   Usage and storage of tools ❏

4. PERSONAL PROTECTIVE EQUIPMENT
   Goggles or face shields ❏
   Safety shoes ❏
   Gloves ❏
   Respirators or gas masks ❏
   Protective clothing ❏

5. MATERIAL-HANDLING EQUIPMENT
   Power trucks, hand trucks ❏
   Elevators ❏
   Cranes and hoists ❏
   Conveyors ❏
   Cables, ropes, chains, and slings ❏

6. BULLETIN BOARDS
   Neat and attractive ❏
   Display changed regularly ❏
   Well illuminated ❏

7. MACHINERY
   Point of operation guards ❏
   Belts, pulleys, gears, shafts, etc. ❏
   Oiling, cleaning, and adjusting ❏
   Maintenance and oil leakage ❏

8. PRESSURE EQUIPMENT
   Steam equipment ❏
   Air receivers and compressors ❏
   Gas cylinders and hose ❏

9. UNSAFE PRACTICES
   Excessive speed of vehicles ❏
   Improper lifting ❏
   Smoking in danger areas ❏
   Horseplay ❏
   Running in aisles or on stairs ❏
   Improper use of air hoses ❏
   Removing machine or other guards ❏
   Work on unguarded moving
     machinery ❏

10. FIRST AID
   First aid kits and rooms ❏
   Stretchers and fire blankets ❏
   Emergency showers ❏
   All injuries reported ❏

11. MISCELLANEOUS
   Acids and caustics ❏
   New processes, chemicals, and
     solvents ❏
   Dusts, vapors, or fumes ❏
   Ladders and scaffolds ❏

Signed _____

USE REVERSE SIDE FOR DETAILED COMMENTS OR RECOMMENDATIONS

Figure 4.2 Safety inspection checklist

SUMMARY OF UNSAFE PRACTICES

Area or Division _____ Force _____
District _____ Period Covered _____

	GROUP (FORCE, DISTRICT, DIVISION OR AREA)						TOTAL
1	SUPERVISORS REPORTING UNSAFE PRACTICES						
2	SUPERVISORS NOT REPORTING UNSAFE PRACTICES						
3	TOTAL NO. OF SUPERVISORS						
4	TOTAL NO. OF EMPLOYEES IN GROUP						
5	NUMBER OF UNSAFE PRACTICES REPORTED						

CAUSE OF UNSAFE PRACTICES

6	SUPERVISION	LACK OF ANALYZING, OR PLANNING THE WORK						
7		INADEQUATE TASK TRAINING						
8		LACK OF DEFINITE OR SPECIFIC INSTRUCTIONS						
9		IMPROPER ASSIGNMENT OF EMPLOYEE						
10		FAILURE TO SEE THAT INSTRUCTIONS WERE FOLLOWED						
11		OTHER						
12	EMPLOYEE	LACK OF ANALYZING, OR PLANNING THE WORK						
13		DISREGARD FOR KNOWN SAFE PRACTICES						
14		LACK OF EXPERIENCE						
15		ABSTRACTION OR FORGETFULNESS						
16		HASTE						
17		OTHER						
18	TOTAL							

UNSAFE PRACTICES

19	MOTOR VEHICLES—OPERATION AND MAINTENANCE						
20	POLES—WORKING ALOFT						
21	ACTION, BOTH IN AND OUT OF BUILDINGS THAT MIGHT RESULT IN SLIPS OR FALLS						
22	LADDERS—EXTENSION, STEPLADDERS, AND MOBILE PLATFORMS						
23	BODY HARNESSES AND LANYARDS						
24	CLIMBERS, PADS, AND STRAPS						
25	GUARDING EMPLOYEES AND PUBLIC						
26	TOOLS AND MATERIALS						
27	GOGGLES						
28	USE OF RUBBER GLOVES AND OTHER PROTECTIVE DEVICES AND PRECAUTIONS TAKEN AROUND LIVE WIRES						
29	MANHOLES, CONDUIT AND EXCAVATIONS						
30	FIRST AID FOR AND CARE OF INJURIES						
31	MISCELLANEOUS						
32	TOTAL						

RECOMMENDATIONS _____

Observed by _____
Title _____

Figure 4.3 Summary of unsafe practices (From *Accident Prevention Manual for Industrial Operations*, 7th ed., 1974. Copyright © National Safety Council. Used with permission.)

Category	REF.	NO.	Category	REF.	NO.
19. MOTOR VEHICLES · OPERATION AND MAINTENANCE			**26. TOOLS AND MATERIALS**		
Improper Parking			Improper Use of Tools and Materials		
Failure to Conform to Traffic Laws			Use of Defective or Unauthorized Tools		
Stepped Off or On Vehicle in Motion			Tossing Tools and Materials		
Backing Up Without Taking Proper Precautions			Dropping Tools and Materials from Aloft		
Poor Housekeeping on Truck or Car			Unsafe Lifting or Handling		
Lights, Brakes, Horn, etc. Not Tested			Unsafe Carrying of Tools, Nails, Tacks, etc.		
Unsafe Handling of Derrick			Improperly Stored or Placed		
Under Derrick in Operation			Unsafe Use of Cable Car		
Hands On or Near Winch Line Sheave or Drum			Handline Dangling		
Unsafe Handling and Use of Trailer			Tools and Materials Left Lying Around		
Unsafe Performance of Maintenance Operations			Failure to Use Tree Sling		
			Unsafe Cutting of Wire — Flying Ends or Pieces		
			Not Using Flashlight Where Required		
20. POLES · WORKING ALOFT			**27. GOGGLES · FAILURE TO USE WHEN:**		
Failure to Test or Make Safe before Climbing			Drilling Concrete Brick or Other Masonry		
Failure to Compensate for Unbalanced Load			Grinding, Chipping, Handling Brush, etc.		
Working in Dangerous Position					
Lack of Care in Climbing					
Standing Under Workman Aloft			**28. USE OF RUBBER GLOVES, ETC. AND PRECAUTIONS TAKEN AROUND LIVE WIRES**		
Lack of Care Approaching or Leaving Pole					
21. ACTION BOTH IN AND OUT OF BUILDINGS THAT MIGHT RESULT IN SLIPS OR FALLS			Failure to Use Rubber Gloves When Required		
			Failure to Test and Maintain Properly		
Unnecessary Running, Stairs and Across Floors			Working Too Close, Live Wires When Aloft		
Lack of Ordinary Care Outside Building			Lack of Precaution to Prevent Wire From	xxx	xxx
Sitting on Tilted Chairs			Flipping Up Into Live Wires		
Standing on Chairs, Boxes, Cans, etc.			Sagging or Falling Into Live Wires		
			Reel Tender Not Protected		
22. LADDERS · EXTENSIONS, MOBILE AND STEP LADDERS			Unsafe Use of Chain Hoist, Tent, Steel Tape, etc.		
			Incomplete Survey After Suspected E.L. Contact		
Failure to Make Secure (Footing Lashing, Holding)			Carelessness around Electric Circuits or Equipment		
Failure to Place Leg thru Ladder or Use Safety			Failure to Use Adequate Protective Devices		
Pull Rope Not Tied					
Defective Ladder, Spurs Not Turned, etc.			**29. MANHOLES, CONDUIT, AND EXCAVATIONS**		
Overreaching Too High Up on Ladder, etc.			Failure to Do Proper Tests for Gas or Oxygen Deficiency		
Improper Angle for Climbing			
Failure to Inspect			Insufficient Ventilation (with Sail or Blower)		
Unguarded at Hazardous Location			Entered Manhole Without Manhole Guard		
Failure to Use Where Required or Used Wrong Kind			Failure to Use Ladder in Manhole or Excavation		
Not Lashed to Motor Vehicle or Carried Properly			Insufficient Guarding, Manholes or Excavations		
Failure to Extend Spreaders of Stepladder			Unsafe Removal and Handling of Cover		
Tools or Material Left on Steps or Top			Smoking or Open Flames Near or in Manholes		
Shoved Mobile Ladder Endangering Person on Ladder					
			30. FIRST AID AND CARE OF INJURIES		
23. HARNESSES AND SAFETY STRAPS			Failure to Give Proper First Aid		
Failure to Use While Aloft (On Pole, Platform, etc.)			Did Not Continue Proper Care of Injury		
Failure to Look, Feel, and Know Snaphook Is Secure			Failure to Report Injury		
Not Inspected or Properly Maintained			First Aid Kit Not Properly Maintained		
24. CLIMBERS, PADS, AND STRAPS			**31. MISCELLANEOUS**		
Wearing in Trees, Vehicles; on Ladder, Ground, etc.			Horseplay on the Job		
Failure to Inspect and Maintain Properly			Debris Left Lying Around		
Unsafe Climbing Habits			Unsafe Position on St., Hwy, Rd., R.R. Track, etc.		
			Handling of Hot Solder, Paraffin, etc.		
25. GUARDING EMPLOYEES AND PUBLIC			Poison Ivy or Oak — Lack of Protection or Care		
Failure to Use Adequate Warning Signs or Flags			Clothing and Shoes — Poor, Insufficient		
Keeping Children and Others Away from Operation			Trees or Brush — Cutting and Handling		
Guarding Public at Dangerous Location					

Figure 4.4 Unsafe practices observed (From *Accident Prevention Manual for Industrial Operations*, 7th ed., 1974. Copyright © National Safety Council. Used with permission.)

FOREMAN'S INSPECTION FORM

Name _____ Date _____

Symptom noted Act/Condition/Problem	Causes Why — What's Wrong	Corrections made or suggested By you — By others

Figure 4.5 Suggested inspection form (From *Techniques of Safety Management* by Dan Petersen. Copyright © 1989 by Dan Petersen. Used with permission.)

Systematic Inspection by Supervisors

Supervisors should continuously make sure that PPE, tools, technology, machines, robotics, and other departmental equipment are maintained properly and are safe to use.

To do this effectively, use systematic inspection procedures and delegate authority to others in your department. For instance, tool-room attendants might inspect all hand tools to ensure they are kept in safe condition. Some companies require portable electric tools to be turned in to the electrical department for a monthly check.

Inspection programs should be set up for new equipment, materials, technology, and processes. You should ensure that nothing is put into regular operation until it has been checked for hazards, its operation studied, additional safety devices installed, if necessary, and safety instructions developed.

You might give your team leaders responsibility for inspecting equipment and for ensuring their workers observe safe practices. If you do, make certain all inspections by persons other than you are up to your standards. Spot check periodically to make sure assignments are being carried out, safety and health precautions are being observed, and equipment is running efficiently and safely.

Inspection of Work Practices

You should regularly observe your people to determine whether they are working in the safest way and complying with your rules and objectives. You should also be on the lookout for barriers and obstacles in the work environment that prevent employees from working safely and perhaps trigger shortcuts or improvisations. As you look over your area, keep in mind questions such as:

- Do employees operate machinery or use tools, appliances, or other equipment without authority?
- Are they working or operating at unsafe speeds?
- Have guards been removed, or have guards or other safety devices been rendered ineffective?
- Do people use defective tools or equipment, or use tools or equipment in unsafe ways, or use their hands or body instead of tools?
- Do they overload, crowd, arrange, or handle objects or materials unsafely?
- Do people stand or work under suspended loads, open hatches, shafts, or scaffolds; ride loads; get on or off equipment or vehicles in motion; walk on railroad tracks; or cross car tracks or vehicular thoroughfares except at crossings?
- Do they repair or adjust equipment in motion, under pressure, when electrically charged, or when containing dangerous substances?
- Are safety procedures being followed as written? Are shortcuts being taken to get the job done quicker?
- Does anyone or anything distract the attention of or startle workers?
- Do workers fail to use safety equipment, or do they use inadequate, badly adapted, or wrongly chosen personal protective equipment (PPE) or safety devices?
- Do employees have poor housekeeping habits or fail to remedy unsanitary or unhealthful conditions?
- Is horseplay activity a common occurrence?

Be sure to recognize positive safety efforts by your employees. Do not go out on the floor simply fishing for faults. Give positive reinforcement when employees wear PPE, follow inconvenient procedures, take extra steps to ensure safety, and watch out for the safety and health of their co-workers, for example. When needed, provide corrective coaching when a task is being performed in an unsafe manner. Coaching should be delivered in a positive manner—aim to teach, not accuse.

Your regular inspections should also focus on ergonomics. Ergonomics is looking at how your machines, systems, and procedures interact with your people. For instance, many people in their normal work must use parts of their body repetitively. Over time, this can result in back problems, arm and shoulder pains, wrist injuries, etc. Much of this can be reduced through an ergonomic analysis.

This ergonomic analysis has as its primary focus preventing repetitive motion injuries, commonly called musculoskeletal disorders (MSDs).

MSDs are occupational injuries and illnesses that develop over time, affecting the musculoskeletal and peripheral nervous systems. They can develop in any part of the body, but are most prevalent in the arms, back, knees, and shoulders. These disorders are caused by jobs that require repeated exertions and movements near the limits of the individual's strength and range-of-motion capability. These movements, although not initially painful, cause micro-traumas to the soft tissues. Over time, small strains to the muscle/tendon/ligament system build up, resulting in fatigue and soreness. If the individual continues the action causing the pain, cumulative trauma disorders are likely to develop. MSDs can have the following effects on individuals:

- pain
- numbness or loss of sensation
- reduced strength
- degraded ability to perform work
- degraded ability to participate in leisure activities

Other Approaches to Hazard Identification

Other approaches for pinpointing hazards, inspections aside, are:
- job safety analysis
- hazard hunts
- OSHA compliance checks
- ergonomic analysis

Each is described, should you choose to use the technique, in chapter 10. How objectives can be set and how your performance can be measured is also spelled out.

Should you choose to do straight inspections as described in this chapter, objectives and measures like number of inspections, number of hazards removed, etc., can be used in your company's accountability system and as leading indicators of safety and health performance.

HAZARD PREVENTION AND CONTROL

The third core responsibility of a supervisor in a safety and health system is hazard prevention and control. Identify your control options by:
- reviewing sources, such as OSHA standards and guidance documents; industry consensus standards, such as those promulgated by the American National Standards Institute (ANSI), the National Fire Protection Association (NFPA), and the International Organization for Standardization (ISO); the National Institute for Occupational Safety

and Health (NIOSH) publications; manufacturers' literature; and engineering reports to identify potential control measures. Keep current on relevant information from the safety trade media and professional safety and health associations.
- investigating control measures used in other workplaces and determining whether they would be effective at your workplace
- soliciting input from employees who may be able to suggest and evaluate solutions based on their knowledge of the facility, equipment, and work processes

Select controls that are most feasible, effective, and permanent.
- Immediately eliminate or control all serious hazards (hazards that are causing or are likely to cause death or serious physical harm).
- Use interim controls while you develop and implement long-term solutions.
- Select controls according to a hierarchy that emphasizes engineering solutions (including elimination or substitution) first, followed by safe work practices, administrative controls, and finally the use of personal protective equipment.
- Don't select controls that may directly or indirectly introduce new hazards.
- Review and discuss control options with employees to ensure controls are feasible and effective.
- Use a combination of control options when no single method in the hierarchy of controls fully protects employees.

Pay particular attention to precursors of serious injuries and fatalities.
- Precursors are often unusual, nonroutine work. This is the job that pops up only occasionally, or the one-of-a-kind type of situation. These situations may arise in production or nonproduction departments. The normal controls that apply to routine work have little effect in the nonroutine situation.
- Precursors can be nonproduction activities. Much of our safety effort has been directed to production work. But there is tremendous potential exposure for loss in nonproduction activities, such as maintenance, vehicle transportation, and research and development facilities. In these types of situations, most work tends to be nonroutine. As it is nonproduction, it often does not get the attention from safety, and it is not usually subject to developed procedures. Severity is predictable here.
- Sources of high energy are another category of precursors. In general, we can associate high energy with severity. Electricity, steam, compressed gases, and flammable liquids are examples.

- Certain construction activities are precursors: high-rise erection, communication towers, wind turbines, other work at heights, tunneling, working over water, etc. (Actually, construction severity is an amalgam of the previously described high-severity situations.)

These are just a starting point. A long list could be made that more extensively specifies the areas where serious injuries or fatalities are predictable.

Develop and update a hazard control plan.
- Prioritize the hazards needing controls.
- Assign responsibility for installing or implementing the controls to a specific person or persons with the power or competency to implement the controls.
- Plan to track progress toward completion.
- Plan to verify the effectiveness of controls after they are installed or implemented.

Implement selected controls.
- Install hazard control measures according to your priorities.
- Implement measures on a "worst-first" basis when resources are limited, according to the hazard ranking priorities (risk) established during hazard inspection and risk assessment.
- Promptly implement any measures that are easy and inexpensive, such as general housekeeping, removal of obvious tripping hazards, basic lighting; regular, top-to-bottom housekeeping is important to find and eliminate combustible dust, as well as many other hazards.

The 5S System

The 5S system of work organization is closely related to housekeeping. 5S methodology uses a list of five Japanese words: *seiri* (sort), *seiton* (set in order), *seiso* (shine), *seiketsu* (standardize), and *shitsuke* (sustain). The 5S list describes how to organize a workspace for efficiency and improved productivity and quality by identifying and storing tools and materials used, emphasizing housekeeping to clear and maintain the workspace, and making these practices standard and sustainable.

Safety is implied in every step of the 5S method (Semiklose 2014):

1. Safety is improved and hazards reduced when you *sort through* a workspace, removing what's unnecessary and improving accessibility and visual communications.
2. Safety benefits from *setting* an orderly workflow and ensuring work is not conducted in a haphazard manner or by taking shortcuts.
3. *Housekeeping*, or putting a *shine* on things, is fundamental to safety—it's a basic tenet. You can't have a zero-accident culture or any type of

100% safe culture without an emphasis on an orderly, organized, clean workspace and workflow. Housekeeping is a shared safety responsibility, ongoing and never-ending; it is a safe behavior that is an essential first step in developing a culture of safety.
4. *Standardizing* work practices establishes conformity. Conformity is critical to safety success. For work to be done safely, it must be done in compliance with a set of standards. OSHA regulations are all about establishing conformity in how safety is practiced.
5. These work practices—removing waste and unnecessary tools and materials, setting a clean and orderly workspace and workflow, effective housekeeping, and compliance with work norms and rules—all must be *sustainable*. They are behaviors that must become routine, embedded habits. The 5S practices are also a mindset or attitude that is ingrained in employees as "the way things are done around here." This, by the way, is the definition of culture: acceptance and ownership of the way things are done.

Validating Hazard Controls

Confirm that your hazard controls are effective.
- Track progress and verify implementation by asking the following questions: Have all control measures been implemented according to the hazard control plan? Have engineering controls been properly installed and tested? Have employees been appropriately trained so that they understand the controls, including how to operate engineering controls, safe work practices, and PPE use requirements? Are controls being used correctly and consistently?
- Conduct regular inspections (and industrial hygiene monitoring, if indicated) to confirm that engineering controls are operating as designed.
- Evaluate control measures to see if they are effective or need to be modified. Involve your employees in evaluating controls. If controls are not effective, identify, select, and implement further control measures that will provide adequate protection. Set a target completion date.
- Invite experienced employees to develop a solution (control) for a task being performed that has been deemed unsafe and have those individuals train less-experienced team members on the new procedure (control).
- Confirm that work practices, administrative controls, and personal protective equipment usage policies are being followed.
- Conduct routine, preventive maintenance of equipment, facilities, and controls to prevent incidents due to equipment failure.

Install Emergency Controls

Select controls to protect your employees during any nonroutine operations and emergencies.

- Develop procedures to control hazards that may arise during nonroutine operations.
- Develop or modify plans to control hazards that may arise in emergency situations.
- Procure any equipment needed to control emergency-related hazards.
- Assign responsibilities for implementing the emergency plan.
- Conduct emergency drills to ensure that procedures and equipment provide adequate protection during emergency situations.

INVESTIGATING INCIDENTS

Incident investigation (either of injuries or near injuries) is the fourth core supervisory responsibility. It is fundamental in preventing additional incidents and near misses. The aims of your investigations are to determine direct causes, uncover contributing incident causes, prevent similar incidents, document facts, provide information on costs, and, in general, promote safety and health.

A good safety system deals positively with the investigation of incidents and thus minimizes any attempt to cover up causes and effects. A high positive score in this category indicates a program in which thorough investigations are made and supervisors and employees freely discuss causes and circumstances.

In a quality incident investigation process, the search for cause goes beyond identifying the unsafe act and condition; it searches for multiple causes, including weaknesses of the management system as well as organizational influences (i.e., lack of safety funding, a production-over-safety mentality, lack of involvement of executives in the safety and health system, conflicting messaging from management). It also searches for the reasons that unsafe acts are committed—the causes of human error.

A quality incident investigation process is not designed to find fault or assess blame.

The form shown in figure 4.6 for the supervisor's investigation concentrates on the identification of the unsafe mechanical/physical/environmental condition and any unsafe behavior. The identification of these factors is based on a theory of incident causation defined by H.W. Heinrich (Heinrich 1969): "The occurrence of an injury invariably results from a completed sequence of factors, the last one of these being the injury itself. The incident that caused the injury is in turn invariably caused or permitted directly by the unsafe act of a person and/or a mechanical or physical hazard."

This is known as the Domino Theory of Incident Causation. It urges us to find an act and/or a condition behind every incident and remove it. This approach is quite limiting, however. Behind every incident lie many contributing factors, causes, and subcauses. Multiple Causation Theory states that factors combine in random fashion to cause incidents.

Let us briefly look at the contrast between the Multiple Causation Theory and the Domino Theory. Take, for example, this common incident: a worker falls off a stepladder. If we investigate this incident using the Domino Theory, we are asked to identify one act and/or one condition.

- the unsafe act: climbing a defective ladder
- the unsafe condition: a defective ladder
- the correction: getting rid of the defective ladder

Investigating the same incident in terms of Multiple Causation, we ask about some of the contributing factors surrounding this incident:

- Why was the defective ladder not found in normal inspections?
- Why did the supervisor allow its use?
- Did the injured employee know they should not use it?
- Were they properly trained?
- Were they reminded?
- Did the supervisor examine the job first?

The answers to these and other questions would lead to the following kinds of corrections:

- an improved inspection procedure
- improved training
- a better definition of responsibilities
- prejob planning by supervisors

With this incident, as with any accident, we must find some fundamental root causes (emphasis on the plural) and remove them if we hope to prevent a recurrence. Defining an unsafe act, "climbing a defective ladder," and an unsafe condition, "a defective ladder," has not led us very far toward any meaningful safety corrections. When we look at the act and the condition, we look at symptoms, not at causes. If we deal only at the symptomatic level, we end up removing symptoms but allow root causes to remain to cause another incident or some other type of operational error.

Root causes often relate to the management system. They may be due to management's decisions, policies and procedures, and budgets; supervision and its effectiveness; or training. Root causes are those that would affect permanent results when corrected. They are weaknesses that not only affect the single incident being investigated, but also might affect future incidents and operational problems.

SUPERVISOR'S ACCIDENT REPORT   OSHA File _____
(To be completed immediately after accident, even when there is no injury)   (Yr. – Mo.)

Company name and address _____

Business SIC code _____

Plant or location address _____
(if different from above)

Accident date _____/_____/_____ Time _____

Day of week ☐ Sun. ☐ Mon. ☐ Tue. ☐ Wed. ☐ Thur. ☐ Fri. ☐ Sat.

1. Name and address of injured (or ill) person _____
   _____

   SSN_____ 2. Age _____ 3. Sex _____

4. Years of service _____ 5. Time on present job _____ 6. Title/occupation _____

7. Department _____ 8. Location _____

9. Accident category (check) ☐ Motor vehicle ☐ Property damage ☐ Fire ☐ Other _____

10. OSHA recordable? ☐ Yes ☐ No

11. Severity of injury ☐ FATALITY ☐ Lost workdays ☐ Restricted workdays ☐ Medical treatment
    ☐ First-aid, return to work ☐ Other, specify_____

12. Amount of damage $ _____

13. Estimated number of days away from job _____

14. Nature of injury or illness _____

15. Part of body affected _____

16. Degree of disability ☐ Temporary total ☐ Permanent partial ☐ Permanent total

17. Describe in detail what happened _____
    _____
    _____
    _____

    Witness(es) _____

18. Describe any unsafe mechanical/physical/environmental condition at time of accident (be specific)
    _____
    _____
    _____

19. Describe any unsafe act by employees or others. (Be specific; must be answered.)
    _____
    _____
    _____

Figure 4.6 Sample supervisor's accident report form

20. Describe any personal factors that contributed to accident.

   _____
   _____
   _____
   _____

21. What applicable personal protective equipment (PPE) was being used? _____
   _____Did PPE fail? ☐ Yes ☐ No

22. What personal protective equipment should have been used? _____
   _____Was proper PPE available? ☐ Yes ☐ No

23. Corrective actions: what can be done to prevent a recurrence of similar incidents? _____
   _____
   _____
   _____
   _____

24. Describe in detail what happened. (Specify all machinery, chemicals or tools involved.) _____
   _____
   _____
   _____
   _____
   _____
   _____
   _____
   _____
   _____
   _____
   _____
   _____
   _____
   _____
   _____
   _____
   _____

PREPARED BY   DATE: / /   APPROVED BY   DATE: / /
NAME _____   NAME: _____
TITLE _____   TITLE _____
SIGNATURE _____   SIGNATURE _____

Figure 4.6 Sample supervisor's accident report form *(continued)*

```
Name of Injured _____ Date of Accident _____ Time _____
Seriousness:    ☐ Lost Time    ☐ Doctor    ☐ First Aid Only    ☐ Near Miss
Nature of Injury_____
What Happened? _____
_____
_____

What acts and conditions were involved (use back also)?
What caused them? How were they corrected?
```

Unsafe Act/Condition/Symptom	Possible/Probable Cause	Correction/Suggested Correction
1.		
2.		
3.		
4.		
5.		

Supervisor _____ Department _____

Figure 4.7 Supervisor's report of accident investigation

	Circle One	
1. Was it on time?	Yes – 5 pts.	No – 0 pts.
2. Was seriousness indicated?	Yes – 5 pts.	No – 0 pts.
3. Does it say where it happened?	Yes – 5 pts.	No – 0 pts.
4. Can you tell exactly what the injury is?	Yes – 5 pts.	No – 0 pts.

	Circle One
5. How many acts and conditions are listed?	5 4 3 2 1 0
6. How many causes are identified?	5 4 3 2 1 0
7. How many corrections were made or suggested?	5 4 3 2 1 0
8. How many of the listed corrections would have prevented this accident?	5 4 3 2 1 0
9. How many corrections are permanent in nature?	5 4 3 2 1 0
10. In how many of the corrections listed is the supervisor now doing something differently?	5 4 3 2 1 0

Total of Circled Points _____
Multiply X 2 _____

Reviewed by _____ SCORE _____
General Manager

Figure 4.8 Investigation rating sheet

In this chapter, we'll ask you to investigate incidents under the Multiple Causation Theory rather than the Domino Theory. The form used should be similar to the one shown in figure 4.7. This form, we believe, will force you to look for as many as five underlying causes for the incident investigated. We also urge your boss to rate your identification of causes (see figure 4.8).

What Should Be Investigated?

An incident that causes death or serious injury obviously should be thoroughly investigated. The "near incident" that might have caused death or serious injury is equally important from a safety standpoint and should be investigated; for example, the breaking of a crane hook or a scaffold rope or an explosion associated with a pressure vessel.

Each investigation should be made as soon after the incident as possible. A delay of only a few hours may permit important evidence to be destroyed or removed, intentionally or unintentionally. Also, the results of the investigation should be made known quickly to the entire workforce; their "lessons learned" value is greatly increased by promptness.

Any epidemic of minor injuries demands study. A particle of emery in the eye or a scratch from handling sheet metal may be a very simple case. The immediate cause may be obvious, and the loss of time may not exceed a few minutes. But if cases of this or any other type occur frequently in the plant or in your department, an investigation might be made to determine the underlying causes.

The Key Facts in Safety Incidents

We have concentrated up to this point on root causes. But, it could be your company needs additional information in an investigation. There is no federal OSHA standard on incident investigation. Practices are explained in the American National Standards Institute (ANSI) standard Z16.2-1995, *Information Management for Occupational Safety and Health* (the most recent update).

ANSI/ASSP/ISO 45001-2018, clause 8, provides guidance on the operational planning and control requirements relating to the OH&S management system. And, according to Clause 10.2 Incident, nonconformity and corrective action, the organization should have a process in place for reporting and investigating incidents and other nonconformities, and for taking action to correct them and deal with their consequences. Incidents include near misses, injuries, ill health, and damage to property and equipment. Nonconformities include protective equipment malfunctioning, failure to follow legal requirements, failure to follow prescribed procedures, and a contractor behaving in an unsafe manner on-site.

Also, robust systems need to be in place to ensure that accidents are adequately investigated and appropriate lessons are learned. ISO 14001 and ANSI/ASSP/ISO 45001 both require the organization to put in place procedures to respond to environmental and safety-related nonconformances.

The system needs to take account of injury or damage to employees, visitors, contractors, and members of the public, as well as looking at property damage. There needs to be a thorough investigation of all incidents so that the root causes of the problem may be properly understood.

Data needs to be gathered and records maintained of all stages in the investigation process. It is vital that relevant corrective action be put in place to address problems that have arisen. This action should be reviewed through the risk assessment process prior to implementation; after all, the intention is not to make an unsafe situation worse (ISO 45001-2018).

The ANSI/ASSP Z10-2019 *Occupational Health and Safety Management Systems* standard requires "a process shall be established and implemented to assess health and safety hazards and the level of risk for identified hazards. Priorities are to be set based on the level of risk, potential for system improvements, standards, regulations and potential business consequences. Underlying causes related to system deficiencies are to be identified as well" (Johnson 2019).

Identifying Patterns

You should identify certain key facts about each injury or illness and the incident that produced it. These facts are to be recorded on a form that will permit summarization to show general patterns of injury and incident occurrence in as great analytical detail as possible. These patterns are intended to serve as guides to the areas, conditions, and circumstances to which incident prevention efforts may be directed most profitably. Today, predictive analytics software allows patterns to be plotted and analyzed to be proactive in targeting preventive measures. Analytics include:

1. *Nature of injury/illness*—the type of physical injury/illness incurred
2. *Part of body*—the part of the injured person's body directly affected by the injury
3. *Source of injury/illness*—the object, substance, exposure, or bodily motion that directly produced or inflicted the injury/illness
4. *Event or exposure*—the manner in which the injury/illness was produced or inflicted by the source of the injury/illness
5. *Secondary source of injury/illness*—the machine, equipment, object, or substance that either generated the source of the injury/illness or was related to the event or exposure
6. *Occupation of employee*—uses the US Bureau of the Census occupational classification system to describe the kind of work in which the employee is engaged

7. *Industry of worker*—describes the kind of business in which the employer is engaged according to the North American Industrial Classification System (NAICS)
8. *International Statistical Classification of Diseases and Related Health Problems (ICD) coding*—it is suggested (though not required) that for a more comprehensive recordkeeping and surveillance system, injuries/illnesses should also be classified according to the World Health Organization's International Statistical Classification of Diseases and Related Health Problems (ICD). The 11th revision of the ICD was released in June 2018.

As you can see, these categories are included in the form in figure 4.4.

Figure 4.9 is a checklist of these categories. In addition to unearthing causes in your investigations, your company may want additional information from this checklist so it can better see patterns of incidents in the company as a whole.

Costs of Safety Incidents

Cost information about incidents is often needed. Some proposed safety corrections may be accepted or rejected on the basis of their return on investment (ROI). While most executives want to make their company a safe place to work, they are also responsible for profits. Usually executives are, and should be, reluctant to spend money for incident control unless they can save at least as much as they spend. Former Alcoa CEO Paul O'Neill is an exception. For example, when asked if improving productivity was part of his plan when replacing equipment so people didn't get hurt, O'Neill said: "I think that had the benefit of improving productivity, but that was not the primary objective; it was a secondary consequence. But, yes, oftentimes when you take risk out, you take out unexpected events."

O'Neill's primary objective was (Friedlander 2016):

> I started by articulating the idea that we should be an injury-free workplace, because almost every organization that I know really well, like Alcoa, believes that accidents are inevitable. I don't believe that's right. (Injury-free) is a beginning place for providing an idea that everyone in an organization can be connected to, because, in truth, nobody really wants to be hurt. . . . If you can connect with people on the level that is innately human, it establishes kind of a first link in a highway that can connect aspirational goals for everything in an organization: to be the best in the work at everything you do. And personal safety, individual safety, is kind of the first step.

Still, most organizations today operate on the premise that without information on the costs of incidents, it is impossible to estimate the savings through incident control.

1. NATURE OF INJURY

Foreign body	Strain and sprain	Amputation	Dermatitis
Cut	Fracture	Puncture wound	Ganglion
Bruises and contusions	Burns	Hernia	Abrasions
			Others_____

2. PART OF BODY

Head and Neck	**Upper Extremities**	**Body**	**Lower Extremities**
Scalp	Shoulder	Back	Hips
Eyes	Arms (Upper)	Chest	Thigh
Ears	Elbow	Abdomen	Legs
Mouth, teeth	Forearm	Groin	Knee
Neck	Wrist	Others_____	Ankle
Face	Hand		Feet
Skull	Fingers and thumb		Toes
Others_____	Others_____		Others_____

3. ACCIDENT TYPE

Struck against (rough or sharp objects, surfaces etc., exclusive of falls)	Struck by sliding, falling or other moving objects	Overexertion (resulting in strain, hernia. etc.)	Inhalation, absorption, ingestion. poisoning, etc.
Struck by flying objects	Caught in (on or between)	Slip (not a fall)	Contact with electric current
	Fall on same level	Contact with temperature extremes, burns	Others_____
	Fall to different level		

4. HAZARDOUS CONDITION

Improperly or inadequately guarded	Defective tools, equipment, substances	Hazardous arrangement	Poor housekeeping
Unguarded	Unsafe design or construction	Improper illumination	Congested area
		Improper ventilation	Others_____.
		Improper dress	___No unsafe condition

5. AGENCY OF ACCIDENT

Machine	Can and end conveyors (belt, cable, can dividers, chain, twisters, drops, can elevators, etc.)	Hoists and Cranes	Chemicals
Vehicles		Elevators (passenger and freight)	Ladders or scaffolds
Hand tools			Electrical apparatus
Tin and black plate (sheet, stock, or scrap)		Building (door, pillar, wall, window, etc.)	Boilers, pressure vessels
Material work handled (other than tin and black plate)	Conveyors (chutes, belt, gravity)	Floors or level surfaces	Others_____
		Stairs, steps. or platforms	

6. UNSAFE ACT

Operating without authority	Using equipment, tools, materials or vehicles unsafely	Unsafe loading, placing and mixing	Adjusting, clearing jams, cleaning machinery in motion
Failure to warn or secure		Unsafe lifting and carrying (including insecure grip)	
Operating at unsafe speed			Distracting, teasing
Making safety devices inoperative	Failure to use personal protective equipment	Taking an unsafe position	Poor housekeeping
Using defective equipment, materials, tools or vehicles	Failure to use equipment provided (except personal protective equipment)		Others_____.
			___No unsafe act

CONTRIBUTING FACTORS

Disregard of instructions	Lack of knowledge or skill	Failure to report to medical department	Others_____.
Bodily defects	Act of other than injured		___No contributing factor

Figure 4.9 Checklist for identifying key facts (From *Accident Prevention Manual for Industrial Operations*, 7th ed., 1974. Copyright © National Safety Council. Used with permission.)

Work incidents for the purpose of cost analysis fall into two general categories: (1) incidents resulting in work injuries and (2) incidents that cause property damage or interfere with production. No matter what category it falls into or how severe it is, every incident costs every company money. In 2005, the US Department of Labor determined that there were 4.6 injuries per 100 full-time employees in the workplace. Injured employees required an average of 19 therapy visits (Workers' Compensation Research Institute). The average number of workdays lost due to work injuries was nine days and sprains/strains accounted for 40% of the injuries. A work-related injury resulted in an average loss of approximately $38,000, including wages, productivity loss, and medical expenses (National Safety Council 2005). The National Safety Council also documented that the longer you wait to treat workers' compensation injuries, the greater the cost. The average back injury (sprain/strain) can cost more than $10,000 in direct costs (NSC Statistics) and anywhere from $30,000 up to $100,000 in indirect costs (Gagne 2011).

There are two categories of costs: insured and uninsured.

Every organization paying compensation insurance premiums recognizes such an expense as part of the costs of incidents. In some cases, medical expenses, too, may be covered by insurance. These costs are definite, and they are known; they are insured costs.

Insured costs can be obtained directly from the insurance company or they can be estimated by a predetermined formula. Your company may use a system for determining those costs.

Sometimes referred to as "hidden costs," uninsured costs include such expenses as:

- cost of wages paid for time lost by workers who were not injured (These are employees who stopped work to watch or to assist after the incident or to talk about it or who lost time because they needed equipment damaged in the incident or because they needed the output or the aid of the injured worker.)
- cost of damage to material or equipment
- cost of wages paid for time lost by the injured worker, other than workers' compensation payments (Payments made under workers' compensation laws for time lost after the waiting period are not included in this element of cost.)
- extra cost of overtime work necessitated by the incident
- cost of wages paid supervisors for time required for activities necessitated by the incident
- wage cost caused by decreased output of injured worker after return to work
- cost of learning period of a new worker

- uninsured medical cost borne by the company (This cost is usually for medical services provided at the plant dispensary or a local occupational health service provider.)
- cost of time spent by higher supervision and clerical workers on investigations or in the processing of compensation forms
- Other possible costs are damage to the corporate brand, damage to corporate reputation and social responsibility perception, negative media coverage, negative social media posts by employees, public liability claims, rental fees for equipment, loss of profit on contracts canceled or orders lost if the accident causes a net long-term reduction in total sales, loss of bonuses by the company, wages of new employees if the additional hiring expense is significant, excess spoilage (above normal) by new employees.

Figure 4.10 is a form to assist you in estimating the uninsured incident costs. Your company may require you to use such a form.

DEPARTMENT SUPERVISOR'S ACCIDENT COST REPORT

Injury Accident _____

No-injury Accident _____

Date_____ Name of injured worker _____

1. How many other workers (not injured) lost time because they were talking, watching, helping at accident? _____

    About how much time did most of them lose? ____ hours ____ minutes

2. How many other workers (not injured) lost time because they lacked equipment damaged in the accident or because they needed the output or aid of injured worker?
    _____

    About how much time did most of them lose? ____ hours ____ minutes

3. Describe the damage to material or equipment. _____

    Estimate the cost of repair or replacement of above material or equipment $_____

4. How much time did injured worker lose on day of injury for which he was paid?

    _____ hours _____ minutes

5. If operations or machines were made idle:
    Will overtime work be necessary to make up lost production?...............Yes ❑, No ❑.
    Will it be impossible to make up loss of use of machines or equipment?... Yes ❑, No ❑.

    Contractual penalties or other special nonwage costs due to stopping an operation $___

6. How much of supervisor's time was used assisting, investigating, reporting, assigning work, training or instructing a substitute, or making other adjustments? _____ hours _____ minutes

    Name of supervisor _____

    Fill in and send to the safety department no later than day after accident.

Figure 4.10 Department supervisor's accident cost report

Other Approaches to Incident Cause Identification

In chapter 10, other techniques are described that you can use for cause identification and removal. These are:
- Safety Sampling
- Statistical Safety Control
- Technique of Operations Review
- Incident Recall Technique
- Root-Cause Analysis
- Issue-Based Information System
- Function Analysis Diagram
- Fault Tree Analysis
- Fishbone Diagram
- Failure Modes and Effects Analysis
- The Cause Map
- Apollo Root-Cause Analysis
- The Accimap
- STAMP—Systems-Theoretic Accident Model and Process

When your organization holds you accountable for safety performance, it must measure whether you are actually doing the activities expected of you. If you are expected to do traditional incident investigation, you will also be measured, as indicated earlier, by metrics such as number of investigations performed, timeliness, quality of the investigation, corrective actions implemented to prevent recurrence, and so on.

REFERENCES

Friedlander, Adam. 2016. *Safety and Workers' Compensation Strategies to Unleash Productivity and Profits*. CreateSpace Independent Publishing Platform.

Gagne, R. 2011. "What does a workplace injury cost? Direct Versus Indirect Cost and Their Affect to the Bottom Line." Fit2WRK. http://www.dorn companies.com/downloads/articles/cost_of_a_work_place_injury.pdf.

Heinrich, H.W. 1969. *Industrial Accident Prevention*. New York: McGraw-Hill.

ANSI/ASSP/ISO 45001-2018. 2018. *Occupational Health and Safety Management*. Park Ridge, IL: American Society of Safety Professionals.

Johnson, Dave. 2019. "ANSI-ASSP Z10 *Safety and Health Management System*." *Industrial Safety & Hygiene News*, January 2019.

Krieger, Gary R., and Montgomery, John F. 1997. *Accident Prevention Manual for Business and Industry, Administration & Programs*, 11th ed. Itasca, Illinois: National Safety Council.

National Safety Council. 1974. *Accident Prevention Manual for Industrial Operations*, 7th ed. Chicago: National Safety Council.

Petersen, Dan. 1989. *Techniques of Safety Management: A Systems Approach*. Goshen, NY: Aloray.

Robson, Lynda S., Amick III, Benjamin C., Moser, Cindy et al. 2016. "Important factors in common among organizations making large improvement in OHS performance: Results of an exploratory multiple case study." *Safety Science* 86 (July): 211–227.

Semiklose, Tom. 2014. "Safety: Is It the Sixth "S" in a 5S System?" *Plant Engineering*, May 2014.

CHAPTER 5

Accountability

For more than 80 years, safety professionals have preached the principle of line responsibility in safety work, and yet there are still supervisors today who say, "Safety is the safety manager's job," or "If that's a safety problem, take it up with the safety committee."

Worse yet, when an incident occurs, it goes on the safety specialist's record instead of the record of the line supervisor in the department where it occurred.

Instead of preaching that the line has responsibility, safety professionals should be devising procedures to fix such accountability. When a person is held accountable (is measured) by the manager or supervisor for something, he will accept the responsibility for it. If not held accountable, he will not accept the responsibility. As a result, effort will always be expended in the area being measured.

The attitude of most supervisors today lies somewhere between total acceptance and flat rejection of comprehensive safety incident prevention programs. In her book, *Fierce Conversations*, Susan Scott describes the "accountability ladder," which covers the range, or steps, of accountability: unaware, blame others, excuses, wait and hope, acknowledge reality, "own it," find solutions, and get on with it (Scott 2002).

Most typical is the organization in which line supervisors do not shirk their safety responsibility but do not fully accept it either, nor treat it as they would any of their defined production responsibilities. In most cases, their "safety hat" is worn far less often than their "production hat," their "quality hat," their "cost control hat," or their "performance improvement hat."

In many organizations, safety is not considered as important to the line manager as many other duties that are being performed. In a 2017 survey of safety and health professionals, 43% said making safety part of a supervisor's daily job was one of their biggest challenges. Making supervisors accountable for safety was a challenge for 54% of survey respondents (Johnson 2017).

What shapes a supervisor's attitude toward safety? It depends on abilities, role perception, and effort. All are important, and a supervisor will not turn in the kind of performance we want unless we take all three into account (see figure 5.1).

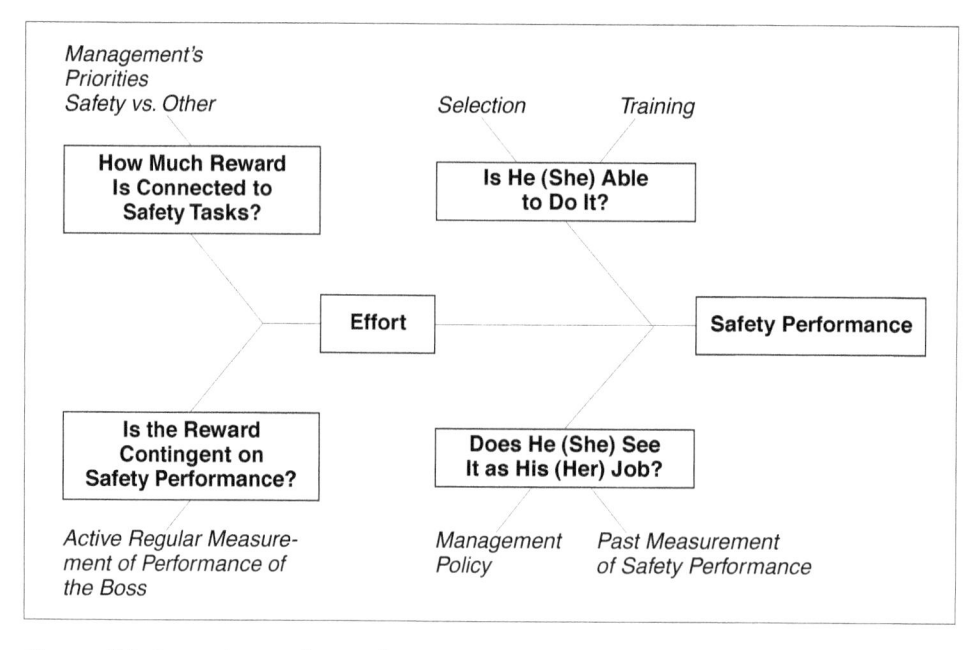

Figure 5.1 Supervisory safety performance model (Adapted from the Lawler and Porter model.)

Two basic factors determine how much effort a person puts into a job: (1) his or her opinion of the value of the rewards, recognition, and positive reinforcement and (2) the connection the person sees between effort and those positives. This is true of a supervisor's total job, as well as of any one segment of it, such as safety.

THE PERFORMANCE MODEL

The Value of Rewards

Rewards for safety performance are no different from rewards for performance in any other area where management asks for performance from the supervisor. While our model focuses primarily on positive rewards (peer acceptance, subordinate approval, enhancing the likelihood of promotion, merit salary increase, a higher bonus, intrinsic feelings of accomplishment, a pat on the back, a compliment from the manager), it also could mean negative rewards (chew-out, lower and harder pat on the back, reprimand).

The main difficulty in developing a reward system is not determining what the rewards will be for performance, but determining when the reward should be given, when the supervisor has "earned" it. When it comes to safety, we have precious few good measurement tools to tell us when a supervisor is performing as expected.

The supervisor looks at the work situation and asks, "What will be my reward if I expend effort and achieve a particular goal?" If supervisors consider the value of the reward that management will give for achieving the goal is great enough, they will decide to expend the effort.

"Reward" here means much more than just financial reward. It includes all the things that motivate people: recognition, chance for advancement, increased pay. Most research into supervisory motivation today indicates that advancement and expanded responsibility are the two greatest motivators. According to a 2015 Gallup survey, nonmonetary motivating factors include: managers communicate clearly and often, managers help set performance goals, managers are open and approachable, and managers focus on developing the strengths of individuals (Harter and Adkins 2015).

In assessing whether rewards really depend upon effort, supervisors might ask themselves the following kinds of questions:

1. Will my efforts here actually bring about the results wanted, or are factors involved that are beyond my control? (The latter seems a distinct possibility in safety.)
2. Will I actually get that reward if I achieve the goal?
3. Will management reward me better for achieving other goals?
4. Will it reward another supervisor (in terms of promotion) because of seniority, regardless of my performance?
5. Is safety really that important to management or are other areas more crucial right now?
6. Can management really effectively measure my performance in safety, or can I let it slide a little without management's knowing?
7. Can I show better results in safety or in some other area?

Line supervisors unconsciously asks these questions and others before determining how much effort to expend on safety and health activities. Supervisors must get the right answers before deciding to make the effort needed for results. Often line supervisors decide that their personal goals would be better achieved by expending efforts in nonsafety areas, and too often their analysis is correct because management is rewarding other areas more than safety.

Changing this situation—this form of culture—is the single greatest task for any organization (management and safety professionals). Change can be achieved by instituting better measurement of line safety performance; by offering better rewards for line safety achievement; and by ensuring that accountability for safety activities is in place at all the levels of the organization, including for the senior executives.

Ability

Job performance does not depend simply on the energy and effort that supervisors expend. It also depends on the abilities they bring to the task, both inherent capabilities and specialized knowledge in the particular field of endeavor. In safety incident prevention, this means that we must ensure, through training, that line supervisors have sufficient safety knowledge to oversee their employees and the conditions under which these people work. In most industries, lack of knowledge is not a problem, because line supervisors usually know far more about safety than they apply. Supervisors can achieve remarkable results on their incident records merely by applying their supervisory knowledge, even if they have little safety knowledge. If a manager does not have adequate safety knowledge, the problem is easily remedied through training.

Role Perception

Role perception is even more important than ability. Line supervisors' perceptions of their safety role determine the direction in which they apply their efforts. Lawler and Porter describe a good role perception as one in which supervisors' views concerning placement of effort correspond closely with the views of those who will be evaluating performance (Porter and Lawler 1968).

In safety, role perception has to do with whether line supervisors know what management wants in terms of incident prevention and whether they know what their duties are. In evaluating role perception, the safety professional should search for answers to some questions about the organization and about each line supervisor in it. These questions concern the content and effectiveness of management's policy on safety, the adequacy of supervisory training, company safety procedures, and the systems used to fix accountability. There are four key considerations.

1. Is the required performance clearly defined?
2. Is the accountability system in place? (Here we are looking at how the person is measured and rewarded.)
3. Does each person know how to do what is expected (self-efficacy)?
4. Is the perceived reward enough to capture the person's attention and ensure performance?

Supervisory Performance

What drives performance is supervisors' perceptions of what the boss wants done—their perception of how the boss will measure them, and their perception of how they will be rewarded for that performance. Research shows these questions dictate supervisory performance (Myers 1966):

- What is the expected action?
- What is the expected reward?
- How are the two connected?
- What is the numbers game? (How is performance measured?)
- How will my actions affect me today and in the future?

Accountability Systems

Any accountability system that defines, validly measures, and adequately rewards will work. Here are some positive results of practicing a constructive approach to accountability (Performance Management n.d.):

- improved performance
- more employee participation and involvement
- increased feelings of competency
- increased employee engagement to the work
- more creativity and innovation
- higher employee morale and satisfaction with the work

The following are some accountability system examples.

SCRAPE

The System of Counting and Rating Accident Prevention Effort (SCRAPE) is a systematic method of measuring the safety incident prevention effort. It involves tight accounting for safety and health tasks. Most companies measure accountability through analysis of results. Monthly incident reports at most plants suggest supervisors should be judged by the number and the cost of incidents that occur under their jurisdiction. We should also judge line supervisors by what they do to control losses. SCRAPE is one simple way of doing this. It is as simple as deciding what supervisors are to do and measuring to see that they do it.

The first step in SCRAPE is to determine specifically what the line supervisors are to do in safety. Normally, this falls into the categories of (1) making physical inspections of the department, (2) training or coaching people, (3) investigating accidents, (4) attending meetings of the employees' manager, (5) establishing safety contacts/one-on-one conversations with the people, and (6) orienting new people. There could be many other tasks, however.

Every week, each supervisor will fill out a small form (see figure 5.2).

Management, on the basis of this form, spot-checks the quality of the work done in all six areas and rates the incident prevention effort.

With a SCRAPE system, there is tight accountability and little to no flexibility. Each supervisor is required to engage in the same activities, as indicated in

```
Department _____ Week of _____
(1) Inspection made on _,_____ # corrections _____
(2) 5-minute safety talk on _____ # present _____
(3) # accidents _____ # investigated _____
    Corrections _____
(4) Individual contacts
Names _____
    _____
    _____
(5) Management meeting attended on _____
(6) New person (names):          Oriented on (dates):
    _____            _____
    _____            _____
    _____            _____
```

Figure 5.2 The SCRAPE system

the paragraph above. Obviously, SCRAPE fits well in a top-down company with a relatively direct, authoritarian style. It can also be used in early installation of an accountability system, and flexibility can follow later.

SAFETY BY OBJECTIVES (SBO)

Safety and health processes have failed in some essential ways. Many processes are far from producing behavior that could be considered goal-directed. Responsibilities, even with a written policy, are often unclear. Participation in goal-setting and decision-making is almost nonexistent. Feedback and reinforcement are slow and often not connected to the amount of effort expended in safety (especially when the number or the severity of incidents is the measuring stick). Planning is minimal, and while results are often measured, freedom of decision or control is seldom left to the lower levels. And imagination and creativity are rare commodities in most safety and health processes. The principles of management by objectives (MBO), adapted to safety processes (SBO), can overcome some of these failings (see figure 5.3).

These are the steps of SBO:

1. Obtain management supervision agreement (with staff safety consultation) on objectives. In the implementation stages of an SBO process, the agreement will emphasize not only *results* objectives but also *activities* objectives. Initially, the agreement reached will be on strategies and objectives (what practices, tools, and resources to be used, as well as results). Once the process is under way, only objectives are agreed to.

2. Give each supervisor an opportunity to perform. Once agreements are completed, leave supervisors alone to proceed with their action plans. Require only progress reports.
3. Let supervisors know how they are doing. With quantified objectives (either result or activity objectives must be quantified) give regular, current, and pertinent feedback so supervisors can adjust their plans when they see the need.
4. Help, guide, and train supervisors. Both management and safety staff fulfill this role. The safety staff provides the subject matter and safety technical expertise, while management provides managerial help when asked, guiding supervisors when indicated, and training at the outset.
5. Reward supervisors according to their progress. This requires a reward system that is geared to the progress made toward agreed-upon objectives. The various managerial rewards should be used: pay, status, advancement, recognition.

Going back to the 1960s, the SBO approach has been installed in a variety of different industries: brewing (Adolph Coors Company), chemical (DuPont Corp.), railroading (Union Pacific, Santa Fe), paper (Hoerner-Waldorf), and others (Petersen 1996).

The results, of course, are not uniform. There are some successes and some less successful applications; much depends on the implementation, the commitment of management, and the meaningfulness of the objectives that were set. SBO has, of course, been implemented differently in each organization. Some have left the objective-setting areas wide open—totally up to the supervisors and their managers. Others have limited supervisory choices to certain allowable strategies. One organization's management spelled out 12 areas that were believed to be areas of

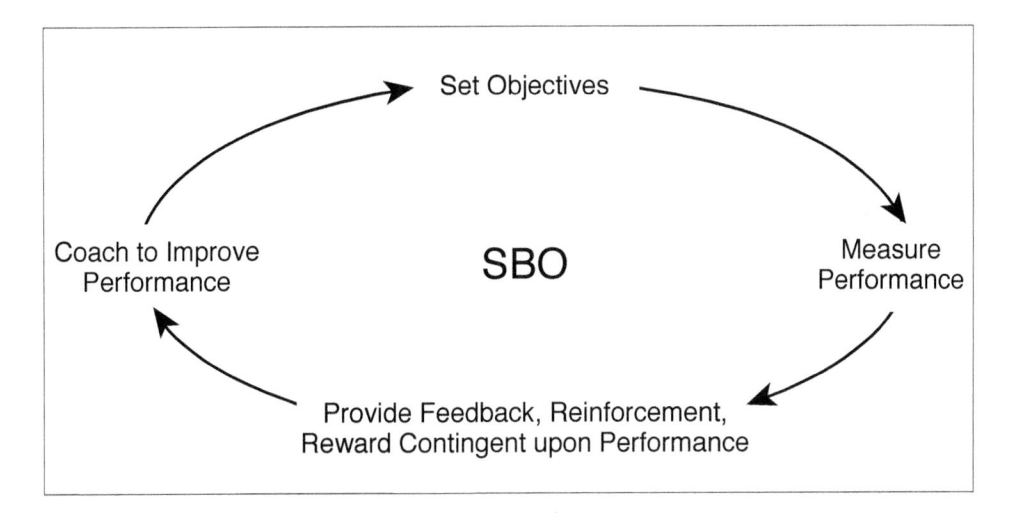

Figure 5.3 The SBO system

slippage in safety efforts. Most have required tasks and also offer additional, optional tasks that a supervisor can select from a menu. Supervisors then set goals for those optional tasks selected.

For the most part, SBO works and continues to work once implemented. One company reported a 75% reduction in the frequency rate of recordable incidents in the first three months of the process. One claimed a six-month savings of $2.3 million. One reported a 67% reduction in incident frequency continuing after three years.

With an SBO system, there is tight accountability and almost total flexibility. Supervisors can select any activities to engage in to satisfy their safety responsibilities, as long as there is mutual agreement with their managers.

A MENU SYSTEM

Many organizations find SCRAPE too top-down in style and SBO too loose and opt for a system halfway between the two known as a Menu system. Here certain tasks are deemed to be mandatory, and others are optional, to be selected from a menu of activities provided by the organization. Figure 5.4 shows the Menu system for

---

XYZ COMPANY
ACCOUNTABILITIES--FIRST LINE SUPERVISOR

GENERAL

The key accountability of the First Level Manager is to carry out the tasks defined below.

TASKS

Required tasks are:

- Hold periodic safety meetings with all employees.
- Include safety status in all work group meetings.
- Inspect department weekly and write safety work orders as required.
- Have at least five one-to-one contacts regarding safety with employees each week.
- Investigate injuries and accidents in accordance with Managing Safety guidelines within 24 hours.

In addition, in agreement with Department Head:

- Select at least two other tasks from a provided list and agree on what measurable performance is acceptable.
- Report on these activities weekly.

WEEKLY SAFETY REPORT

The First Level Manager shall prepare and distribute a Weekly Safety Report in accordance with the format shown in Exhibit 4-6.

MEASURE OF PERFORMANCE

- Successful completion of tasks.

REWARD FOR PERFORMANCE

Safety will be listed as one of the key measures on the Accountability Appraisal Form.

Figure 5.4 First-line supervisor accountabilities—Menu system

one organization, figure 5.5 for shows a system used by another. Figure 5.6 shows the weekly report a supervisor might fill out to send his or her manager that shows task completion.

These are examples employed at the first-line supervisory level. Obviously, the accountability system must be in place at all other levels of the organization.

```
                        ABC COMPANY
            ACCOUNTABILITIES—FIRST LINE SUPERVISOR

• ACCOUNTABILITIES              —STOP Program
   —Accident Investigation       —Safety Improvement Teams
   —Continuous Departmental Inspection  —Positive Reinforcement
   —Employee Communications    • PERFORMANCE MEASUREMENT
   —Employee Training             —100%, Based on Activities
• OPTIONAL ACTIVITIES           • PERFORMANCE WEIGHTING
   —One-to-One Contacts           —20% of Total Performance Appraisal
   —Group Meetings
```

Figure 5.5 First-line supervisor accountabilities

```
            FIRST-LEVEL MANAGER'S WEEKLY SAFETY REPORT
From _____ To _____ Week Ending _____
1. Working Group Safety Meeting
   Date _____ Subject _____
   _____
   _____

2. Department Safety Inspections
   Date _____ Findings _____
   _____
   _____

3. One-To-One Contacts
   Employee _____ Date _____
   Employee _____ Date _____
   Employee _____ Date _____
   Employee _____ Date _____
   Employee _____ Date _____
   Employee _____ Date _____
4. Injury Status
   Name _____ Date _____
   Injury Description _____
   _____
   _____

5. Other Safety Tasks
         Description          Action       Compliance To Goal
   _____
   _____
   _____

Report Distribution: _____ Staff Manager
                     _____ Employee Relations Manager
```

Figure 5.6 First-level manager's safety report

Middle Management

The basic performance model applies here also. Middle managers also must have clearly defined roles, valid measures of performance, and rewards contingent on performance sufficient to get their attention.

Performance at this level is critical to safety success. Middle managers (the persons to whom the first-line supervisors report) play a more central role than the supervisors because they make the system run or allow it to fail. The middle manager's role is threefold:
- to ensure subordinate performance
- to ensure the quality of that performance
- to do some things that visually say safety is important

In reality, very little is known about how middle managers take safety into account in their daily operations and the challenges they face. It has been suggested that middle managers act as "informal safety auditors" who are able to provide "soft" alarm systems in safety management. This is also referred to as middle managers' safety wisdom—the ability to judge, make decisions, influence others, and manage quantitative and qualitative information in order to maintain safety (Callari, Bieder, and Kirwan 2019).

Examples of accountability systems at the middle-management level are shown in figures 5.7 and 5.8.

Top Management

At the executive level, we have a different ball game. While the basic performance model may be similar, it is certain that some inputs are more important at the top. The executive's individual traits (genuine executive interest) are a large factor, and role perception (believing they personally have a role) is crucial. Clearly, visibly demonstrated management commitment to safety and health is essential. But what drives performance? The classic answer is money—though that answer is probably less true than we think. Different executives are driven to achieve successful safety and health performance for different reasons.

There is probably more interest and commitment at the executive level today than we have ever seen before. Research supports this. In 2017 research, 58% of safety and health professionals surveyed said senior executives spend more time on safety and health issues and activities than they did 10 or 15 years ago (Johnson 2017).

Perhaps catastrophic incidents such as Bhopal (1984), Chernobyl (1986), space shuttle Challenger (1986), space shuttle Columbia (2003), the Texas City refinery explosion (2005), Deepwater Horizon (2010), the Rana Plaza factory collapse

```
ABC COMPANY
DEPARTMENT MANAGER
```

- ACCOUNTABILITIES
    - Assure Supervisory Performance by Receiving and Reacting to Reports
    - Audit Performance Through Spot Checks
    - Maintain Departmental Budget
    - Visibly Participate in Programs
    - Develop Safety Management Knowledge and Skills in Subordinates
- OPTIONAL ACTIVITIES
    - Participate in Audits
    - Participate in Inspections
    - Initiate One-to-One Contacts
    - Create Ad Hoc Committees
    - Support Recognition Programs
- PERFORMANCE MEASUREMENT
    - 25-50%, Numbers
    - 50-75%, Audit & Activities
- PERFORMANCE WEIGHTING
    - 20% of Total Performance Appraisal

Figure 5.7 Department manager's accountabilities

```
ABC COMPANY
DEPARTMENT MANAGER
```

GENERAL

The key accountability of the Department Managers is to ensure that the plans and programs of the XYZ Company Safety System are carried out in their area.

TASKS

- Review reports from their area on task accomplishments and act accordingly.
- Assess task performance defined for subordinate managers and feedback as appropriate.
- Engage in some self-defined tasks that can readily be seen by the work force as demonstrating a high priority to employee safety.
- Develop safety management knowledge and skills in subordinate managers.
- Make one-to-one safety contacts with hourly employees.
- Participate in department safety inspections.

PERIOD SAFETY REPORT

Department Managers shall prepare and distribute a periodic safety report in accordance with the format shown.

MEASURES OF PERFORMANCE

- Safety audit results for area(s) of accountability.
- The 13-period rolling total injury frequency record for area(s) of responsibility.

REWARD FOR PERFORMANCE

- Safety will be listed as one of the key measures on the Accountability Appraisal Form.

Figure 5.8 Department manager accountabilities and performance measures

(2013), and Amtrak fatal accidents (2015, 2016) explain some of this increased commitment. The safety professional who does not take advantage of this interest is missing a major opportunity.

While interested in safety and health, an executive typically does not have the foggiest idea of how to ensure safety and health performance. This is the safety professional's job—to spell out the role and to spell out the system.

A SAFETY BALANCED SCORECARD

The trend today is toward using multiple measures to assess safety system effectiveness. These usually include at least three measures:

1. the accident record
2. the audit score
3. perception survey results

There could be other measures in a scorecard, for instance:

4. behavior sampling results
5. percentage to goal on system improvements
6. dollars spent (claim costs, total costs of safety, etc.)

Procter & Gamble's scorecard contains two measures: the OSHA incident rate and Key Element ratings (basically an audit score).

Other organizations are experimenting with other mixes for their scorecard of metrics to assess safety system effectiveness:

- Navistar uses eight: incident frequency rate, lost-time case rate, disability costs, percent improvement in safety performance, actual healthcare costs, absenteeism, short-term disability, and long-term disability.
- Kodak sets goals and measures in seven areas: lost time, plant operations matrix (percent to goal), employee surveys, assessment findings, integration matrix, vendor selection, and "best in class" (a benchmark metric).

Many other possible metrics, both leading and trailing, are discussed in detail in a new book on metrics from the Metrics Task Force of Organization Resources Counselors (now known as ORCHSE Strategies). What is true of safety system content, is also true of safety metrics: there is no one right way to do things. Each organization must determine its own "right way."

In addition, after deciding the components to be included in the scorecard, you must decide how each component should be weighted, making it possible to come up with a single metric, if so desired.

We have two serious problems. One, we must figure out what should go into our scorecard and two, we must convince our middle and upper management about the appropriateness of the scorecard elements. Safety professionals must create dissonance in their organizations with status-quo metrics from the CEO down. Then, they must install the selected scorecard to replace what is most often the current, single metric—the accident record.

As Petersen noted (Petersen 2001), "At some point, we will have to do this. Probably, the sooner we start down this route, the better."

No matter which system an organization uses to assess safety system effectiveness, the entire accountability system starts with a clear definition of roles.

LINE HIERARCHY ROLES

The roles of several layers of the line hierarchy are as follows:

1. The role of the first-line supervisor is to carry out some agreed-upon tasks to an acceptable level of performance.
2. The roles of middle and upper management are to
    (a) ensure subordinate performance
    (b) ensure the quality of that performance
    (c) personally engage in some agreed-upon tasks
3. The role of the executive is to visibly demonstrate the priority of safety and health.
4. The role of the safety and health staff is to advise and assist each of the above.

The supervisor's role as defined above is relatively singular and simple—to carry out the safety and health tasks agreed upon. What are those tasks? While it may depend upon the organization, safety and health tasks might fall into these categories:

Traditional Tasks	Nontraditional Tasks
inspect	give positive strokes
hold meetings	ensure employee participation
perform one-on-ones	do worker safety analyses
investigate incidents	do force-field analyses
do job safety and health analyses	assess climate and priorities
make observations	perform crisis intervention
enforce rules	
keep records	

In addition to the above, supervisors no doubt will be responsible for certain day-to-day actions not easily spelled out or measured, following standard operation procedures (SOPs). How well do they understand their responsibilities? Supervisors often simply do not know what is expected of them, particularly in safety and health. Almost always they have no idea of the extent of their authority, and usually they are unclear as to how their performance is being measured, again particularly in safety and health.

As mentioned earlier, the role of the supervisor is to engage regularly (daily) in some predefined tasks. What are those tasks? There are many that have been traditionally perceived as crucial and others thought of today as very meaningful while somewhat nontraditional. For the most part, all of this is based mostly on tradition and opinion.

What are the crucial safety and health tasks for a supervisor? What must a supervisor do regularly to achieve safety and health success? The answer to this is that we do not know. Research does indicate there are some common expectations. A 2017 survey (Johnson 2017) revealed:

- 85% expected supervisors to find and fix hazards
- 84% expected them to observe employee safety-related behavior
- 77% expected supervisors to conduct accident investigations
- 74% expected them to conduct safety meetings, daily briefings, and toolbox talks
- 72% expected supervisors to conduct department inspections
- 69% expected them to conduct employee safety training
- 64% expected supervisors to discipline employees for at-risk behavior and safety rules violations

An important point to remember: don't overload supervisors with safety and health commitments. Overloading can lead to the assertion, "You're not being accountable." Mark Samuel, author of the article "Unleash the Power of an Accountable Organization," lists these ways to keep commitments (Samuel 2012):

- Identify the desired outcomes for your performance and communication at work.
- Develop a select number of "nonnegotiable" commitments.
- Create "recovery plans" or your best responses that you will use if you find yourself in jeopardy of breaking one of these commitments or agreements.
- Assess any new commitments that might interfere with existing commitments.
- Acknowledge yourself for every commitment you keep and every commitment you break.

Safety and health-related activities for supervisors will vary widely organization by organization. As previously stated, there is no one-size-fits-all, magic safety and health process. In reality, it does not make any difference what a supervisor does, as long as something is done regularly, daily, to emphasize the importance of safety and health. (Review chapter 3 on the safety and health job and chapter 4 on key safety and health tasks.)

THE BOTTOM LINE REGARDING RESPONSIBILITY AND ACCOUNTABILITY

Supervisors are agents of the legal entity of an employer; therefore, supervisors of employees are responsible for protecting the safety and health of employees. It is well established in the historical management of safety and health in the workplace that the primary responsibility of the protection of an employee falls to the direct employer. This is well established by a century of history of workers' compensation practices in the United States and was clearly recognized by the OSH Act in 1970. Section 4, Applicability, reads,

> Nothing in this Act shall be construed to supersede or in any manner affect any workmen's compensation law or to enlarge or diminish or affect in any other manner the common law or statutory rights, duties, or liabilities of employers and employees under any law with respect to injuries, diseases, or death of employees arising out of, or in the course of, employment. Section 5. Duties. (a) Each employer—(1) shall furnish to each of his employees employment and a place of employment which are free from recognized hazards that are causing or are likely to cause death or serious physical harm to his employees; (2) shall comply with occupational safety and health standards promulgated under this Act (OSHA 1970; Henshaw et al. 2007).

Employers are generally considered sophisticated users of tools, materials, and processes and have care, custody, and control of employer workplaces. Such employers are to take whatever measures necessary based upon the available knowledge at the time to protect their employees in any and all employer-controlled workplaces even if the employees are operating onsite at other employer premises.

With the changing nature of today's multi-employer worksites, OSHA has continued to maintain its longstanding policy that the employer (and no one else) continues to be responsible for the protection of its employees. One of the first citations issued by OSHA regarding multi-employer worksites, subsequently challenged by a party of a multi-employer worksite, appears to have been in 1975, when such OSHA citations were dismissed (OSHRC 1975). With multi-employer worksites more common by the 1990s, OSHA has taken various actions to address this fundamentally changing structure of employer relationships at many industrial and commercial worksites in the United States. However, while recognizing that on multi-employer worksites there may well be multiple "exposing, creating, correcting, or controlling" employers that might simultaneously be cited by OSHA for violation of any particular OSHA standard, OSHA has continued to maintain its longstanding, important social policy that the employer (and no one else) continues to be responsible for the protection of its employees (OSHA 1999). Summarizing the bottom line, the supervisor of an employee is the person in the best position to protect the safety and health of an employee and is recognized as the agent or representative of the legal entity with the responsibility for protecting the safety and health of employees. Top management can mandate protection and provide resources, and safety departments can help with programs, processes, and systems, but at the end of the day the responsibility for the protection of the safety and health of employees falls on the supervisor.

REFERENCES

Callari, Tiziana C. , Corrine Bieder, and Barry Kirwan. 2019. "What is it like for a middle manager to take safety into account? Practices and challenges." *Safety Science* 113 (March): 19–29. https://doi.org/10.1016/j.ssci.2018.10.025.

Harter, Jim, and Amy Adkins. 2015. "Employees Want a Lot More From Their Managers." Gallup News, April 8, 2015. http://news.gallup.com/businessjournal/182321/employees-lot-managers.aspx.

Henshaw, John L., Shannon H. Gaffney, Amy K. Madl et al. 2007. "The Employer's Responsibility to Maintain a Safe and Healthful Work Environment: An Historical Review of Societal Expectations and Industrial Practices." *Employee Responsibilities and Rights Journal* 19 (3): 173–192.

Johnson, Dave. 2017. "State of the EHS Nation 2017." Reader Survey. *Industrial Safety & Hygiene News*, October 2017.

Scott, Susan. 2002. *Fierce Conversations: Achieving Success at Work & Life, One Conversation at a Time.* New York: Viking.

Myers, M. Scott. 1966. "Conditions for Manager Motivation." *Harvard Business Review*, January 1966.

Performance Management. n.d. US Office of Personnel Management. Accessed March 3, 2020. https://www.opm.gov/policy-data-oversight/performance-management/.

Petersen, Dan. 1996. *Safety by Objectives: What Gets Measured and Rewarded Gets Done*, 2nd ed. New York: Van Nostrand Reinhold.

Petersen, Dan. 2001. "The Safety Scorecard: Using Multiple Measures to Judge Safety System Effectiveness." *EHS Today*, May 2001.

Samuel, Mark. 2012. "Being Indispensable: When Keeping Commitments Undermines Your Accountability." Huffington Post blog, June 6, 2012. Accessed March 27, 2019. https://www.huffingtonpost.com/mark-samuel/accountability_b_1408758.html.

Occupational Safety and Health Administration (OSHA). 1970. US Occupational Safety and Health Act. Public Law 91-596. 84 STAT. 1590. 91st Congress, S.2193. December 29, 1970.

Occupational Safety and Health Administration (OSHA). 1999. US Department of Labor. OSHA Instruction. Multi-Employer Citation Policy. CPL 02-0.124, 12/10/1999.

Occupational Safety and Health Review Commission (OSHRC).1975. *Secretary of Labor v Grossman Steel and Aluminum Corp.* OSHRC Docket No. 12775.

Porter, Lyman W., and Edward E. Lawler, 1968. *Managerial Attitudes and Performance.* Homewood, IL: R.D. Irwin.

CHAPTER **6**

Leadership

Much has been written about leadership and what makes a good leader. It seems the more we read about leadership, the more confusing it gets.

Let's try to cut through this confusion right from the start of this chapter.

Without writing an entire book on leadership, here are the ten most common leadership styles ("10 Common Leadership Styles" n.d.):

- coaching leadership—underutilized because it is time-intensive
- visionary leadership—the ability to set goals and drive progress through trust
- servant leadership—emphasis is on employee satisfaction and collaboration
- autocratic leadership—expect employees to do exactly what they're asked
- hands-off leadership—delegate many tasks, spend little time on supervision
- democratic leadership—ask for input, consider feedback, then make your decision
- pacesetter leadership—short on mentorship, focus on high standards and hitting goals
- transformational leadership—clear communication, employee motivation, commitment to the big picture
- transactional leadership—reward for success, discipline for failure
- bureaucratic leadership—focus on responsibilities, little need for collaboration

TRANSFORMATIONAL LEADERSHIP

Of the ten leadership styles, transformational leadership is the most discussed in safety today. Why? We are in the era of fast-paced business change. Change is a constant. Many organizations are undertaking fundamental, strategic, systemwide transformation to keep pace with disruptive forces and to keep aligned with changing business conditions. And safety and health, to remain integrated with overall organizational transformation, must be in alignment with this leadership style.

Supervisors are critical lynchpins in transformational leadership, because engagement is key to transformational success, and supervisors are on the front lines of engaging employees. A transformational leader empowers workers to engage in the work process, in the safety and health processes—to go beyond their own self-interest. This is accomplished when the leader personally cares about each worker.

The critical skills of transformational leadership are listening, communicating, caring, collegiality, and engagement. You listen for meaning and feeling, not just facts. You speak in the language of your employees. You're open to feedback and criticism and start meetings with safety staff to communicate its importance.

Caring is the most important characteristic of transformational leadership. You demonstrate genuine, visible concern for your employees. You're sensitive to their needs and empathetic, and you interact with all levels of the workforce.

Demonstrating a sense of equality among those you supervise is also key. You can mix with all levels in a friendly manner; relate to all levels and make them feel at ease; and show gratitude, sympathy, or empathy at all levels.

Finally, transformational leaders demonstrate a personal connection with their subordinates. You help them to commit and achieve goals, link workers' needs with the organization's needs, and convey a sense of worth to those you supervise—they are not just cogs in a wheel (Fulwiler 2013).

Embrace Your Role

It's clear today that the best supervisors really operate as leaders. They see their role, without getting much training, and figure out their job has evolved into being performance managers and team builders. They are charged, formally or informally, with developing knowledge and skills and collaboration. They are comfortable with professional relationships with their people that involve sincere caring.

Supervisors are often business leaders, helping their people understand the business impact of their actions, such as cutting corners or not wearing PPE. They help their people understand the big picture—the business they are part of.

How do you lead your employees to be safe and engage in safe behaviors?

Leadership is crucial to positive safety results. Leadership creates and maintains the culture that determines what *will* and *will not* work in safety and health efforts. Leadership is infinitely more important than policy—at all levels of the organization.

A leader can be staff or line. The focus is not on power but on the ability to influence others within the organization. Through actions and decisions, a leader sends clear and consistent messages to his area of the organization regarding which policies are important. Through his actions, systems, measures, and rewards, a leader clearly determines whether desired safety outcomes will be achieved in his area of responsibility (Petersen 2003).

Leading Change

Dr. John Kotter outlined his now famous eight-step process for leading change (which would include leading safety) in his book *Leading Change* (Kotter 1996):

1. Establish a sense of urgency; identify realities; identify and discuss crises, potential crises (safety incidents), or major opportunities (to improve safety).
2. Create the guiding coalition, a group, or a team with enough power to lead the change.
3. Develop a vision and strategy to direct the change and achieve the vision.
4. Communicate the change vision; constantly communicate (the safety message); have your guiding team (perhaps the safety committee) model the behavior expected of employees.
5. Empower broad-based action; eliminate obstacles; change systems or structures that undermine the change vision; encourage nontraditional ideas, activities, and actions.
6. Generate short-term wins, visibly recognize and reward those who made the wins possible.
7. Consolidate gains and produce more change; reinvigorate (the safety process) with new projects, themes, and change agents.
8. Anchor new approaches in the culture, articulate the connections between new (safe) behaviors and organizational success.

Impact Skills

Zenger/Folkman, a leadership development consultancy, conducted a survey of 332,860 bosses, peers, and subordinates and asked what skills have the greatest impact on a leader's success (Zenger and Folkman 2014). The same competencies were selected as most important for supervisors, middle managers, and senior managers. The top eight, in rank order are:

1. inspires and motivates others
2. displays high integrity and honesty
3. solves problems and analyzes issues
4. drives for results
5. communicates powerfully and prolifically
6. collaborates and promotes teamwork
7. builds relationships
8. displays technical or professional expertise

No one has the magic key to understanding all people—knowing how to get them to want to do what needs to be done. All we can do is attempt to gain some insights.

Insights from Coaching

Didier Deschamps, the coach of France's national men's World Cup 2018 winning soccer team, says you gain insight into your people by knowing how to adapt (Lyttleton 2017): "Adapting to the group that you have at your disposal; adapting to the place where you are working; adapting to the local environment. This is crucial: adaptability. It means being aware of the strengths and weaknesses inside the group; being aware of all the outside factors that can influence your sphere; and adapting to all of that, then modifying what you've done and not being afraid to change."

Deschamps thinks about every word he utters and is acutely aware of his body language and how he delivers his message. "It's not just the words you use, but the way you use them, and the message that puts over. Also, your face, too, and the way you project your message."

Deschamps takes in as much as he can. He has created a circle of trust that both empowers the group and provides him with more information to make better decisions. Every new player called up to the French squad has a one-on-one chat with Deschamps. He tells them what he thinks of them as athletes and what he wants from them. "You have to put time in, to get to know your people better. They have different lives, personalities, cultures, backgrounds, even views on life. So you have to be able to tune into their station. What interests me is to know the person behind all that."

Supervisory Leadership Influences

Let's look at what leadership influences you have as a supervisor. These influences help to mold and shape an employee's decision about how that person will work. Each individual must make this decision, management cannot. But your leadership skills can wield considerable influence.

For example, let us imagine a factory employee named Jim, who slaves over a hot machine all day to produce 275 Super Speed Fishing Worm Untanglers, Size 4. One day, management hands out booklets telling Jim and his fellow workers how they can produce 300 untanglers instead of 275. Nobody in his right mind enjoys making fishing worm untanglers. So Jim hastily skims through the booklet, throws it away, and keeps right on turning out 275 a day.

Management, through you as the supervisor, then sends down an order warning that any employee who fails to produce 300 untanglers a day will be fired. Jim is now powerfully motivated. He finds the booklet is interesting reading after all, and he learns everything in it with ease. He also produces 300 untanglers. You have thus extended an influence that has motivated Jim. You have not only changed his production level, you have also made him interested in reading.

Leaders from top management on down, through stated values, policies, and organizational culture, show that safe performance from employees is desirable. Leadership cannot, however, force a safe performance. Each employee decides for himself whether he will work, how hard he will work, and how safely he will work.

His attitudes shape his decision—attitudes toward himself, his environment, his boss, his company, his entire life situation. His decision is based on his knowledge, his skills, and his peer's attitude toward safety and health, as well as his personal value for safety. As a leader, you can recognize those influences over which you have control as a supervisor and extend your influence wherever possible.

The Influence of Supervisors

Practically all your company's attempts to engage employees go through supervisors. You are, among other things, a funnel. You direct all material and information to the employee. You also direct or carry out the vast majority of training. Everything that is designed to engage employees is applied by you. Obviously, your leadership role is crucial. The supervisor is the key person in any program to create and maintain interest in safety because the supervisor is responsible for translating management's policies into action and for promoting safety activities directly among the employees. How well you meet this responsibility will determine to a large extent how favorably the employees receive the safety activities.

The supervisor's attitude toward safety is a significant factor in the success, not only of specific promotional activities, but also of all safety and health processes, because his or her views will be reflected by the employees in that department.

The supervisor who is sincere and enthusiastic about incident prevention can do more than the safety director to maintain interest.

Conversely, if the supervisor pays only lip service to the program or ridicules any part of it, such an attitude offsets any good that might be done by the safety professional.

Setting a good example—for instance, wearing safety glasses and other personal protective equipment whenever it is required—is one of the most effective ways the supervisor can promote safety.

Teaching safety is an important function of the supervisor. You cannot depend upon safety posters, a few warning signs, or even general rules to do your job of training and supervision. A good balance of basic training and supervision and judicious use of promotional material proves effective. However, the supervisor must first be trained if the supervisor is to be competent.

Supervisors can be most effective in giving facts and personal reminders on safety to employees. This procedure is particularly necessary in the transportation, energy, and utility industries where remote crews and lone workers are on their own.

In any case, supervisors should be encouraged to take every opportunity to exchange ideas on incident prevention with employees, to commend them for their efforts to do the job safely, and to invite them to submit safety suggestions.

Your leadership role is indeed crucial to the success of your company's safety and health results. And your success in carrying out this role depends almost entirely on your leadership skills in dealing with your people. You cannot succeed in safety and health, or in anything else, without people. You need them. You need to understand them, and they need to understand you.

The following are some leadership tools you can employ to improve and sustain safety and health performance.

Employee Safety Analysis

Safety and health professionals and supervisors are generally aware of the concept of job safety analysis: the systematic analysis of specific jobs to spot situations with accident potential. Worker Safety Analysis (WSA) is the systematic analysis of a worker. One tool we can use in worker safety analysis is shown in figure 6.1. Management can devise a form to assist the supervisor in looking systematically at each worker to determine whether an individual is highly likely to make human errors. Are there logical reasons why any particular employee is likely to make such errors? Worker safety analysis can uncover these reasons.

Some of the subjects covered on the form in figure 6.1 are optional; for example, information about life change units (LCUs). These items can be left off a form if the information is not available, although LCU information might be available to a supervisor who knows the people on his team.

A life change unit is a component the Holmes and Rahe Stress Scale developed in the 1960s. Thomas Holmes and Richard Rahe were interested in the influence of stress on the incidence of illness in an individual. They asked participants (who were medical patients) if they had experienced 43 stressful life events. These were the LCUs, and each was given a score that weighted how stressful the event was. Each LCU has a different value of stress. The more LCUs an individual experiences, the higher the score. Higher scores and higher weighted LCUs contribute to a greater likelihood that illness will occur.

LCUs range from the death of a spouse (the highest score) to a minor law infraction (the lowest score). Other examples include pregnancy, beginning or ending school/college, retirement, trouble with work, divorce, being fired, being incarcerated, marriage, vacation, the holiday season, and changes in residence (Holmes and Rahe, 1967).

Worker Safety Analysis (WSA)

Personality type and safety incident risk are also optional in the Worker Safety Analysis and might not be filled in by many. These items may be less valuable, from a safety and health standpoint, than the other items on the form. The value analysis is quite arbitrarily decided by the supervisor and might or might not be useful.

Current motivational analysis is the most valuable item in this form (figure 6.1). The supervisor should look at each item listed and determine what motivational pull it will have on the employee. Included are most of the important determinants of employee performance we have discussed in this book.

The supervisor should consider the current job assignment in terms of the load it places on the person. The last item on the form is force-field analysis; the supervi-

WORKER SAFETY ANALYSIS

Name_____Date _____

Long-term analysis
   Biorhythmic Information (dates to watch): _____
   LCU Information; approximate units accumulated now: _____

Personality and value analysis:
   Personality type _____
   Accident risk _____

                             Key Importance   No Importance
   Value of work
   Value of safety

Current motivational analysis _____Turn ons _____Turn offs
   Peer group _____
   Me (boss relations) _____
   Company policy _____
   Self (personality) _____
   Climate_____
   Job-motivation factors _____
      Achievement_____
      Responsibility _____
      Advancement _____
      Growth _____
      Promotion _____
      Job _____
   Participation _____
   Involvement _____

Current job assignment_____High _____Low
   Pressure involved _____
   Worry or stress
   Information processing need _____
   Hazards faced _____
   Other _____

Force-field analysis:

  Pulls to safety
  ↑
  ↓
  Pulls away from safety

Current assessment:
❏ OK   ❏ Discuss with worker   ❏ Training   ❏ Crisis intervention
                    ❏ Contract   ❏ Behavior modification
❏ Crisis intervention

Figure 6.1 Supervisor's Worker Safety Analysis form

sor may choose to perform a small force-field analysis to determine the current pulls on the employee. The entire worker safety analysis might lead to some disposition, as shown at the bottom of the form.

Obviously, the supervisor who fills out this kind of form will need considerable training in order to understand the concepts involved. The purpose of worker safety analysis is to help the worker, its intent is to spot the causes of human error before an incident can occur.

Use the form to assess each employee. If you choose, use it only as a guideline to your thinking, not as a check-off sheet without any names. Assure over time that each employee is assessed by you.

How to Set Objectives with WSA:
- number of WSAs completed
- percentage of people analyzed, etc.

Measurement:
completion to goal

Reward:
- Performance Appraisal System
- daily numbers game

Dealing with Human-Error Causes

The bottom of the form offers several dispositions. If no real problem is unearthed and no action is indicated, the "OK" box is checked. Other disposition options are: to discuss the analysis with the person, as in the case of a relatively minor problem; to send the person to receive additional training, or to give it yourself; to administer crisis intervention in the event that the analysis reveals something crucial and critical that must be dealt with; to use behavior-based safety; or to draw up a contract for behavioral change. Some of these dispositions will usually require additional comment.

Human error results from one or a combination of three things: (1) overload, which is defined as a mismatch between a person's capacity and the load placed on him/her in a given state; (2) a decision to err; and (3) traps that are left for the worker in the workplace (Petersen 2003).

Overload: A human being cannot help but err if given a heavier workload than a person has the capacity to handle. This overload can be physical, physiological, or psychological.

Decision to err: Reasons for this might include:

1. Due to the employee's current motivational field, it makes more sense to operate unsafely than safely. Peer pressure, pressure to produce, and many other factors might make unsafe behavior seem preferable.
2. The employee's mental condition might lead that person to have a safety incident.
3. The employee just does not believe that he or she will have an accident (low perceived probability).

Traps: Here we're talking about human factors concepts. One trap is incompatibility. The employee errs because his work situation is incompatible with the employee's physique or with what he is used to.

A second trap is the design of the workplace.

A third trap is the culture of the organization—what behaviors it encourages or discourages. Human errors at lower levels of the organization are symptoms of things that are wrong in the organization at higher levels. Much more progress can be made by changing the situation rather than by preaching or discipline.

Training

This is one of the simplest solutions, and usually one of the most *ineffective*. It assumes that we have identified a lack of knowledge or skill. If this assumption is correct, training is the proper solution and will be effective. If, however, the assumption is not correct; that is, the problem is not a lack of knowledge or skill, a different solution is indicated.

Crisis Intervention

Obviously, crisis intervention is indicated only if a severe, immediate problem exists.

Behavior Change

Behavior change is not new, and it is relatively simple to understand. The basic process involves systematically reinforcing positive behavior while correcting at-risk behavior. Feedback is essential. The end result is the creation of a more acceptable response to a given situation. The technique concentrates on a person's observable behavior and an analysis of its underlying system causes (Ludwig 2017).

Contracts

A contract can also affect behavior change in an employee. A contract is an agreement to do something about something—an agreement between the supervisor and the employee. Contracts can be established to change behavior; to change feelings; or to change physical conditions, such as high blood pressure or obesity. In a work situation, contracts are primarily used for the purpose of changing behavior. According to the book *The OK Boss* by Muriel James, there is a five-step process for making contracts (James 1975):

1. The establishment of a goal: James suggests the employee asks the question, "What do I want that would enhance my job?"
2. The definition of what needs to be changed to achieve the goal: "What would I need to change so that I can reach my goal?"

3. The determination of how much the person is willing to do to achieve the goal: "What would I be willing to do to make the change happen?"
4. The determination of measurement and feedback needed to accomplish the change: "How would others know when I have affected the change?"
5. What pitfalls are there in the way? "How might I sabotage or undermine myself so that I would not achieve my goals?"

Muriel James states that each of the five points should be discussed when a contract is made. Written answers to each of the questions are also helpful.

The contract is an excellent management tool for dealing with employees. The employee is allowed to participate in what is going on, which is always preferable to authoritarian enforcement.

Inverse Performance Appraisal

Inverse Performance Appraisals (IPAs) are a way any supervisor can get accurate information as to his/her management effectiveness. This is done through systematically asking his/her people on a regular schedule what they think are his/her strengths and weaknesses when it comes to safety performance.

The IPA Procedure

Reproduce the form in figure 6.2 so that each of the employees who report to you has a copy. Call a meeting of your staff/team and explain that you would like their honest opinion of the way they are being managed by you when it comes to safety. Pass out the form. Suggest that they select one person to collect them and tabulate the results for you. Assure that no names are asked for or should be used. Leave the group to complete the forms.

Report back to the group the results of the appraisal in another meeting. Use the results to set objectives on improvement.

How to Set Objectives with IPA:
- number of times completed
- percentage of employees involved
- analysis of results
- changes made, etc.

Measurement:
- completion to goal
- analysis of results and changes made
- improvement over time

```
Department_____

Note:  Do not sign your name. Your boss will not see this sheet. He or she will receive a
       summary of responses from this department.

Consider your boss and how he or she performs compared to your expectations.

Does your boss:           Better than I would expect      Worse than I would expect
                                      10                              1

Know you? _____
Understand you? _____
Know what your needs are? _____
Write any comments here you wish:_____
_____
_____
_____

Back you?_____
Listen to you? _____
Talk to you? _____
Write any comments here you wish:_____
_____
_____
_____

All your input? _____
Ask for your ideas? _____
Use your ideas? _____
Write any comments here you wish:_____
_____
_____
_____

Remove any barriers in your way? _____
Have enough influence with his or her boss?_____
Have enough influence with other departments _____
Write any comments here you wish:_____
_____
_____
_____

Talk down to you?_____
Treat you as a child? _____
Treat you as a subordinate?_____
Write any comments here you wish:_____
_____
_____
_____
```

Figure 6.2 Inverse performance standards form

Reward:
- Performance Appraisal System
- daily numbers game

Safety Improvement Teams (SITs)

Employee participation and involvement is one of the best ways to provide an environment that is engaging and motivational. When people have a piece of the action, are involved, it positively affects their behavior.

SIT Procedure

Call your people together and suggest you need their help in safety. Ask them to join with other workers of their choice to help solve problems in the department. Allow them to work with people of their choice and select problems of their choice. Provide them with any technical help they ask for. Ask for a monthly (regular) progress report.

> *How to Set Objectives with SIT:*
> - number of teams
> - percentage of people involved
> - number of projects worked on, solved, etc.
>
> *Measurement:*
> - completion to goal
>
> *Reward:*
> - Performance Appraisal System
> - daily numbers game

Climate Analysis (CA)

Climate Analysis (CA) is a technique to assess your staff's/team's perception of your organization at a given point in time. Safety climate research has been based on prior work on organizational climate, which, like the weather, changes regularly. The safety climate can be influenced by an external context, such as OSHA regulations; an internal context, such as the nature of organizational change and employees' perceptions; the content of change, such as changes in organizational structure and leadership; and process-oriented factors, such as the sequence of action an organization takes to make change (Robson et al. 2016).

Asking employees can be very useful in assessing the real corporate climate—assuming they will level with you. Whether this happens probably depends on trust and spending enough time in the process to get to where they will be honest with you regarding what they really think.

A note about the difference between organizational climate and culture: *Climate* has less to do with an organization's values and more to do with workers' shared perceptions, which often change like the weather. Climate is the process of quantifying the culture of an organization, and climate precedes culture. It is a set of properties of the work environment, perceived directly or indirectly by the employees, that is assumed to be a major force in influencing employee behavior (Ivancevich, Konopaske, and Matteson 2008).

Management sets the vision and values and makes decisions that create a culture. *Culture* has nothing to do with safety per se. Safety is not a subfunction of culture. Culture is one of the things that establishes what goes on in an organization for everything—including safety. Culture is how we work with each other.

Culture is a major factor in the causes of human behavior. Considerations that determine culture include (Petersen 2003):

- How are decisions made?
- How are people measured?
- How are people rewarded?
- Is teamwork fostered?
- What is the history and what are the traditions of the organization?
- Who are the corporate heroes and why?
- Is the safety system intended to save lives or to comply with regulations?
- Are supervisors required to perform safety tasks daily? This says that safety is a true value.
- Do big bosses wander around and talk to people?
- Is using the brain allowed on the workfloor?
- Has the company downsized?
- Is the company profitable? Too much? Too little?

Surveys

The climate analysis survey gathers a lot of data quickly and can be processed rapidly by software. But the survey instrument is crucial. It must be constructed by people who know what they are doing, and that takes time. Each question must be carefully constructed and validated by a professional test-development person working with subject experts. Figure 6.3 is a short, quick rating your employees can give you, however.

Procedure

First, fill out the form in figure 6.3. Ask each of your people to assess the climate as you explain each of the factors. Once they understand each factor, ask them to assess again quarterly. Work on the weak spots between each assessment for the areas you have some control over.

	Organizational variables					Item no.
LEADERSHIP	How much confidence and trust is shown in subordinates?	Virtually none	Some	Substantial amount	A great deal	1
	How free do they feel to talk to superiors about job?	Not very free	Somewhat free	Quite free	Very free	2
	How often are subordinate's ideas sought and used constructively?	Seldom	Sometimes	Often	Very frequently	3
MOTIVATION	Is predominant use made of 1 fear, 2 threats, 3 punishment, 4 rewards, 5 involvement	1, 2, 3 occasionally 4	4, some 3	4, some 3 and 5	5, 4, based on group	4
	Where is responsibility felt for achieving organization's goals?	Mostly at top	Top and middle	Fairly general	At all levels	5
	How much cooperative teamwork exists?	Very little	Relatively little	Moderate amount	Great deal	6
COMMUNICATION	What is the usual direction of information flow?	Downward	Mostly downward	Down and up	Down, up, and sideways	7
	How is downward communication accepted?	With suspicion	Possibly with suspicion	With caution	With a receptive mind	8
	How accurate is upward communication?	Usually inaccurate	Often inaccurate	Often accurate	Almost always accurate	9
	How well do superiors know problems faced by subordinates?	Not very well	Rather well	Quite well	Very well	10

1 2 3 4 5 6 7 8 9 10 11 12 13 14 15 16 17 18 19 20

	Organizational variables					
DECISIONS	At what level are decisions made?	Mostly at top	Policy at top, some delegation	Broad policy at top, more delegation	Throughout but well integrated	11
	Are subordinates involved in decisions related to their work?	Almost never	Occasionally consulted	Generally consulted	Fully involved	12
	What does decision-making process contribute to motivation?	Not very much	Relatively little	Some contribution	Substantial contribution	13
GOALS	How are organizational goals established?	Orders issued	Orders, some comments invited	After discussion, by orders	By group action (except in crisis)	14
	How much covert resistance to goals is present?	Strong resistance	Moderate resistance	Some resistance at times	Little or none	15
CONTROL	How concentrated are review and control functions?	Very highly at top	Quite highly at top	Moderate delegation to lower levels	Widely shared	16
	Is there an internal organization resisting the formal one?	Yes	Usually	Sometimes	No—same goals as formal	17
	What are cost, productivity, and other control data used for?	Policing, punishment	Reward and punishment	Reward, some self-guidance	Self-guidance, problem-solving	18

1 2 3 4 5 6 7 8 9 10 11 12 13 14 15 16 17 18 19 20

Figure 6.3 An organizational profile

How to Set Objectives with CA:
- number of times CAs completed
- number of CAs
- percentage of people involved
- analysis of results
- changes from CAs, etc.

Measurement:
- measure completion of goal
- changes made from results.

Reward:
- Performance Appraisal System
- daily numbers game

REFERENCES

Fulwiler, Richard. 2013. "Transforming Leaders Drive Excellence." *Industrial Safety & Hygiene News*, June 2013.

Holmes, Thomas, and Richard Rahe. 1967. "The Holmes-Rahe Stress Inventory." The American Institute of Stress. Accessed December 3, 2019. https://www.stress.org/holmes-rahe-stress-inventory/.

Ivancevich, John M., Robert Konopaske, and Michael T. Matteson. *Organizational Behavior & Management*, 8th ed. New York: McGraw-Hill/Irwin.

James, Muriel. 1975. *The OK Boss*. Reading, MA: Addison-Wesley Publishing Co.

Kotter, John. 1996. *Leading Change*. Brighton, MA: Harvard Business Publishing.

Ludwig, Tim. 2017. "You Can't Fix Stupid, Fix the Environment." *Industrial Safety & Hygiene News*, June 2017.

Lyttleton, Ben. 2017. *Edge: What Business Can Learn from Football*. New York: HarperCollins.

Petersen, Dan. 2003. "Human Error." *Professional Safety*, December 2003.

Robson, Lynda S., Benjamin C. Amick III, Cindy Moser et al. 2016. "Important factors in common among organizations making large improvement in OHS performance: Results of an exploratory multiple case study." *Safety Science* 86 (July): 211–227.

"10 Common Leadership Styles (With Examples)." n.d. Indeed Career Guide. Accessed 10.16.19. https://www.indeedm/career-advice/career-development/10-common-leadership-styles.

Zenger, Jack, and Joseph Folkman. 2014. "The Skills Leaders Need at Every Level." *Harvard Business Review*, July 2014.

PART III

Techniques that Work

CHAPTER 7

Coaching

Coaching today is one of a supervisor's core competencies, and it most certainly applies to safety and health. We use the term coaching instead of training because coaching connotes a wider range of activities than training does. We are interested in all activities you should consider to improve specific job performance. We're not interested in a dry, classroom approach that the term training often brings to mind. Or for that matter, online training that can leave participants "on their own" without interaction.

Supervisors are positioned well on the front lines to provide coaching. Supervisors have "their finger on the pulse of operations," and more than any other leaders in an organization, supervisors most often attend safety meetings and workshops and develop personal relationships with individual employees and team members (Callari, Bieder, and Kirwan 2019).

In an article, "Helping Mining Superintendents Become Effective Safety Coaches," author Michael Hajaistron points out critical activities when coaching your people (Hajaistron 2018):

- safety contacts
- job safety briefings
- life-saving procedure application and verification (addressing shortcuts taken by employees when trying to work with complicated life-saving procedures, such as confined space entry)

According to Dekra (n.d.), "In recent decades, coaching has emerged as one of the most noteworthy changes in supervisor responsibilities. At leading companies supervisors have stopped thinking of themselves as traffic cops or umpires and now conduct themselves more like coaches of athletic teams. A coach provides a combination of advice, motivation, direction, and team skill development. To help their supervisory personnel succeed as coaches, organizations have begun to train supervisors in personal interaction and communication."

To coach means to help a person perform better. Some organizations have extensive coaching training programs, and others have very limited training. In either case, you have to be a coach on your job. Any supervisor will readily admit having a responsibility to help his people be better, safer performers.

For our purposes, we'll say that coaching consists of doing these kinds of things: explaining, demonstrating, correcting, encouraging, and reprimanding. Putting the coaching process in its simplest form, we can say that it has three steps: (1) finding out where the employee is now in terms of skill performance, behaviors, and attitudes toward the job; (2) finding out where we want the person to be; and (3) providing the difference.

Unfortunately, we usually spend almost all our time in safety determining content and methods to improve performance. Theorists tell us to spend the bulk of our effort and concentration on (1) and (2) above. If we do a good job in analyzing these, the third step usually falls into place naturally. Theorists tell us that content—the methodology of coaching—is no more than the difference between the first two steps and that the method of presentation is almost immaterial to learning.

Notice that the coaching elements of explaining, demonstrating, correcting, encouraging, and reprimanding share a common thread: all involve having conversations. Here are tips for effective one-on-ones or safety contacts (Moussa, Boyer, and Newberry 2016):

- listen and inquire
- ask questions
- listen carefully (active listening)
- avoid reacting (getting emotional)
- show humility
- ask for feedback—"What can I do better?"
- accept criticism
- solicit advice on changing your behavior
- know your default style of supervising
- ask yourself which style would work best in this conversation and adapt

What are the most common mistakes supervisors make during these one-on-one conversations? (Scott 2002)

- doing most of the talking
- taking the problem away from someone
- not inquiring about emotions—ask, "What are you feeling?"
- delivering unclear messages, unclear coaching, and unclear instructions
- canceling the one-on-one meeting
- allowing interruptions
- running out of time
- moving too quickly from question to question
- coaching in areas in close proximity to co-workers
- assuming your one-to-ones are effective

To avoid these mistakes and be an effective coach requires a certain amount of emotional intelligence. Instead of how smart you may be, emotional intelligence is about having empathy and showing a willingness to cooperate. Emotional intelligence is being able to manage yourself as a coach, being mature in one-to-one conversations, and seeking first to understand the other person's point of view (Williamsen 1997).

According to research, employers seem to want it both ways when it comes to supervisors and safety—they want supervisors to be both coaches and enforcers.

Seventy percent of respondents in one survey said one of their biggest challenges is to develop supervisors as leaders, not just as rule and behavior enforcers. Ninety percent said supervisors today must give positive reinforcement to employees. But asked how supervisors' safety-related jobs are evolving, less than half of respondents (42%) said supervisors today act more like coaches than cops (Johnson 2017).

Sometimes supervisors may think they are acting as safety coaches, but that's not the perception of employees. One supervisor who attended a leadership safety coaching workshop always thought he was perceived as a coach. Then once, while conducting a safety audit, he heard over the loudspeaker, "Charlie 2-2-3, Charlie 2-2-3." Someone pulled him aside and explained, "that's the code" for you doing your safety work. This supervisor reflected and realized he was never provided the skills or training to actually coach for performance or give feedback to facilitate desired behavior (Galloway 2015).

TWO COACHING TASKS

Every supervisor has two divergent coaching tasks: (1) to coach each person individually and (2) to coach the team collectively. Let's look at some tools you can use to improve your coaching.

Coaching the Individual

The supervisor must look at each person individually and go through the process of finding out the person's needs—where the person is now in comparison to where you want him to be in terms of skill development, technical knowledge, and behavior and attitude toward work responsibilities. Then, with explanations, demonstrations, corrections, encouragements, and reprimands, each individual must receive ongoing coaching to achieve the performance level you want.

When should the individual be coached? Obviously, coaching should occur whenever you feel the person needs to perform better in any area. Or when you catch them doing something well. Coaching seems to be particularly appropriate in the following kinds of situations.

When a new person is assigned to you. You need to show them around, introduce them to people; explain the purpose of your department or team; instruct them on safety rules and regulations, safety goals, expectations, and safety-related activities; point out special hazards; and, in other ways, get them oriented to the job to be done. This is a task you are already doing. By giving it conscious attention, you'll do it better and improve the person's performance.

When you see an unsafe act. Often a word or comment or brief explanation is sufficient to correct it. Sometimes there is a need for greater explanation or demonstration. At the back of our minds is the thought that an unsafe act continued long enough will finally produce a safety incident. Safety is not a goal that can be measured in daily or hourly figures. Your people know safety is important by what you do in your daily and hourly contacts with them. What you "do" is much more influential that what you "say." Actions speak louder than words. When you turn your back on unsafe acts, when you fail to do the coaching at-risk behavior calls for, your people quite readily accept the fact that safety is not an important goal or important in their work.

When you see anything performed well. It is easier to improve performance by praise of a job well done than it is by criticism. Individuals react positively to compliments and want to continue to receive them. Regarding safety, this can include everything from acknowledging when an employee is wearing the proper PPE; when an employee reports a hazard, incident, or near miss; when you observe safe work behaviors; and when an employee makes a safety suggestion, offers a problem-solving solution, or goes out of the way to help a co-worker.

When we give orders or work assignments. Our orders should clearly express the fact that we want something accomplished safely. When you don't get the performance you expect, this situation is a red flag that should alert you to give additional coaching at this time.

When you see anything being done incorrectly. If we coach when we see jobs performed well, our people are more ready to accept our coaching when we observe work done incorrectly. When we praise, we establish what we do want. When we see anything done incorrectly, we can establish what it is that we do not want and use the opportunity to establish what we do want. We want safe behaviors and work practices. We don't want shortcuts, risk-taking, or horseplay.

Whenever you assign an unusual job. Much of our work falls into rather routine patterns, but in every organization there are some situations that are unusual. Every unusual situation or unusual job, infrequently performed, suggests to us that we have a need to coach, to explain, to demonstrate, to make sure that people know what we want, for it is in these nonroutine circumstances that we often experience a severe injury.

This is especially true when you have employees performing unusual assignments in their first few months on the job. Research clearly shows that newly hired employees have an increased risk of work injury. The capacity to master unusual jobs requires coaching to increase competency to a high level. Effective one-on-one coaching can mitigate the risks of new hires (or even experienced employees) using a different work method, doing an unusual task, being distracted, and being rushed (Laberge et al. 2016).

Coaching the Team

The supervisor must also look at the team as a whole and assess its needs. The supervisor should look for occasions or situations when this can be most effective. Some of these circumstances are:

When you see a better (safer) way to do things.

When new products, methods, machines, or technologies are introduced. Even though only some of your people will operate the machines or use a technology, it is smart to acquaint the whole group with the new product, method, machine, or technology. Everyone should understand how it fits into the total group effort.

When unsafe conditions crop up. An unsafe act is performed by an individual. But unsafe conditions might require the group or team's attention, because many unsafe conditions are system deficits—failing equipment, poor housekeeping, process bottlenecks, unacceptable noise and/or lighting levels, toxic substance overexposures, and so on. You cannot see or be present every time an unsafe condition crops up. Such conditions must be seen and corrected or reported on as a group effort.

When establishing your goals. Supervisors often do not clearly establish and explain their goals to their people. Usually, you have a general idea of the outcome desired by the work of the whole group and a general idea of the performance required and desired by the whole group. This needs to be explained and discussed with your group. The supervisor's job is to get the group to want to achieve his goals or (more precisely) to cause the supervisor's goals to become the goals of the group.

When any unusual condition affects the whole group. This may come about as the result of a safety incident, a slowdown in work with necessary layoffs, a work interruption, an unusual or special job, or any occasion in which the understanding of the whole group and the cooperation of the whole group is important to accomplish the end result desired.

How to Coach

While we won't discuss specific methods here (a book in itself), we do want to bring up a few ideas on human learning. There has been more research on human learning than on almost any other topic in psychology. Here are some of the "knowns":

- *Motivation and learning*—Learning theorists agree that an individual will learn best if the person is motivated toward some goal that is attainable by learning the subject matter presented. People's behavior is oriented toward relevant goals, whether these goals are safety, increased recognition, production, or simply socializing. People attempt

to achieve those goals that are important to them at the moment, regardless of what's important to you.
- *Reinforcement and learning*—Positive recognition for certain behavior increases the probability that the particular behavior will occur again. Negative recognition decreases that probability. Reinforcement is most important to learning.
- *Practice and learning*—An individual learns best through hands-on practice and involvement.
- *Feedback and learning*—Informing an employee about how they are doing is essential for the learning process. It is difficult for an employee to improve his performance unless he is given some knowledge of the current status of his performance. What is he doing well? What skills have been mastered? What errors need to be pointed out? How can the person correct the errors? This is essential.
- *Meaningfulness and learning*—In general, meaningful material is learned better than material that is not meaningful. In order to simplify an employee's learning task, make the material as personally meaningful and relevant to him as possible.

Later we'll discuss a number of different ways of coaching you may wish to consider. Safety meetings are only one way—there are a number of other methods that have been found to be much more effective. One-on one-contacts typically get much better results, for example.

In addition, the following techniques will be described:
- job safety observations
- safe behavior reinforcement
- one-minute safety contacts
- prejob and postjob briefings
- stress assessment techniques

For each objective, setting and measurements will be spelled out.

JOB SAFETY OBSERVATION (JSO)

A Job Safety Observation (JSO) provides you with a device to learn more about the work habits of each of your people. Following the procedures described below, you can use this opportunity to check on the results of past training; make immediate, on-the-spot corrections and improvements in work practices; and compliment and reinforce safe behavior. Through your conversations, you can encourage proper behavior and attitudes toward safety. Follow these steps when implementing a JSO process in your department.

1. Select the worker and job to be observed; the job should have tight, operational definitions of how it should be done.

2. Make the observation.
3. Record safe and at-risk behaviors.
4. Review the results with the employee observed.
5. Follow up.

Worker Selection

Eventually, you'll observe all your people. But you might consider the following possibilities when determining which person to observe first:
- the new person on the job
- people recently out of training programs
- below-average performers
- accident repeaters
- risk takers
- employees presenting problems unique to them

Making the Observation

In most cases, you should inform the person who will be observed of what you are doing prior to the JSO and explain why you are making an observation. Then simply observe the employee in his normal operation, making any applicable notes on the worksheet about his normal work practices and procedures, as well as safe behaviors and any unsafe behavior exhibited. Be careful to stay out of the employee's way and don't distract him or her. And be careful not to go on a "fishing for faults" expedition, looking only for problems, errors, and risks. This biased "fishing trip" can ruin trust between you and your employee and put the employee on the defensive (Ludwig 2018).

Recording Work Practices

Fill out the Job Safety Observation Worksheet during the JSO after reviewing it with the employee. File it in any manner that suits your needs.

The Review

When you have completed the JSO, sit down with the employee and give your conclusions. Express appreciation to the employee for cooperating and lay out your honest feelings about work habits and practices. The first time you go through this with an employee both of you will be nervous and your employee may be concerned or apprehensive. Keep the person at ease and keep the discussion informal and friendly. Do not let the discussion be a one-way communication. Don't do all the talking. Encourage the person to talk and give you his or her views on the job, as well as any problems or barriers the person sees to working safely. Be careful not to play the "blame game" or label the employee as "careless" or "distracted." One, you want to focus on behaviors not the behaver (the "sin," not the "sinner"). And two, you need to ask why an individual may seem careless or distracted. The "why" question is crucial in conversations and getting to "the ground truth" and reality.

The Follow-up

Follow up on the observation as needed. In some cases, follow-up will be often. In other cases, it will be seldom. How often you follow up depends on the person and on the job. Follow-up JSOs are usually a good idea after a job change or changing work conditions.

Benefits of JSOs

The JSO is a feedback device. It provides excellent information on the effectiveness of your training and on the adequacy of your job procedures. Through the JSO, any substandard practices or system risk factors can usually be identified before an incident happens. JSOs also give you the opportunity to sit down with your people individually to discuss their performance and to compliment or correct their work habits. In addition, you get to know each worker better and thus can spot any physical or psychological issues more readily.

JSO Procedure

Reproduce figure 7.1 in sufficient quantity so all supervisors involved in the JSO program will have at least 25 copies. Then set a schedule for your department as follows:

1. List those activities performed in your department that you feel warrant a JSO.
2. Schedule the JSOs. Do no more than one per day. Do no less than one per week.
3. Carry out each observation as outlined in this section.
4. Upon completion of each JSO, review it with the employee observed.
5. Provide the employee with a copy of the completed form.
6. Keep several copies in your files for future training purposes.

How to Set Objectives with JSO:
- number of JSOs made
- percentage of people covered
- number of suggestions made
- number of positive strokes given, etc.

Measurement:
- completion to goal

Reward:
- Performance Appraisal System
- daily numbers game—recordkeeping of JSOs

JOB SAFETY OBSERVATION		
Employee:	Supervisor:	
Job:	Date:	Time:
Notes on any job practices that are unsafe:		
Notes on any practices that need change or improvement:		
Notes on any practices that deserve complimenting:		
Notes on the review and discussion:		

Figure 7.1 Worksheet for observation

ONE-ON-ONE CONTACTS (OO)

The one-on-one contact (OO) is a personal conversation between you, the supervisor, and each person who works for you. The conversation can be safety-related, or it can be used simply as an opportunity for you to get to know each person who works for you a little better. Conversations must occur regularly to be useful.

Contact Procedure

Schedule yourself time each day to make your contacts. Contact at least one person each day. Keep a list of your people to ensure you miss no one over time. If you wish, use the Worker Safety Analysis Form in chapter 6 to assist.

How to Set Objectives with OO:
- number of OOs per day
- number of OOs per week, etc.

Measurement:
- completion to goal

Reward:
- Performance Appraisal System
- daily numbers game—recordkeeping of contacts

SAFE BEHAVIOR REINFORCEMENT (SBR)

It has been known through research for many years that positive reinforcement immediately following a desired behavior is the strongest way to build and maintain safe behavior. Safe Behavior Reinforcement (SBR) is simply a way of utilizing this fact.

SBR Procedure

Each day ensure you schedule yourself some time to observe each person that works for you at least once. When you observe, react to whatever you see. If the person is working unsafely, react as you normally would.

If, however, the person observed is working safely, make an immediate contact with that person and say something positive—pleasurable (an "attaboy" or whatever fits your personality)—attaching it to the behavior you have observed. Make sure the person knows that you desire safe work and will be looking for that each day.

Keep track each day of the number of observations made and the number of positive reinforcements. Total them each week, month, etc., and publish them for your group.

How to Set Objectives with SBR:
- number of observations
- number of positive reinforcements
- percentage of positive reinforcements versus negative reinforcements to achieve desired behavior
- percentage of people covered, etc.

Measurement:
- completion to goal (through self-reporting)

Reward:
- Performance Appraisal System
- daily numbers game—recordkeeping of observations, positive reinforcement, percentage of positive versus negative reinforcement, percent of people covered

ONE-MINUTE SAFETY CONTACTS (OMC)

The one-minute contact (OMC) system is a three-step process.

1. Sit down with each subordinate and agree on what are the key objectives of his/her job. Agree also as to the safety hazards, critical behaviors, and your expectations.
2. Check with each employee at least once each week and spend a minimum of one minute with each on a one-minute praising.
3. Check at least once each week to see if a one-minute reprimand is in order—make it positive by using only 15 seconds to point out the behavior you want changed.

Schedule yourself to ensure each person who works for you is checked each week. Keep track to ensure this happens.

How to Set Objectives with OMC:
- number of people with objectives agreed to
- percentage of people with objectives set
- number of one-minute praisings
- number of one-minute reprimands
- ratio of praisings to reprimands

Measurement:
- completion to goal

Reward:
- Performance Appraisal System
- daily numbers game—recordkeeping of one-minute observations, number of praisings, number of reprimands, ratios

PREJOB AND POSTJOB BRIEFINGS

These briefings are important tools used in the increasing popular Human and Organizational Performance (HOP) safety procedures. Prejob briefings are expected before work begins and can take the form appropriate to the situation using the graded approach—from an informal supervisor-to-worker discussion to a formal, structured, and documented meeting. The prejob briefing is the last confirmation of readiness before performing individual work activities/tasks and provides the job participants with a collective understanding of the task to be completed. Topics typically include requirements for performing the task, identified hazards and necessary controls, environmental impacts, facility conditions, emergency contingency actions, and individual roles/responsibilities.

Postjob review is a discussion between workers and the field work supervisor following a specific work activity, which could be an entire job or a discrete part of a larger job. Postjob reviews evaluate the entire work planning and execution process. If a *formal* postjob review is conducted, it is documented on specific forms, depending on the driver for the postjob review (Hanford Mission Support Contract 2011).

How to Set Objectives with Prejob and Postjob Briefings:
- number of people participating in prejob and postjob briefings
- number of prejob briefings
- number of postjob briefings

Measurement:
- completion to goal

Reward:
- Performance Appraisal System
- daily numbers game

STRESS ASSESSMENT TECHNIQUE (SAT)

You can assist your staff tremendously by giving attention to them and putting your focus on stressors they face on the job. You can also assist them by focusing on whether they are exhibiting any of the telltale warning signs that show they are heading toward stress-related illnesses.

The Stress Assessment Technique (SAT) utilizes a number of different assessment approaches to evaluate an individual's likelihood of becoming fatigued, distracted, or ill from experiencing distress. Use the following steps in assessing the individuals who work for you.

1. Check for the warning signs. They are:
    - general irritability, hyperexcitation, or depression
    - pounding of the heart
    - dryness of throat and mouth

- impulsive behavior, emotional instability
- overpowering urge to cry or run and hide
- inability to concentrate
- feelings of unreality, weakness, dizziness
- predilection to becoming fatigued
- floating anxiety
- tension and alertness
- trembling or nervous ticks
- tendency to be easily startled
- high-pitched nervous laughter
- stuttering or other speech difficulties
- bruxism (grinding teeth together)
- insomnia
- hypermotility, moving for no reason, cannot relax
- sweating
- frequent need to urinate
- diarrhea, indigestion, queasiness, vomiting
- migraine headaches
- pain in neck and lower back
- loss of, or excessive, appetite
- increased smoking
- increased use of drugs or alcohol
- drug or alcohol addiction
- nightmares
- neurotic behavior
- psychosis
- safety incident proneness

2. Are your employees in any of the following "high-stress" job categories?
    - laborer
    - lone worker
    - long-haul trucking
    - express delivery trucking
    - office assistant
    - inspector
    - lab technician
    - office manager
    - foreman
    - manager
    - machine operator
    - farm owner
    - mine operator
    - printer

3. Are your workers expressing any stressors regarding these categories?
   - job satisfaction
   - physical work conditions
   - organizational factors
   - workload
   - work hours
   - work task
   - career development
   - downsizing
   - big brother syndrome (the feeling of always being monitored)
   - acquisitions and mergers
   - too much responsibility
   - the "ostrich syndrome" (denying or refusing to acknowledge something that is blatantly obvious)
4. Following are typical strategies that reduce job stress. How many are you using now?
   - job redesign, modifying the content of work, enriching the tasks done, rotation
   - organizational modification; giving greater autonomy, more ownership, more delegation of decision-making and problem-solving to the employee
   - ergonomic redesign, using what we know to make the job user friendly
   - modifying the working space and time demands, removing crowding or isolation, allowing rest periods
   - reducing forced overtime through better manpower planning and better scheduling
   - providing more information on everything; being transparent, so the employees can feel they are a part of the organization
   - allowing employee input before changes are made in the work setup
   - allowing employee participation in most decision-making
5. From all of the above, write an objective on how you can help those under your supervision or within your group.

How to Set Objectives with SAT:
- number of people assessed
- percentage of people assessed

Measurement:
- completion to goal

Reward:
- Performance Appraisal System
- daily numbers game

REFERENCES

Callari, Tiziana C. , Corrine Bieder, and Barry Kirwan. 2019. "What is it like for a middle manager to take safety into account? Practices and challenges." *Safety Science* 113 (March): 19–29. https://doi.org/10.1016/j.ssci.2018.10.025.

Dekra. n.d. "The Secret of Supervisors Leading Safety." Accessed March 27, 2019. https://dekra-insight.com/en/topic/the-secret-of-supervisors-leading-safety.

Galloway, Shawn. 2015. "Are Your Supervisors Cops or Coaches?" *BIC Magazine*, October 2015.

Hajaistron, Michael. 2018. "Helping Mining Superintendents Become Effective Safety Coaches." Dekra/BST. Accessed January 10, 2020. http://dekra-insight.com/images/white-paper-documents/wp_helping_mining superintendents_become_effective_safety_coaches_8.5x11_us_2016.pdf.

Hanford Mission Support Contract. 2011. "Conducting Pre-Job Briefings and Post-Job Reviews." April 28, 2011. https://www.hanford.gov/pmm/files.cfm/msc-pro-14047.pdf.

Johnson, Dave. 2017. "State of the EHS Nation 2017." Reader Survey. *Industrial Safety & Hygiene News*, October 2017.

Laberge, Marie, Calvert Benedicte, Mark Fredette et al. 2016. "Unexpected events: Learning opportunities or injury risks for apprentices in low-skilled jobs? A pilot study." *Safety Science* 86 (July).

Ludwig, Tim. 2018. *Dysfunctional Practices that Kill your Safety Culture (and what to do about them)*. Blowing Rock, NC: Calloway Publishing.

Moussa, Mario, Madeline Boyer, and Derek Newberry. 2016. *Committed Teams*. Hoboken, NJ: Wiley.

Scott, Susan. 2002. *Fierce Conversations: Achieving Success at Work & Life, One Conversation at a Time*. New York: Viking.

Williamsen, Mike. 1997. "The Culture of Safety: An interview with safety pioneer Dan Petersen." *Professional Safety*, March 1997.

CHAPTER **8**

Hazard Identification and Mitigation

One of the "root causes" of workplace injuries, illnesses, close calls, and incidents is the failure to identify or recognize hazards that are present or that could have been anticipated. A critical element of effective safety and health processes is a proactive, ongoing activity to identify and assess these hazards.

IDENTIFYING HAZARDS

To identify and assess hazards, employers, and workers:
- collect and review information about the hazards present or likely to be present in the workplace
- conduct initial and periodic workplace inspections to identify new or recurring hazards
- investigate injuries, illnesses, incidents, and close calls/near misses to determine the underlying hazards, their causes, and safety and health process shortcomings
- group similar incidents and identify trends in injuries, illnesses, and hazards reported
- consider hazards associated with emergency or nonroutine situations
- determine the severity and likelihood of incidents that could result for each hazard identified, and use this information to prioritize corrective actions

This practice is called risk assessment. Risk ratings can be immediately dangerous, high risk, medium risk, low risk, or very low risk.

There is a difference between a hazard and a risk. A *hazard* can cause harm, such as electricity, chemicals, working at height, noise, machinery, and so on. The *risk* of personal harm—severity and probability—posed by these hazards varies depending on controls and procedures put in place (CCOHS n.d.-a).

The International Organization for Standardization (ISO) published ISO 31000 *Risk Management—Guidelines* in 2018. The American adoption of this standard is

ANSI/ASSP/ISO 31000-2018 *Risk Management—Guidelines*. OSHA does not have a risk management standard.

CORRECTING HAZARDS

Some hazards, such as housekeeping and tripping hazards, can and should be fixed as they are discovered. Fixing hazards on the spot emphasizes the importance of safety and health and takes advantage of a safety leadership opportunity. To learn more about fixing hazards identified, consult OSHA's *Hazard Prevention and Control* (OSHA n.d.-a).

OSHA (2016) maps out six action steps: (1) collect existing information about workplace hazards; (2) inspect the workplace for safety hazards; (3) identify health hazards; (4) conduct incident investigations; (5) identify hazards associated with emergency and nonroutine situations; and (6) characterize the nature of identified hazards, identify interim control measures, and prioritize the hazards for control.

According to OSHA, you might find information pertaining to your workplace hazards from these sources (OSHA 2016):

- equipment and machinery operating manuals
- Safety Data Sheets (SDS) provided by chemical manufacturers
- self-inspection reports and inspection reports from insurance carriers, government agencies, and consultants
- records of previous injuries and illnesses, such as OSHA 300 and 301 logs and reports of incident investigations
- workers' compensation records and reports
- patterns of frequently occurring injuries and illnesses
- exposure monitoring results, industrial hygiene assessments, and medical records (appropriately redacted to ensure patient/worker privacy)
- existing safety and health processes (lockout/tagout, confined spaces, process safety management, personal protective equipment, etc.)
- input from workers, including surveys or minutes from safety and health committee meetings
- results of job hazard analyses, also known as job safety analyses

Typical hazards, according to OSHA, fall into several major categories (though each workplace will develop its own list):

- general housekeeping
- slip, trip, and fall hazards
- electrical hazards
- equipment operation
- equipment maintenance
- fire protection
- work organization and process flow (including staffing and scheduling)

- work practices
- workplace violence
- ergonomic problems
- lack of emergency procedures

Many hazards can be identified using front-line knowledge. You can easily identify and correct hazards associated with broken stair rails, broken lighting, blocked aisles and exits, and frayed electrical cords. Employees are very useful internal resources, especially if they are trained in how to identify and assess risks (OSHA 2016).

Health hazards are more difficult to inspect for and include chemical hazards (solvents, adhesives, paints, toxic dusts, etc.), physical hazards (noise, radiation, heat, etc.), biological hazards (infectious diseases), and ergonomic risk factors (heavy lifting, repetitive motions, vibration). Reviewing employees' medical records (appropriately redacted to ensure patient/worker privacy) can be useful in identifying health hazards associated with workplace exposures (OSHA 2016).

Foreseeable emergency scenarios and nonroutine tasks take into account the types of material and equipment in use and the location within your facility. Scenarios such as the following may be foreseeable (OSHA 2016):

- fires and explosions
- chemical releases
- hazardous material spills
- startups after planned or unplanned equipment shutdowns
- nonroutine tasks, such as infrequently performed maintenance activities
- structural collapse
- disease outbreaks
- weather emergencies and natural disasters
- medical emergencies
- workplace violence

Finally, you want to evaluate each hazard by considering the severity of potential outcomes, the likelihood that an event or exposure will occur, and the number of workers who might be exposed.

OSHA recommends using interim control measures to protect employees until more permanent solutions can be implemented. Prioritize the hazards so that those presenting the greatest risk are addressed first. OSHA emphasizes that employers have an ongoing obligation to control all serious recognized hazards and to protect employees (OSHA 2016).

Job Safety Analysis (JSA)

Job Safety Analysis (JSA), also known as Job Hazard Analysis, is a procedure that identifies the hazards associated with each step of a job and develops solutions for

JOB:		
What to Do (*Steps in sequence*)	**How to Do It** (*Instructions*) (*Reverse hands for left-handed operator.*)	**Key Points** (*Items to be emphasized.* *Safety is always a key point.*)
1.	1.	1.
2.	2.	2.
3.	3.	3.
4.	4.	4.
5.	5.	5.
6.	6.	6.

Figure 8.1 Job analysis worksheet

each hazard that either eliminate or control it. A job safety analysis worksheet is illustrated in figure 8.1. In the left column, the basic steps of the job are listed in the order in which they are performed. The middle column describes how to perform each job step. The right column gives the safety procedures that should be followed to guard against hazards. The basic steps in making a JSA are:

1. Select the job to be analyzed.
2. Break the job down into sequential steps.
3. Identify the hazards and potential for incidents.
4. Develop ways to eliminate the hazards listed.

A blank worksheet used for OSHA compliance is shown in figure 8.2.

Selecting the Job

According to the Canadian Centre for Occupational Health and Safety, all jobs should be subject to a JSA. Constraints posed by the time and effort required will limit your ability to do some JSAs. Factors to be considered in setting a priority for analysis of jobs include (CCOHS n.d.-b):

```
Job operation _____
Presently required personal protective equipment _____
Sequence of job steps              Hazards or OSHA violations
1.                                 1.
2.                                 2.
3.                                 3.
4.                                 4.
Recommended safe procedure
1.
2.
3.
4.
```

Figure 8.2 OSHA job safety analysis worksheet (From *The OSHA Compliance Manual* by Dan Petersen. Copyright © 1975 by McGraw-Hill. Used with permission.)

- *Incident frequency and severity:* jobs where safety incidents occur frequently or where they occur infrequently but result in serious injuries.
- *Potential for severe injuries or illnesses:* the consequences of an incident, hazardous condition, or exposure to harmful products are potentially severe.
- *Newly established jobs:* due to lack of experience in these jobs, hazards may not be evident or anticipated.
- *Modified jobs:* new hazards may be associated with changes in job procedures.
- *Infrequently performed jobs:* employees may be at greater risk when undertaking nonroutine jobs, and a JSA provides a means of reviewing hazards.

Breaking Down the Job

After a job has been chosen for analysis, the next stage is to break the job into steps. According to the Canadian Centre for Occupational Health and Safety, a job step is defined as a segment of the task necessary to advance the work (CCOHS n.d.-b).

Do not make the steps too general. Missing specific steps and associated hazards will not help. But if they are too detailed, there will be too many steps. A rule of thumb is that most jobs can be described in less than ten steps.

Remember to keep the steps in their correct sequence. Any step that is out of order may miss serious potential hazards or introduce hazards that do not actually exist.

Record each step in sequence. Make notes about *what* is done rather than *how* it is done. Each step starts with an action verb.

This part of the analysis is usually prepared from knowing the job or watching a worker do the job. The observer is normally you, the immediate supervisor. You might want to have a member of the health and safety committee participate in the observation. Key points are less likely to be missed this way.

The job observer should have experience and be capable in performing all parts of the job. To strengthen full cooperation and participation, the reason for the exercise must be clearly explained. The JSA is neither a time and motion study nor an attempt to finger individual unsafe acts. The job, not the individual, is being studied.

The job should be observed during normal times and situations. For example, if a job is routinely done only at night, the JSA review also should be done at night. Similarly, only regular tools and equipment should be used. The only difference from normal operations is the fact that the worker is being observed.

When completed, the breakdown of steps should be discussed by all the participants (always including the employee) to make sure that all basic steps have been noted and are in the correct order (CCOHS n.d.-b).

Identifying Hazards

After the breakdown, you should analyze each step in detail to identify hazards and potential safety incidents. Each should be recorded on the worksheet in the center column. Keep hazards parallel with the steps recorded. Check with the employee you're working with for ideas. Also, check with other employees who have knowledge of that job.

Developing Solutions

When hazards have been identified, your next step is to begin developing solutions to the problems you've identified. Solutions might incorporate:
- an entirely different way to do the job
- a change in physical conditions, layout, or environment
- a changed job procedure
- a change in frequency or how often the job is performed

For each hazard on the sheet, ask "What can be done differently and how should it be done?" Answers and solutions should be very specific and very concrete to be of value. Solutions that merely state "Be more alert" or "Use more caution" or something similar are worthless. Solutions should state exactly what to do and how to do it.

While performing the JSA, you'll learn more about the job observed than ever before. You also will have involved an employee and demonstrated to your employ-

JOB SAFETY ANALYSIS

Job Steps	Hazards/Potential Accidents	Controls

Job: _____   Date: _____
Employee: _____   Supervisor: _____

Figure 8.3 Worksheet for analyzing job safety

ees and the department that you care about the safety of that job. And you'll be creating safer conditions for the job observed.

JSA Procedure

Reproduce figure 8.3 in sufficient quantity. Then set a schedule for your department as follows:

1. List all jobs in the department.
2. Schedule them for analysis. Take no more than perhaps three per week. Take no less than one per week.
3. Carry out each analysis as outlined in this section.
4. Upon completion of each analysis, review it in detail with the employee involved for valuable additional input.
5. Provide the observed employee with a copy of the final analysis.
6. Keep several copies yourself and use these in future orientation and training sessions.

How to Set Objectives with JSA:
- number of JSAs to be completed

Measurement:
- completion of objective

Reward:
- Performance Appraisal System
- recognition of the number of JSAs completed, which is a leading indicator of safety and health performance

Hazard Hunt (HH)

Another method used successfully to spot possible causes of safety incidents is the Hazard Hunt. It is also good for engaging your people. To implement the procedure, follow these steps:

1. Make copies of the Hazard Hunt form (figure 8.4) available to all of your people.
2. Hold a short session with them to explain the form and the reasons for using it.
3. Have employees jot down anything they feel is a hazard and return the form to you.
4. Review the forms, correct those hazards you can, and initiate action when closure is out of your control.
5. Inform employees of your actions. Always tell them what you are doing, even if you decide the hazards they mention are not really problems. Then hash over any disagreements with individuals to clear the air.
6. If you agree something is a hazard and must be corrected, assign a priority to it and schedule it for abatement. The matrix in figure 8.5 provides a good guide for prioritizing.

The HH Procedure

Reproduce figure 8.4 in sufficient quantity so that each participating supervisor can have several hundred copies. Then

1. Hold a short meeting with all the employees in your department. Explain that you are asking for their help in finding hazards and OSHA violations. Ask them to look around their area and the whole department and jot down on the Hazard Hunt form any problems they see. Have them return the forms to you.
2. Give five to ten copies of the form to each employee.

Hazard Identification and Mitigation

```
To: _____
From: _____
                        HAZARD HUNT
I think the following is a hazard: _____
_____
_____

DO NOT WRITE BELOW HERE—TO BE FILLED IN BY SUPERVISOR
Supervisor:
    Agree this is a hazard.
        Corrected by Supervisor on _____ Discussed on _____
        If can't correct, sent to Personnel on _____
        Job order on _____ Scheduled _____ Discussed on _____
    Do not agree this is a hazard.
        Discussed _____ Conclusion _____
        To Personnel _____ Conclusion _____
DO NOT WRITE BELOW HERE—FOR PERSONNEL USE.
Supervisor _____ HH # _____
Matrix # _____ (Seriousness)
```

Figure 8.4 A hazard hunt form (From *The OSHA Compliance Manual* by Dan Petersen. Copyright © 1975 by McGraw-Hill. Used with permission.)

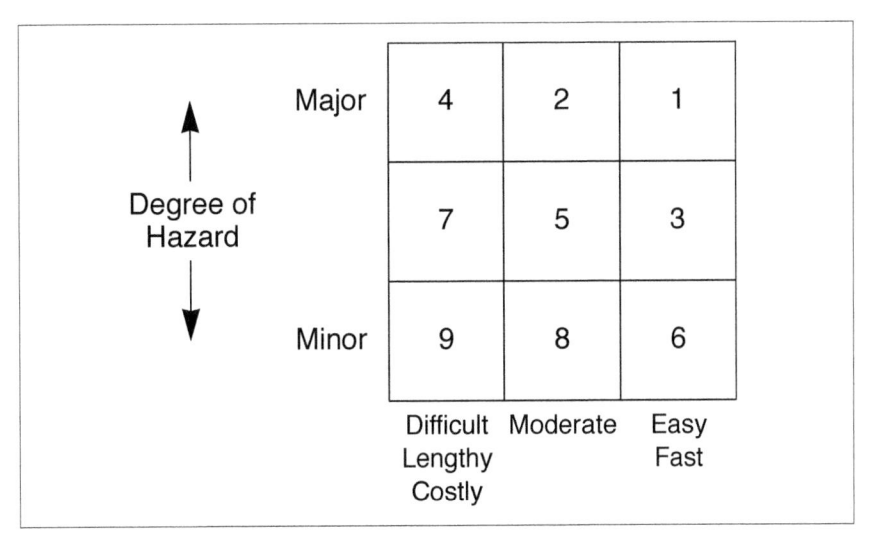

	Difficult / Lengthy / Costly	Moderate	Easy / Fast
Major	4	2	1
(Degree of Hazard)	7	5	3
Minor	9	8	6

Figure 8.5 Safety matrix (From *The OSHA Compliance Manual* by Dan Petersen. Copyright © 1975 by McGraw-Hill. Used with permission.)

3. React to every form you get back—give a response to each employee who turns in a form. Tell every employee what the company will do about each hazard listed. If nothing can be done, explain why.
4. Use the matrix to explain to an employee why it will take a while to correct the problem listed if it has a low priority.
5. Keep the forms on file for future training purposes.

How to Set Objectives with HH:
- number of HHs submitted

Measurement:
- percentage to objective

Reward:
- Performance Appraisal System
- recognition of the number of HHs completed, which is another leading indicator of safety performance

OSHA Compliance Check (OCC)

In addition to preventing incidents, as a supervisor, you also have a responsibility to ensure your organization complies with the law. This is a shared responsibility. It should not be off-loaded on the safety and health professional. Compliance should be a collaborative effort. The OSHA Compliance Check (OCC) is a tool to assist in this effort.

OCC Procedure

You can go to the OSHA website (www.osha.gov) and search for specific standards, most frequently violated standards, interpretations and clarifications of standards, and training requirements by standard.

It's also worthwhile to check on OSHA's website for the current list of National Emphasis Programs, representing standards and incidents (such as falls or amputations) targeted for enforcement. You want to make sure if any of those standards and incident hazards apply to your work area.

Also check OSHA's A–Z topic index (osha.gov/a-z). Many OSHA standards are explained in full with overviews; standards language (full text) and enforcement guidance; hazards and solutions applicable to the standard; plus additional resources, such as any compliance directives and letters of interpretation relating to specific standards. OSHA's vast resources on its website give you many tools for conducting comprehensive compliance audits.

How to Set Objectives with OCC:
- the number of checks made
- the number of checks per week

- whether the checklist, based on OSHA standards applicable to your workplace, is completed
- the number of violations found
- the number of violations corrected, etc.

Measurement:
- completion to objective

Reward:
- Performance Appraisal System
- recognition of completed OSHA audits, which is another leading indicator of safety performance

Ergonomic Analysis (EA)

An ergonomic analysis (EA) is a way of reducing the probability that your people will be injured (usually over a period of time—the injury is most often a cumulative trauma, back injuries from a single lift being an exception) through exposure to musculoskeletal disorders (MSDs). Each job your people do should be analyzed.

The OSHA website provides valuable information on ergonomic hazards by identifying problems, solutions to control hazards, and enforcement FAQs (OSHA n.d.-b).

This ergonomic analysis has as its primary focus preventing MSDs. These MSDs are, as stated, mostly cumulative occupational injuries that develop over time affecting the musculoskeletal and peripheral nervous systems. They can develop in any part of the body but are most prevalent in the arms and back. These injuries are caused by jobs that require repeated exertions and movements near the limits of the individual's strength and range-of-motion capability. These movements, although not initially painful, cause micro-traumas to the soft tissues. Over time, small strains to the muscle/tendon/ligament system build up, resulting in fatigue and soreness. If the individual continues the action that is causing pain, musculoskeletal disorders are likely to develop. MSDs can have the following effects on individuals:

- pain
- numbness or loss of sensation
- reduced strength
- degraded ability to perform work
- degraded ability to participate in leisure activities

Here are several good reasons why we should try to eliminate MSDs from the workplace:
- It's the right thing to do.
- It's the humane thing to do.
- MSDs are costly.
- OSHA will make you eliminate them. The agency does not have a specific ergonomics standard but will, under certain circumstances, use its

General Duty Clause Section 5(a)(1) to keep your workplace free from recognized hazards, including ergonomic hazards.

In order to prevent MSDs, we have to understand what causes them. Musculoskeletal disorders have been correlated with hazardous combinations of the following "generic" risk factors:
- forceful exertions
- frequent exertions
- body posture
- mechanical stress
- vibration
- low temperatures

The presence of the above risk factors is related to the design of the job. For example, we can either design a workstation that requires the worker to use a poor posture all day or we can design it so that all operators can do the operation in a good posture. Areas of the design that may expose the worker to these generic risk factors are called "job-specific" risk factors and include these items:
- workplace layout
- tools
- parts
- environment

Figure 8.6 is a table showing, for each involved part of the body, each factor that must be looked at on an ergonomic analysis and at what point you should begin to be concerned that a factor could eventually cause an MSD.

EA Procedure

With the information in figure 8.6 in mind, look at each job to determine the potential of an MSD. It may help to reproduce the form in figure 8.7, which is the checklist you carry with you, with figure 8.6 on the back for your constant reference.

How to Set Objectives with EA:
- number of analyses made
- percentage of jobs completed
- number of suggestions made
- number of job changes made
- number of completions, etc.

Measurement:
- completion to objective

Reward:
- performance appraisals
- recognition of the number of ergonomic assessments completed, which is a leading indicator of safety performance

Hand & Wrist	Possible CTD Problem	Neck	Possible CTD Problem
GRASP • pinch grip • static hold	• prolonged pinch grip • forceful grasp	NECK POSTURE • bend/twist > 20°	• > 50% of time
WRIST POSTURE • flexion/extension • ulnar/radial deviation	• flexion/extension >45° • radial/ulnar deviation	Back LIFTING	Possible CTD Problem • > 90% of Action Limit • non-NIOSH
FREQUENCY • hand or wrist manipulations	• > 10 per minute	TORSO POSTURE • torso bending • torso twisting	• bend > 45° • bend > 20° + twist
MECHANICAL STRESS • localized pressure to palm or fingers • scraping/pumping • strike with hand • single finger trigger	• prolonged exposure • intense exposure	STATIC HOLD/CARRY • > 5 seconds	• > 10 lbs. • 5-10 lbs. with flexed shoulder
		STATIC LOAD • not able to change sit/stand posture over work day	• poor posture
VIBRATION • high frequency vibration	• prolonged exposure		
Arm & Shoulder	Possible CTD Problem	PUSH/PULL • whole body action	• poor conditions
ARM WORK • exertions > 5 lbs.	• little rest between exertions • large exertion	Legs FOOT ACTUATION • foot pedals	Possible CTD Problem • excessive force • extreme posture • high frequency or duration
STATIC LOAD • prolonged holding	• unsupported • large exertion		
ELBOW POSTURE • fully flexed • fully extended • rotated forearm	• repeatedly	LEG POSTURE • knee • ankle	• deep squat • kneeling • 1 legged posture • walk/stand on uneven surface
SHOULDER POSTURE • flexed • extended • abducted	• flex/abduct > 90° • any extension	MECHANICAL STRESS • localized pressure • kicking	• high force • prolonged exposure
MECHANICAL STRESS • sharp edges • hard surfaces	• repeatedly • high force		

Figure 8.6 Ergonomic analysis overview

Failure Modes and Effects Analysis (FMEA)

Failure Modes and Effects Analysis (FMEA) is a systemic, proactive method for evaluating a process to identify where and how it might fail and to assess the relative impact of the various possible failures. This tells you what parts of the process or operation are most in need of change.

FMEA includes these steps:

1. Identify the parts of the process.
2. Identify failure modes—what could go wrong?
3. Identify failure causes—why would the failure happen?
4. Identify failure effects—what would be the consequence of each failure?

Company	**CHECK IF A POSSIBLE CTD PROBLEM**
Dept.	
Supervisor	
Job Name	

LEFT HAND & WRIST	
Grasp	
Wrist Posture	
Frequency	
Mechanical Stress	
Vibration	

Date ....
Time ....
Pace: mach.   self
Job Rotation: yes   no
Regulator Operator yes   no
Tools/Parts   Weight

RIGHT HAND & WRIST	
Grasp	
Wrist Posture	
Frequency	
Mechanical Stress	
Vibration	

ARM & SHOULDERS	
Arm Work	
Static Load	
Elbow Posture	
Shoulder Posture	
Mechanical Stress	

COMMENTS

NECK	
Neck Posture	

BACK	
Lilfting	
Torso Posture	
Static Hold/Carry	
Static Load	
Push/Pull	

LEGS	
Foot Actuation	
Leg Posture	
Mechanical Stress	

Figure 8.7 Ergonomic analysis checklist

FMEA's emphasis on prevention can reduce harm to workers. It is particularly useful in evaluating new processes prior to startup and in assessing the impact of any proposed change to an existing process (Institute for Healthcare Improvement 2017).

FMEA was originally developed by the Society of Automotive Engineers (SAE) for reliability engineers. It continues to be used by reliability engineers for analyzing potential effects caused by system elements ceasing to operate as designed

(Mohr 2002). Today FMEA also is used by hundreds of hospitals for patient and staff safety initiatives.

Process Hazard Analysis (PHA)

A process hazard analysis (PHA) is defined as (OSHA 2013):
- a systematic effort designed to identify and analyze hazards associated with the processing or handling of highly hazardous materials
- a method to provide information that will help employees and employers in making decisions that will improve safety

A PHA analyzes:
- the potential causes and consequences of fires, explosions, and releases of toxic chemicals
- the equipment, instrumentation, human actions, and other factors that might affect the process

A PHA attempts to determine the failure points, methods of operations, and other factors that can potentially lead to incidents.

A PHA team should include engineers, operators, supervisors, and other employees who have knowledge of the standards, codes, specifications, and regulations that apply to the process being studied.

Specific requirements for conducting a process hazard analysis are described in OSHA's *Process Safety Management* standard, the Environmental Protection Agency's Risk Management Plan (RMP) rule, and the NFPA *Standard for the Prevention of Fire and Dust Explosions*. In most cases, PHAs are used to identify, evaluate, and control the hazards of processes involving highly hazardous chemicals.

Hazard and Operability (HAZOP) Study

The Hazard and Operability (HAZOP) analysis methodology is recognized by OSHA as an acceptable methodology for conducting PHAs of processes covered by OSHA's *Process Safety Management* standard. Other regulators also accept the HAZOP methodology for analyzing existing and potential hazards of a complex process that involves a highly hazardous substance.

Dekra uses a structured HAZOP to identify the hazards of a process and to identify potential operating problems. The emphasis is on evaluating the basic control system, providing effective emergency controls, preventing the release of hazardous materials, and mitigating the consequences of a loss of process control or a hazardous material release. A semiquantitative HAZOP risk analysis incorporates the philosophies of Layers of Protection Analysis (LOPA), Safety Instrumented Systems (SIL), and Fault Tree Analysis (FTA) to assess the reliability of process controls and the number and type of risk reduction measures that might be needed.

A HAZOP reviews the available Process Safety Information (PSI) and identifies missing PSI required to support the HAZOP, including hazardous material properties (combustibility, flammability, explosivity, reactivity, self-heating, toxicity, electrostatic properties), process description, process flow sheets, operating procedures, piping and instrumentation drawings (P&IDs), equipment design specifications, pressure relief system specifications, and site and industry data concerning process component failure frequencies and probabilities of failure on demand (PFD).

A HAZOP study establishes the "Design Intent" for the process, including the desired and/or safe ranges for each of the operating parameters, applying guide words (no, less, more, reverse, etc.) to each of the process parameters (temperature, pressure, flow, level, etc.) to identify deviations from the design intent, determining if the control system and emergency systems are adequate and are sufficiently reliable to prevent each deviation from escalating to an undesirable process incident, estimating the severity of the consequences of each undesired incident, estimating the likelihood of occurrence of each undesired incident, utilizing a risk matrix to determine the relative risks of the undesired incidents, comparing the risk of occurrence for each incident with corporate guidelines for process risk, and determining the number and types of safeguards and/or process improvements that would be needed to reduce the risks to negligible or tolerable risks (Dekra 2019).

Other Recommendations

When conducting inspections, OSHA recommends following these basic principles (OSHA 2016):

- Conduct regular inspections of all operations, equipment, work areas, and facilities. Have employees participate on the inspection team and discuss with them all hazards they see or report.
- Be sure to document inspections so you can later verify that hazardous conditions are corrected. Take photos or videos (perhaps using a smartphone) of problem areas to facilitate later discussion and brainstorming about how to control them and for use as learning aids.
- Include all areas and activities in these inspections, such as storage and warehousing, facility and equipment maintenance, purchasing and office functions, and the activities of on-site contractors, subcontractors, and temporary employees.
- Regularly inspect both plant vehicles (e.g., forklifts, powered industrial trucks) and transportation vehicles (e.g., cars, trucks).

Use checklists that highlight hazards, conditions, and locations to assess. As stated earlier, typical hazards fall into several major categories, such as those listed below; each workplace will have its own list. It's worth repeatedly checking for these hazards, and trained workers are your best assets for finding them.

- general housekeeping
- slip, trip, and fall hazards
- electrical hazards
- equipment operation
- equipment maintenance
- fire protection
- work organization and process flow (including staffing and scheduling)
- work practices
- workplace violence
- ergonomic problems
- lack of emergency procedures

Before changing operations, workstations, or workflow; making major organizational changes; or introducing new equipment, materials, or processes; seek the input of employees and evaluate the planned changes for potential hazards and related risks.

REFERENCES

Canadian Centre for Occupational Health and Safety (CCOHS). n.d.-a. "OSH Answers Fact Sheets: Risk Assessment." Accessed December 4, 2019. https://www.ccohs.ca/oshanswers/hsprograms/risk_assessment.html.

Canadian Centre for Occupational Health and Safety (CCOHS). n.d.-b. "OSH Answers Fact Sheets, Job Safety Analysis." Accessed December 4, 2019. https://www.ccohs.ca/oshanswers/hsprograms/job-haz.html.

Dekra. 2019. "Safe Operations with Expert HAZOP Analysis." Accessed March 27, 2019. https://www.dekra.us/en/process-safety-consulting/hazop/.

Institute for Healthcare Improvement. 2017. "QI Essentials Toolkit: Failure Modes and Effects Analysis (FMEA) Tool." Accessed March 27, 2019. http://www.ihi.org/resources/Pages/Tools/FailureModesandEffectsAnalysisTool.aspx.

Mohr, R.R. 2002. *Failure Modes and Effects Analysis*, 8th ed. Jacobs Sverdrup.

Occupational Safety and Health Administration (OSHA). n.d.-a. *Hazard Prevention and Control*. Accessed February 28, 2020. https://www.osha.gov/shpguidelines/hazard-prevention.html.

Occupational Safety and Health Administration (OSHA). n.d.-b. *Ergonomics*. Accessed December 4, 2019. https://www.osha.gov/SLTC/ergonomics/.

Occupational Safety and Health Administration (OSHA). 2013. "Appendix C to §1910.119 — Compliance Guidelines and Recommendations for Process Safety Management (Nonmandatory)." February 8, 2013. Accessed February 27, 2020. https://www.osha.gov/laws-regs/regulations/standardnumber/1910/1910.119Appc.

Occupational Safety and Health Administration (OSHA). 2016. *Recommended Practices for Safety and Health Programs.* OSHA 3885. October 2016. https://www.osha.gov/Publications/OSHA3885.pdf.

Petersen, Dan. 1975. *The OSHA Compliance Manual.* New York: McGraw-Hill.

CHAPTER **9**

Incident Investigations and Root-Cause Analyses

Two of the most documented and publicized incident investigations involving US workplace safety incidents are the 2003 Space Shuttle Columbia Accident Investigation Board (CAIB) independent review conducted by NASA (CAIB 2003) and the 2007 *Report of the BP US Refineries Independent Safety Review Panel*, headed by James A. Baker III, former US Secretary of State for President George H.W. Bush (BP 2019).

The important takeaway from both of these lengthy, far-ranging investigations (the BP report clocks in at 374 pages) is this: there was no singling out of individuals for blame and shame.

As stated in the CAIB findings, "The Board recognized early on that the accident was probably not an anomalous, random event, but rather likely rooted to some degree in NASA's history and the human space flight program's culture" (CAIB 2003). It further reported:

> The organizational causes (include) the original compromises that were required to gain approval for the Shuttle, subsequent years of resource constraints, fluctuating priorities, schedule pressures, mischaracterization of the Shuttle as operational rather than developmental, and lack of an agreed national vision for human space flight. Cultural traits and organizational practices detrimental to safety were allowed to develop, including: reliance on past success as a substitute for sound engineering practices; organizational barriers that prevented effective communication of critical safety information and stifled professional differences of opinion; lack of integrated management across program elements; and the evolution of an informal chain of command and decision-making processes that operated outside the organization's rules.

The BP report arrived at a similar deep-rooted conclusion (BP 2019). "At Texas City, Toledo, and Whiting, BP has not established a positive, trusting, and open environment with effective lines of communication between management and the workforce."

> BP has not provided effective process safety leadership and has not adequately established process safety as a core value across all its five U.S. refineries. While BP has an aspirational goal of "no accidents, no harm to people," BP has not provided effective leadership in making certain its management and U.S. refining workforce understand what is expected of them regarding process safety performance.

Both of these investigations probed more deeply than the obvious mechanical failures or any individual at-risk behavior, finding incident causes ranging from failed leadership to broken lines of communication, lack of employee involvement, the stifling of professional differences, lack of safety as a core value, budget constraints, schedule pressure, and lack of accountability (BP 2019).

You can use these public investigations as models for your own. There was no rush to judgment, no preexisting assumptions or biases about potential causes were made. A cross-disciplinary collaborative team approach was adopted for the investigations. NASA's 13 investigative board members were supported by a staff of 120, along with some 400 NASA engineers. Investigators studied more than 30,000 documents and conducted more than 200 formal interviews (CAIB 2003).

In all likelihood, your incident investigations will have nowhere near the deep pockets, time, resources, and scale described above. But keep in mind the importance of history, context, organizational values, and decision-making—the big picture. After all, it is likely that you will be involved in investigations. According to research, 77% of front-line supervisors are expected to conduct incident investigations, and 75% are expected to determine the root causes of those incidents. These are among the most important safety-related tasks of supervisors (Johnson 2017).

RISK ASSESSMENT TECHNIQUES

The number of risk assessment or incident investigative/root-cause analysis techniques is far beyond the purview of this chapter. A good overall reference is the ISO/IEC Standard 31010:2009 *Risk Assessment Techniques*. It lists 31 methods.

1. Brainstorming
2. Structured or semistructured interviews
3. Delphi method
4. Checklist
5. Preliminary hazard analysis (PHA)
6. Hazard and operability study (HAZOP)
7. Hazard analysis and critical control points (HACCP)
8. Toxicity assessment
9. Structured What If Technique (SWIFT)

10. Scenario analysis
11. Business impact analysis
12. Root-cause analysis
13. Failure modes and effects analysis (FMEA)
14. Fault tree analysis
15. Event tree analysis
16. Cause and consequence analysis
17. Cause-and-effect analysis
18. Layers of protection analysis (LOPA)
19. Decision tree
20. Human reliability analysis (HRA)
21. Bowtie analysis
22. Reliability-centered maintenance
23. Sneak circuit analysis
24. Markov analysis
25. Monte Carlo simulation
26. Bayesian statistics and Bayes nets
27. FN curve (a risk probability curve)
28. Risk index
29. Consequence/probability matrix
30. Cost/benefit analysis
31. Multicriteria decision analysis (MCDA)

Some of these techniques are self-explanatory (e.g., brainstorming, structured or semistructured interviews, checklists). Their complexity ranges from fairly basic to very rigorous. Many could entail a chapter of their own. For example, ISO 31010 *Risk Assessment Techniques* lists Bowtie analysis as a simple diagrammatic way of describing and analyzing the pathways of a risk from hazards to outcomes and reviewing controls. It combines the logic of a fault tree, analyzing the cause of an event, and an event tree, analyzing the consequences.

With the rising popularity of risk assessment and the myriad of methods and techniques, Bowtie analysis is considered medium in complexity. It identifies both the activities that keep a control working and who is responsible for a control. The Bowtie can also be used to assure hazards are managed to a level as low as reasonably practical (ALARP). Bowtie methodology may be appropriate for organizations looking for a more rigorous risk assessment process—one that links causal relationships in high-risk scenarios.

As a front-line supervisor, you are not expected to have knowledge of ISO/IEC's 31 techniques. Safety staff will supply that subject matter expertise. Here we describe several more basic techniques.

Safety Sampling (SS)

Safety Sampling (SS) is a long-time, well-tested technique in incident prevention. It can also be considered a form of behavioral observation. Observing employee safety-related behavior is the second most important safety-related task for supervisors, behind only finding and fixing hazards, according to recent research (Johnson 2017). It is a little different from the other techniques described in this chapter in that it normally is implemented on a companywide basis by management or the safety director rather than within one department by the supervisor. Still, because it has been so effective in safety and health systems, we believe a supervisor can use this tool advantageously within his unit.

What It Is

Safety Sampling measures the effectiveness of the line manager's safety and health activities, but not in terms of how many or how few incidents occur in his area. It measures effectiveness before the fact of an incident by taking a periodic reading of how safely the employees are working.

Like all good accountability systems or measurement tools, SS is also an excellent motivational tool. Each employee finds it important to be working as safely as possible when the sample is taken or the observation conducted. Many organizations that have conducted samplings report a good improvement in their safety and health record as a result of the increased interest in safety and health on the part of employees.

Safety Sampling is based on the quality control principle of random sampling inspection, which is widely used to determine quality of production output without making 100% inspections. The degree of accuracy desired dictates the number of random items selected that must be carefully inspected. The greater the number inspected, the greater the accuracy.

SS Procedure

There are four steps in a Safety Sampling:

1. *Prepare an inventory*—The inventory lists audit categories (position—being in the line of fire or lifting, safe apparel, housekeeping, tools/equipment, and procedures such as lockout-tagout). Sometimes called a Critical Behavior Checklist, it is the key to Safety Sampling (Geller 1996). This list contains specific behaviors that occur in your department that can be observed being performed either safely or when at risk. These are the "incidents waiting to happen." The inventory list is developed from past incident records and from known possible causes. The inventory is then placed in an observation form (see figure 9.1).

2. *Conduct the sample*—The inventory can be attached to a clipboard or loaded on a mobile device. Yes, today you can also do this using a checklist on a mobile device and electronically report and analyze observations. Proceed through your area, observe every employee who is engaged in some form of activity, and record whether the employee is working in a safe or an unsafe manner. Duration, frequency, and scheduling of observations vary widely. First and foremost, the observer must ask permission before beginning an observation. The name of the person observed must never be recorded. To build trust and increase participation, a "no" to a request to observe must be honored (Geller 1996). Each employee is observed only long enough to make a determination. Once the observation is recorded, it should not be changed. If the observation of the employee indicates that they are performing a task safely or unsafely, record the observation appropriately on the checklist. It's important to indicate the type of safe or unsafe practice.
3. *Validate the sample*—The number of observations required to validate the sample is based on the degree of accuracy desired. Count the total number of observations you made. Determine how many unsafe practices you saw. Next, calculate the percentage of unsafe observations. Using this percentage and the desired accuracy, you can calculate the number of observations required by using the data in figure 9.2.
4. *Prepare the report*—Results of your observations can be presented in many different forms, both on paper and electronically. However, the report should include the total percentage of safe and unsafe activities and the number and type of safe and unsafe practices observed.

File paper reports, store software databases of results, and periodically compare your findings to spot trends in the types of both safe and unsafe practices occurring in your unit. This information will help you plan more effective safety training programs. You can also use a database of observations for predictive analytics, employing algorithmic software to identify patterns of safe and at-risk behavior and when and where incidents are most likely to occur.

Benefits

Research has proven that Safety Sampling seems to show the same trends as claim costs, number of incidents, and incident cost per hour worked, although it correlates better with the all-incident rate (all reported incidents per 1000 hours worked).

This seems to indicate SS provides an excellent leading indicator of incident precursors before incidents occur. Of course, by far the greatest benefit of sampling is found in its motivational value. Sampling arouses interest in safety where there has been little interest before.

SAFETY SAMPLING		
A. Number of Safe Observations:		

B. Number of Unsafe Observations:		
Unsafe Act Noted		Sample Date
No safety glasses worn		
Improper use of tools		
Working on unguarded machine		
Not using pushsticks		
Working near tripping hazard		
Improper use of air nozzles		
Using machine improperly		
Wearing loose clothing		
Wearing rings		
Improper lifting		
Improper positioning for lift		
Climbing on racks		
Unsafe loading/piling		
Using defective equipment		
Other: (specify)		

C. Percentage

Sample Date	%	Sample Date	%	Sample Date	%

Supervisor: _____ Department: _____

Figure 9.1 Worksheet for sampling

SS Package

Reproduce figure 9.1 as needed. Then

1. Develop an inventory of unsafe acts you expect to find most often in your department. Record these below the common ones already listed on the form in figure 9.1.
2. For the beginning of the SS program, make trips often throughout the department to build up the number of total observations. Make two or three trips a day at the start. Be sure each employee is observed on each trip.
3. Use figure 9.2 to determine the total number of observations needed to ensure statistical validity. The safer you want your people to work, the more observations you'll need.

Percentage of Unsafe Observations	Observations Needed	Percentage of Unsafe Observations	Observations Needed
10	3,600	30	935
11	3,240	31	890
12	2,930	32	850
13	2,680	33	810
14	2,460	34	775
15	2,270	35	745
16	2,100	36	710
17	1,950	37	680
18	1,830	38	655
19	1,710	39	625
20	1,600	40	600
21	1,510	41	575
22	1,420	42	550
23	1,340	43	530
24	1,270	44	510
25	1,200	45	490
26	1,140	46	470
27	1,080	47	450
28	1,030	48	425
29	980	50	400

Figure 9.2 Number of observations needed for 90% accuracy. (From *Analyzing Safety System Effectiveness*, 3rd ed. By Dan Petersen. Copyright © 1996 by Van Nostrand Reinhold.)

4. If the numbers in figure 9.2 are too high for your department, you may have to cut them down. All this does is reduce your percentage of accuracy. This is not serious since the results are only for your information.
5. Track your findings from week to week. Note progress.
6. Note any trends in types of unsafe acts that are most common. Gear your training to the most common risks.

How to Set Objectives with SS:
- the number of observations you or your team of observers will make
- the percentage of safe and unsafe behaviors you will observe
- the frequency of samples you will take, etc.

Measurement:
- percentage of completion to goal

Reward:
- Performance Appraisal System
- charting and analyzing performance trends

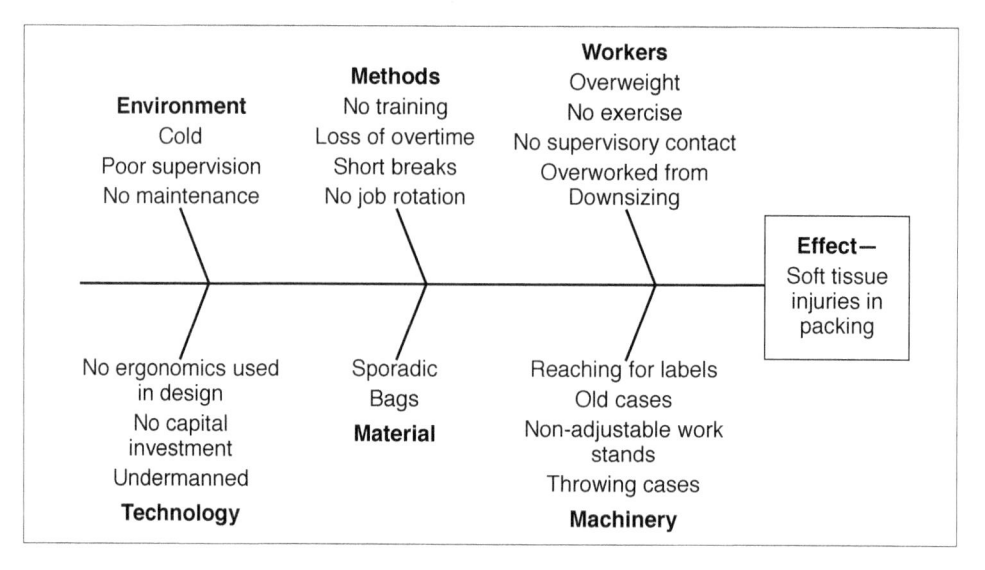

```
                              Workers
              Methods         Overweight
 Environment  No training     No exercise
 Cold         Loss of overtime No supervisory contact
 Poor supervision Short breaks Overworked from
 No maintenance No job rotation Downsizing
                                                    Effect—
                                                    Soft tissue
                                                    injuries in
                                                    packing

 No ergonomics used  Sporadic    Reaching for labels
 in design           Bags        Old cases
 No capital          Material    Non-adjustable work
 investment                      stands
 Undermanned                     Throwing cases
 Technology                      Machinery
```

Figure 9.3 Fishbone chart of conditions contributing to soft tissue injuries in a packing/shipping department

Statistical Safety Control (SSC)

Statistical Safety Control (SSC) applies some common Statistical Process Control (SPC) concepts to safety. The SPC tools used most easily by supervisors are the Pareto Chart, the Fishbone Diagram, the Flowchart, and the Control Chart.

The use of statistical methods is not an all-purpose remedy for every corporate problem. But it is a rational, logical, and organized way to create a system that can assure continuing, ongoing improvements in quality and productivity simultaneously. This is also true for safety.

The SPC method is really a two-pronged approach: (1) increasing employee involvement and (2) problem-solving.

The chart in figure 9.3 was developed by a group of hourly employees to identify why (combinations of reasons) they get soft tissue injuries. The problem was a soft tissue injury in wrists, shoulders, and backs.

Pareto Chart

Paretos can be used in many ways in safety to plot types of injuries that have occurred in your department (see figure 9.4).

In our example, it was decided from Pareto charts that a step change could be made to reduce soft tissue injuries in two departments: the packers in the packaging department and the box handlers in shipping.

The group next used a third SPC tool, a flowchart—basically a step-by-step picture of the step change process (figure 9.5).

Finally, the group decided to concentrate on these factors:
- Get adjustable packing tables.
- Do preshift warm-up exercises.
- Use wrist supports.
- Rotate packers hourly.

A substantial improvement was achieved. The approach became a normal way of life in the plant and was used on other safety, quality, and productivity problems.

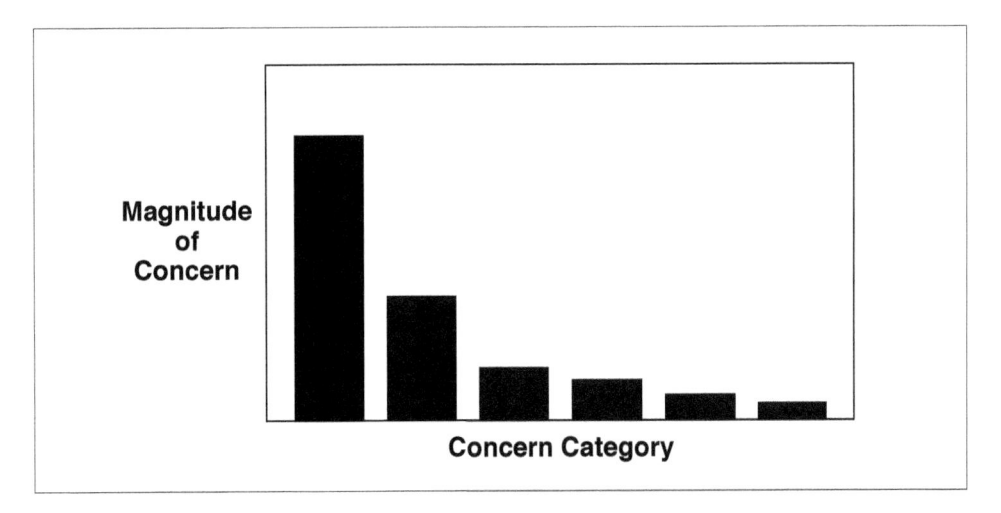

Figure 9.4 Basic Pareto chart: A bar graph of identified causes shown in descending order of magnitude or frequency

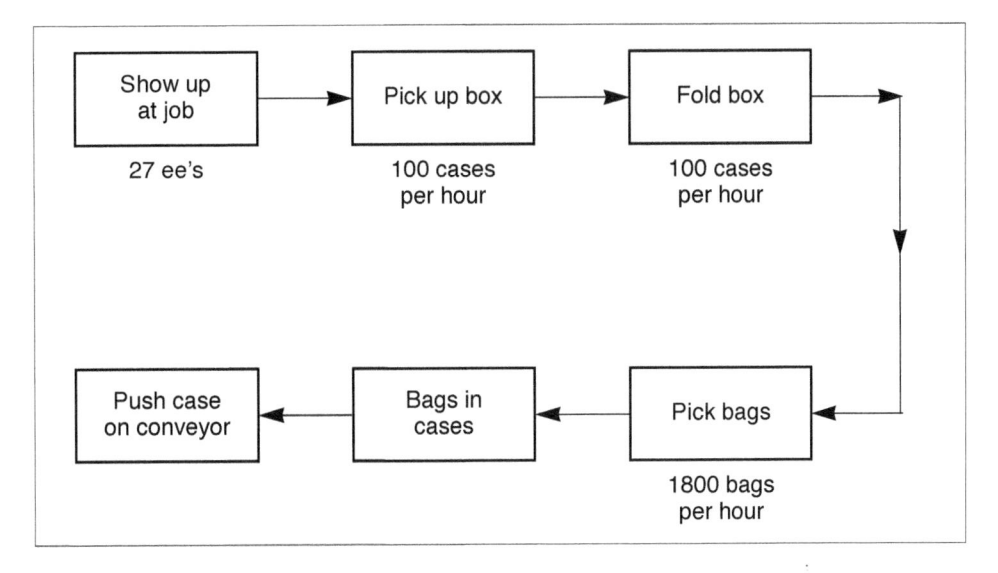

Figure 9.5 Flowchart of a packing process

In using SPC in safety, specific problems can be targeted and solved, and the system can be monitored.

How to Set Objectives with SSC:
- number of times the specific tools have been used (Pareto charts, fishbone diagrams, etc.)
- percentage of incidents where fishbone diagrams were used
- number of problems solved by employee groups using Paretos, flowcharts, etc.

Measurement:
- completion to objectives set

Reward:
- Performance Appraisal System
- tracking and analyzing safety performance trends

Technique of Operations Review (TOR)

The Technique of Operations Review (TOR) was devised to assist you in finding some of the multiple, interrelated causes behind the incidents you are required to investigate. It is basically a tracing system. It also can be used as a training technique in safety.

In a tracing system, the investigator (you) is initially asked to identify what appears to be a major cause or factor behind an event (the incident or close call). You select this cause from a long list of possible causes. Following the description of each major cause are numbers that lead you to other connecting factors, which might also be contributing causes.

The TOR System

The TOR system centers around the Cause Code shown in figure 9.6. The supervisor's incident investigation report in figure 9.7 was developed for use with the TOR by Paul Mueller of the Green Giant Company.

The TOR system begins with an incident or close call. Its purpose is to expose what the real causes are behind this event, which is viewed as a symptom of a more serious problem. These are the steps of the TOR:

1. Describe the event. State clearly what happened.
2. Select one number from the Cause Code (figure 9.6), which seems to be the immediate cause of the event.
3. Trace and eliminate. The initially chosen number is jotted on the form, and the trace step begins. Following this initial number, and in its description, will be other numbers. Jot them down

and read their descriptions. Then decide whether they could also be contributing causes to the event. These numbers lead to additional numbers. List them. Read their descriptions and decide again. Keep tracing and eliminating numbers until you run out of numbers. When the "outs" overtake the "ins," or the final number on the list repeats the number at the top, you have come full circle. The numbers and descriptions that remain are those you have decided are contributing factors.
4. List the contributing factors.
5. Select solutions.

Benefits

The TOR helps identify and define problems by searching for root causes. Such causes, if undetected, might lead eventually to safety incidents and other kinds of losses.

The TOR Package

Reproduce figure 9.8 in sufficient quantities so that all participating supervisors receive 50 copies each. Proceed as follows:

1. Take each event and incident as it occurs in your department and submit it to the TOR analysis using the chart in figure 9.6. Record your findings as you go on figure 9.8.
2. List the contributing factors and corrective actions for each event and incident (see number 3 on figure 9.7).
3. Prioritize the list of actions and set a time schedule to accomplish your goals.
4. Submit to others (and to your boss) the actions that are beyond your direct control.
5. File all figure 9.8s for your future training uses.

Incident Recall Technique (IRT)

The Incident Recall Technique (IRT) has great potential. It is helpful to the line manager and the corporate safety and health program because it is proactive—unearthing many more potential incident causes than most techniques and discovering these causes before they result in incidents of a serious nature. Plus, the IRT involves your workers and demonstrates to them your sincere interest in creating a safe working environment. For these reasons, we have included this technique and urge you to consider its use.

1 TRAINING

10. Training not formulated or need not foreseen 23, 48, 64
11. Instruction was given but results show it didn't take 44, 47, 56, 75
12. Training available but the employee was not assigned or did not attend 26, 35, 87
13. Performance not in accord with policy or procedure 47, 55, 62
14. Failure to provide training whose need had been specified 34, 83, 88
15. Error blamed on faulty training when in fact the error stemmed from deficiencies in management systems 26, 36, 52, 81

3 DECISION & DIRECTION

30. By-passing, conflicting orders, too many bosses 33, 48, 80
31. Decision too far above the problem 34, 83
32. Authority inadequate to cope with the situation 22, 82
33. Decision exceeded authority 13, 47, 86
34. Decision evaded; power to decide not exercised 25, 85
35. Orders or directives failed to produce desired action. Not clear, not understood, or not followed 41, 50, 52
36. Failure to investigate, and to apply the lessons of similar mishaps 26, 43, 61
37. Hazard or problem — controls not developed 26, 64, 66, 86

TRACE GUIDE

| 10 | 11 | 12 | 13 | 14 | 15 |
| 20 | 21 | 22 | 23 | 24 | 25 | 26 |

| 30 | 31 | 32 | 33 | 34 | 35 | 36 | 37 |
| 40 | 41 | 42 | 43 | 44 | 45 | 46 | 47 | 48 |

2 RESPONSIBILITY

20. Duties and tasks not clear, or not accepted 22, 25, 40
21. Conflicting goals 30, 48, 83
22. Dual or overlapping responsibility 25, 30, 48, 80
23. Pressure of immediate tasks obscures full scope of responsibilities 10, 32, 34, 87
24. Buck passing, responsibility not tied down 25, 48, 82
25. Job descriptions inadequate 48, 80, 84
26. Hazard or problem — not recognized .34, 37, 48, 81

4 SUPERVISION

40. Failure to orient or coach — new worker, unusual situation, unfamiliar equipment or process, etc. 23, 24
41. Information provided was insufficient to do the job right 23, 35, 48
42. Lack of two-way communication; failure to listen 15, 36, 82
43. Failure to correct behavior or procedure before accident/incident occurred 26, 36, 61, 73
44. Failure to supervise closely until proficiency was assured 23, 36, 48, 64
45. Honest error. Failure to act, or action turned out to be wrong 14, 15, 20
46. Disorder or confusion in work area 34, 54, 56, 87
47. Job practice out of step with job training 15, 42, 63
48. Initiative. Failure to see problems and exert an influence on them 23, 42, 50, 85

TOR Analysis Worksheets and materials
Licensing arrangements
Management and Employee Training

Available from R. G. Hallock, PhD
Training Consultants to Business and Industry
Business and Technology Center Ste. 211
Pueblo, Colorado 81003
Phone (719) 584-2435

Figure 9.6 TOR Cause Code

Why Accidents Aren't Reported

Confidential perception surveys conducted by consulting firms in a number of companies have revealed that it is fairly common for both supervisors and employees to hide accidents. It is more common among employees. The reasons usually given for not reporting accidents are:

- fear of discipline
- concern about the incident record
- concern about reputation

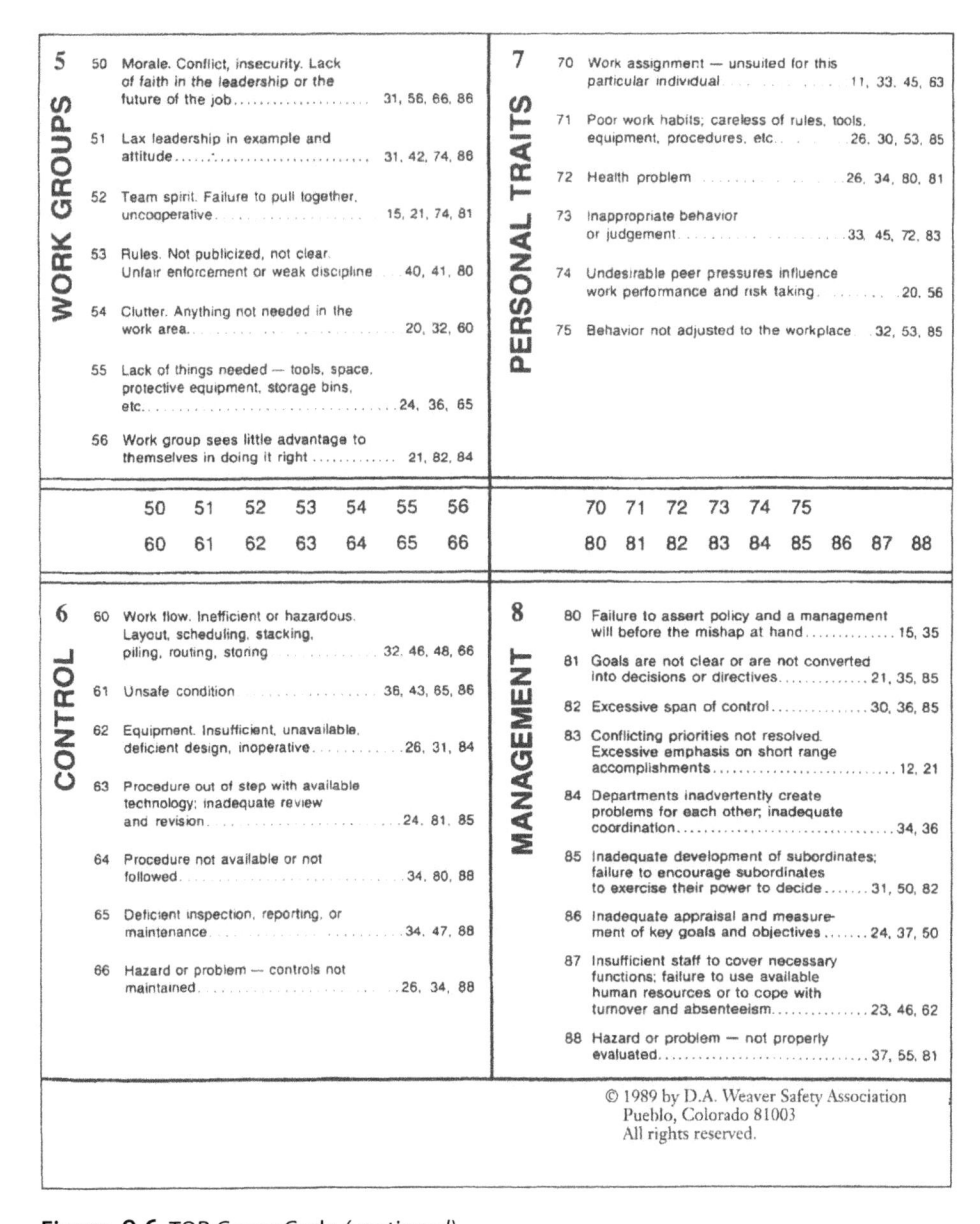

5 **WORK GROUPS**	50 Morale. Conflict, insecurity. Lack of faith in the leadership or the future of the job................. 31, 56, 66, 86 51 Lax leadership in example and attitude........................ 31, 42, 74, 86 52 Team spirit. Failure to pull together, uncooperative................... 15, 21, 74, 81 53 Rules. Not publicized, not clear. Unfair enforcement or weak discipline . . . 40, 41, 80 54 Clutter. Anything not needed in the work area.................. 20, 32, 60 55 Lack of things needed — tools, space, protective equipment, storage bins, etc................ 24, 36, 65 56 Work group sees little advantage to themselves in doing it right......... 21, 82, 84	**7** **PERSONAL TRAITS**	70 Work assignment — unsuited for this particular individual . . . . 11, 33, 45, 63 71 Poor work habits; careless of rules, tools, equipment, procedures, etc. . . . 26, 30, 53, 85 72 Health problem . . . . 26, 34, 80, 81 73 Inappropriate behavior or judgement . . . . 33, 45, 72, 83 74 Undesirable peer pressures influence work performance and risk taking. . . . . . . 20, 56 75 Behavior not adjusted to the workplace . . 32, 53, 85

50	51	52	53	54	55	56		70	71	72	73	74	75		
60	61	62	63	64	65	66		80	81	82	83	84	85	86	87	88

6 **CONTROL**	60 Work flow. Inefficient or hazardous. Layout, scheduling, stacking, piling, routing, storing . . . . 32, 46, 48, 66 61 Unsafe condition . . . . 36, 43, 65, 86 62 Equipment. Insufficient, unavailable, deficient design, inoperative......... 26, 31, 84 63 Procedure out of step with available technology; inadequate review and revision. . . . . 24, 81, 85 64 Procedure not available or not followed. . . . . 34, 80, 88 65 Deficient inspection, reporting, or maintenance. . . . . 34, 47, 88 66 Hazard or problem — controls not maintained. 26, 34, 88	**8** **MANAGEMENT**	80 Failure to assert policy and a management will before the mishap at hand. . . . . 15, 35 81 Goals are not clear or are not converted into decisions or directives. . . . . 21, 35, 85 82 Excessive span of control. . . . . 30, 36, 85 83 Conflicting priorities not resolved. Excessive emphasis on short range accomplishments. . . . . 12, 21 84 Departments inadvertently create problems for each other; inadequate coordination. . . . . 34, 36 85 Inadequate development of subordinates; failure to encourage subordinates to exercise their power to decide. . . . . . . 31, 50, 82 86 Inadequate appraisal and measurement of key goals and objectives. . . . . 24, 37, 50 87 Insufficient staff to cover necessary functions; failure to use available human resources or to cope with turnover and absenteeism. . . . . 23, 46, 62 88 Hazard or problem — not properly evaluated. 37, 55, 81

© 1989 by D.A. Weaver Safety Association
Pueblo, Colorado 81003
All rights reserved.

Figure 9.6 TOR Cause Code *(continued)*

- fear of medical treatment
- dislike of medical personnel
- desire not to interrupt work
- avoidance of red tape involved
- desire to keep personal record clear
- concern about what others might think
- poor understanding of the need to report
- desire to achieve safety incentive rewards

```
                        INCIDENT INVESTIGATION
Employee (if involved)              Dept.           Clock No.
Incident date                       Reported

1. Describe the incident. Include location, witnesses, and circumstances surrounding incident. Try to
   identify the causal factors involved.




2. Subject causes to TOR analysis: state, trace, eliminate.




3. List factors for which you will initiate corrective action.
   Factor:                          Action:


4. List factors which require feasible corrective action by others. Circle routing to their attention.

```

Figure 9.7 Supervisor's incident investigation report

Most of these barriers to reporting incidents are eliminated by the IRT. It takes little effort on your part to gain considerably more incident information on potential causes through the IRT than through more conventional means.

The IRT Procedure

The basic objective of the IRT is to gain the cooperation of employees so they can and will freely recall all incidents from the past. The success of the IRT, in terms of the number of incidents revealed, depends primarily on the skill you use in the interview. Here are the steps of the IRT:

1. Put the employee at ease by ensuring confidentiality.
2. Explain the purpose of the interview and of the IRT.
3. Give assurance that the IRT is totally confidential. Your initial success depends to a great degree on this confidentiality.
4. Point out the benefits of the IRT to everyone—to the employee, his family, his department, his company.
5. Show and explain the report form to him. (See figure 9.9.)

TECHNIQUE OF OPERATIONS REVIEW

Employee involved: Department:

Incident date:

1. Description of the incident:

2. Your TOR Analysis: Trace and Eliminate

3. Causes decided upon:

4. Corrections decided upon:

Figure 9.8 Worksheet for reviewing technique of operations

6. Conduct the interview. Simply ask the employee to recall each incident and near miss seen or heard about on the job. With each incident recalled, be sure to determine how many times the incident was seen or was heard being discussed. Jot down all pertinent information.
7. Probe far and wide. Ask lots of questions to fill in memory gaps. Avoid interrupting but get full information on each incident.
8. Review your understanding of the incident with the employee. Repeat it to make sure you've got it right.
9. Discuss the causes of the incident with the employee and possible remedies. Make it clear you want and need help.
10. Conclude your interviews with "thank you."

Benefits

First and foremost, you are being proactive and may be able to prevent incidents from occurring. Second, you have heightened employee interest in safety and health by asking for and receiving involvement and participation. You have also gotten more information on incident precursors than you would have through a more conventional method. And you have demonstrated to the employee that you care, that you are sincerely interested in safety. Furthermore, the IRT can help you

INCIDENT RECALL TECHNIQUE	
Person interviewed:	Date:
Supervisor:	Department:
Incidents recalled:	
Analysis of causes of recalled incidents:	
Action taken on causes:	

Figure 9.9 Worksheet for incident recall

check your Safety Sampling findings and give you additional input for your safety and health training programs.

The IRT Package

Reproduce figure 9.9 in sufficient quantities so that all participating supervisors can each have 100 for a start. Proceed as follows:

1. Make a list of all employees in your department and schedule one interview per week.
2. Carry out the interviews as scheduled and as discussed in this section.
3. At the end of each interview complete figure 9.9.
4. Let the interviewed employee review the finished report and make any additions.
5. Provide the employee with a copy of the completed form.
6. Keep several additional copies for your records and for future training material.

5-Why Problem-Solving Process

Using this traditional strategy, you want to first identify the problem or incident event involved and grasp the overall situation. Then you dig into the "why" factors. Why was the problem not identified? Why did the system allow the incident to occur? By repeatedly asking "why" five times for each aspect of an incident, you identify incident contributors and/or each cause.

One example: two flow control valves fail. No electric current was received by pumps. (Why did both pumps fail? Why was there no electric current being received by the pumps?) The fuses failed. Voltage, power supply, and relays were functional. (Why did the fuses fail?) The current overloaded the fuse. (Why did the current overload the fuse?) 15 amp fuses had been installed instead of 20 amp fuses. (Why were 15 amp fuses installed?) Because no 20 amp fuses were available at the stores at the time of maintenance, and the electrician used his judgment based on previous experience with these types of pumps.

Gap Analysis

A gap analysis checklist, either on paper or a mobile device, is most often used as a proactive, preincident tool to assess the current state of your safety and health processes. It can also be used postincident to identify gaps or flaws in your processes that contributed to the incident.

Develop your gap analysis checklist of categories based on the most common elements of a safety and health process, such as leadership, training, and hazard prevention and control. When answering questions relating to each category, you must answer simply yes, no, or not applicable.

For example, in the leadership category, one question might be: Is everybody aware of their health and safety responsibilities, accountabilities, and the consequences of nonconformance with the health and safety policy?

In the organizational category, questions could be: Have you identified all jobs and tasks that present a hazard? Have you applied controls to eliminate or reduce the identified risks?

In the hazard prevention and control processes category, you can ask if lockout-tagout, confined spaces, and control of toxic substances procedures are in place—especially important if the incident involved one of these activities. In the training category, you can ask if the type of incident (material handling, vehicle safety, fatigue management, distracted driving, use of PPE, etc.) is regularly covered and documented as a training topic. You can find a sample gap analysis questionnaire at the Canadian Centre for Occupational Health and Safety website (www.ccohs.ca/gapanalysis).

Incident Cause Analysis Method (ICAM)

ICAM draws on the work of organizational psychologist and human error expert Professor James Reason. Its methodology was developed by Gerry Gibb (Safety Wise CEO) with the assistance of Professor Reason, the Australian Transport Safety Bureau (ATSB), and in consultation with safety representatives from industry (Dam 2016).

ICAM does not focus on intentional or unintentional acts of human error that led to an incident. Such a focus is the "person model." Focusing on the individual does not consider the underlying factors that contributed to the actions, or the context in which they occurred. If you consider only the obvious "active" failures and unsafe acts, rather than identifying those potential causes or "latent conditions" within the system, you will limit the potential of your investigation to prevent the same event from recurring.

In Professor Reason's famous Swiss Cheese Model, active failures (holes in the cheese) are the acts or conditions precipitating the incident situation. They usually involve the front-line staff, and the consequences are immediate and can often be prevented by design, training, or operating systems. Latent failures (also holes in the cheese) include contributory factors that may lie dormant for days, weeks, or months until they contribute to the accident. These refer to less apparent failures of organization or design that contributed to the occurrence of errors or allowed them to cause harm to workers.

Every step in a process has the potential for failure, to varying degrees. The ideal safety system is analogous to a stack of slices of Swiss cheese. Consider the holes to be opportunities for a process to fail, and each of the slices as "defensive layers" in the process. An error may allow a problem to pass through a hole in one layer, but in the next layer the holes are in different places, and the problem should be caught. Each layer is a defense against potential error impacting the outcome.

For a catastrophic error to occur, the holes need to align for each step in the process, allowing all defenses to be defeated and resulting in an error. If the layers are set up with all the holes lined up, this is an inherently flawed system that will allow a problem at the beginning to progress all the way through to adversely affect the outcome. Each slice of cheese is an opportunity to stop an error. The more defenses you put up, the better. Also, the fewer the holes and the smaller the holes, the more likely you are to catch/stop errors that may occur (Reason 1990).

ICAM is a holistic analysis method that aims to identify both local factors and failures within the broader organization and production system that contributed to the incident. These factors can include communication, training, operating procedures, incompatible goals, change management, organizational culture, and equipment. The objective is to identify what really went wrong and to make recommendations on necessary remedial actions to reduce risk and build error-tolerant defenses against future incidents.

As mentioned at the start of this chapter, today there are an ever-increasing number of incident investigation techniques. Many are software programs and apps that eliminate pencil-whipping and paperwork. One source lists more than 50 available programs (capterra.com/investigation-management-software/.). Software provider Intelex reports having more than 1000 clients and 1,000,000 users worldwide, including Volvo, Siemens, Nestle, and American Electric Power.

"Managing incident reporting and investigation in your organization has never been easier. Safety Incident Reporting Software lets you easily record, track, trend and investigate all types of incidents, near-misses and dangerous conditions," states the vendor, Intelex.

Employees can access or report information on mobile devices. Incident reporting software documents incidents, near-events, injuries; creates custom reporting forms; assigns corrective/preventive action tasks; shows incident performance metrics using dashboards and reports; identifies contributing factors and root causes of varying complexity; uses multiple cause analysis methodologies (basic checklist, fishbone diagrams, 5 whys, gap analysis, etc.); identifies and implements corrective actions to mitigate root causes; and analyzes trend data to implement preventive measures (Intelex n.d.).

REFERENCES

BP US Refineries Independent Safety Review Panel. 2007. *Report of the BP US Refineries Independent Safety Review Panel.* January 2007. sunnyday.mit.edu/Baker-panel-report.pdf.

Columbia Accident Investigation Board (CAIB). 2003. *Report of Columbia Accident Investigation Board, Volume I.* Washington, DC: NASA. Accessed March 13, 2018. https://history.nasa.gov/columbia/CAIB_reportindex.html.

Dam, Luke. 2016. "The Benefits of the ICAM Incident Investigation Process." *Safety Wise*, Victoria, Australia, February 23, 2016. https://www.safetywise.com/post/2016/02/24/the-benefits-of-the-icam-incident-investigation-process.

Geller, E. Scott. 1996. *Working Safe.* Philadelphia: Chilton Book Company.

Intelex. n.d. "Safety Incident Reporting Software." Accessed March 27, 2019. https://www.intelex.com/landing/safety-incident-reporting-software-0?source=h%2b1cla%2byaKH2gBG7oq333hx90y0Zs0roEexi3cct9Kdand%2bJBePcODv4MYXFEYJOqOmPLwG8q97wQZR5jjFmpw%3d%3d&gclid=EAIaIQobChMI7rS7_9Dh1wIVgbrACh2aTA17EAAYASAAEgK0EvD_BwE.

Johnson, Dave. 2017. "State of the EHS Nation." Reader Survey. *Industrial Safety & Hygiene News.* October 2017.

Petersen, Dan. 1996. *Analyzing Safety System Effectiveness*, 3rd ed. New York: Van Nostrand Reinhold.

Reason, James. 1990. *Human Error.* Cambridge, England: Cambridge University Press.

PART **IV**

Stepping into the Future

CHAPTER **10**

The New Realities of Safety and Health

Safety and health has experienced a shift in paradigms, something most supervisors have not yet realized.

A paradigm can be loosely defined as the rules and beliefs that guide our decisions and actions; the "ground rules," if you will, of the game that we are in. When we live within certain parameters, by certain ground rules, we act in certain ways. We are comfortable; we know "what's right" and "what works." When the rules change, we are usually lost for a while. We cannot cope. Nothing works.

When you go through a paradigm shift, everything you have believed in becomes suspect—you go back to square one. So, you first must realize that a paradigm shift has indeed taken place, that the ground beneath your feet has shifted. Reality has changed. This is not always obvious, particularly to those who have spent a lifetime in safety and health, or to supervisors with limited safety and health responsibilities. But many changes are happening right now. As a supervisor and leader, you need to keep up with the changes.

EXTERNAL ENVIRONMENT CHANGES

External realities have already shifted within our companies. They include:

1. *Workers' compensation is not the "shield" many employers believe it to be.* For instance (Kleiner 2018):
   - Most of us know that injuries that happen at the workplace are covered by workers' compensation, but workers' comp also extends to time on the job spent away from the workplace. Many employees receive compensation for injuries incurred while traveling on business, running a work-related errand, or attending a tradeshow or conference. Employees can also receive compensation for injuries or illnesses that happen over time due to work conditions, like carpal tunnel syndrome, lung disease, and stress-related issues.

- Workers' compensation doesn't cover all on-the-job illnesses and injuries. Not everything that happens in the workplace is covered by workers' compensation. There are a variety of incidents that workers' compensation may not cover, including injuries caused by alcohol or drugs, employee self-inflicted harm, fights started by an employee, violations of company policy, and felonies.
- Workers' compensation doesn't protect employers from every lawsuit. Workers' compensation protects employers in most instances, but there are exceptions that allow employees to sue employers for compensation. If an employee is injured because the employer acted irresponsibly, the employee may be able to sue the business for pain and suffering.

2. *Executives can go to jail today for not dealing with hazards—manslaughter charges, conspiracy charges, willful violations, etc.*
   No executive today (in his right mind) can ignore safety in a commercial enterprise, but executives focused on the many facets of business might have no idea whether safety and health is under control, and they do not learn in business school what questions to ask.

3. *OSHA penalties were significantly increased in 2016.*

Violation Type	Current Maximum Penalty	2016 Maximum Penalty*
Other than serious	$7000	$12,600
Serious	$7000	$12,600
Willful	$70,000	$126,000
Repeat	$70,000	$126,000

   OSHA has instituted a Severe Violator Enforcement Program (SVEP). The SVEP concentrates resources on inspecting employers who have demonstrated indifference to their Occupational Safety and Health Act obligations by willful, repeated, or failure-to-abate violations.

   OSHA fines have reached as high as $81 million—to BP in 2009. The top 25 highest OSHA fines are all above $2.8 million dollars.

4. *The focus has shifted from objective injuries to subjective injuries, from cuts and bruises to back strains, soft tissue injuries, and psychological stress claims.* Guarding machines does not help to reduce frequency rates of many of these injuries.

   The ability to file workers' comp claims for stress due to the job varies by state. In one state, all claims of job-related stress can fall short of the standard of proof that the worker's disability must result from an "objectively verified," job-related stress situation. In another state, a psychiatric injury is compensable if there is a diagnosed mental disorder that caused the disability or the need for treatment. An injured employee must prove that the actual events of employment were the predominant cause (51%) among all of the combined causes of the psychiatric injury. The employee has the burden of proof, which must include the employee's prior medical history, financial/medical issues, and personal/family issues (Schuetz 2013).

5. ***Industries under the microscope have changed from heavy manufacturing to healthcare, energy extraction, retail services, warehousing, and construction*** (which has always been a top OSHA enforcement priority).

6. ***Safety and health performance has become a factor in corporate sustainability ratings and criteria for "green" investing.*** Wall Street analysts, stockholders, and consumers are more interested in corporate safety and health performance than ever before—particularly as it relates to sustainability and a positive brand reputation.

   How do we cope with these external realities? This is what we are trying to determine. Perhaps we need two separate and distinct staffs—one for safety and health, one for compliance. The two functions can in reality have little to do with each other.

7. ***Uncertainty challenges senior leaders in organizations*** due to fast-changing technology disruptions and domestic and global political and economic instability. Howard Schultz, former executive chairman of Starbucks said: "We are living in a world right now where every day, almost, some episodic event is affecting the way we live, the way we think, levels of anxiety, lack of trust, lack of confidence, polarization, dysfunction. How could we ignore what is going on?" (Sorkin 2017)

8. ***We live in anxious times.*** The job market is more uncertain and time demands are expanding. The pressure to be "on call" and available for work is now 24/7/365. Employees feel more stressed to prove their worth and produce, produce, produce, often extending work hours. The price of just about everything—housing, transportation, healthcare—is increasing.

   In 2016, the World Health Organization estimated that without more treatment, 12 billion workdays will be lost to anxiety by the year 2030. Demand for antianxiety and antidepressant medications has skyrocketed. According to Zion Market Research, the "general anxiety disorder market" is undergoing rapid growth and is expected to generate revenue of $3.7 billion by the end of 2020 in the United States (Mahdawi 2018).

9. ***Technological advances demand safety checks.*** Smart robots and complex software systems need to be verified for performance. Safety-critical technology needs to be vetted. Crashes of two Boeing 737 Max 8 jets in 2018–2019 might have been caused by the failure of software intended to prevent the planes from stalling. In 2018, an Arizona woman was

killed by one of Uber's autonomous cars when the vehicle's autonomy systems failed to brake, as did the driver behind the wheel. "As you create more advanced artificial intelligence systems, the harm that can result from the failing can be really large," said Jade Leung, a researcher at Oxford University's Center for the Governance of Artificial Intelligence (Condliffe 2019).

INTERNAL ENVIRONMENT CHANGES

Internal realities continue to shift within our companies. They include:

1. *Changing styles and beliefs of management.* Companies have gone from hierarchal structures to team-based work.
2. *From transactional (focus on the status quo and day-to-day progress toward goals) to transformational leadership* (enhancing the motivation and engagement of followers by directing their behavior toward a shared vision). See chapter 6 for more on transformational leadership.
3. *From treating workers as replaceable cogs to being assets,* partners, and talent.
4. *From focusing on the work to focusing on the worker*—the individual as a whole person, on and off the job. Wellness, well-being, fitness, and lifestyle choices are discussed much more in many companies, with policies and programs being created to boost overall employee health—both physically and mentally.
5. *From compliance, discipline, and maintaining the status quo to maximizing contributions of employees;* to empowering workers to go beyond self-interests; and to demonstrating empathy and caring for workers.
6. *Companies have transitioned from focusing on task behavior and orientation to relationship behavior*—engagement, psychological support, and an emphasis on worker well-being 24/7/365.
7. *Management structures have changed* from autocratic, authoritarian, command and control ("Do as I say") to democratic and employee oriented (with the emphasis on engaging workers, getting their ideas and input).
8. *During these major philosophical management shifts, safety and health has largely gone its own way, ignoring reality.*
9. *Most safety and health processes remain "classical" in nature*—management decides and lectures, and people follow the rules. Especially in small to midsize firms, OSHA compliance remains job one, sometimes the only safety priority.
10. *We still talk about the supervisor as the key person in safety and health;* meanwhile, companies are heading toward having no supervisors. We do not seem to be integrating safety and health into our changing management philosophies.

SAFETY AND HEALTH CHANGES

We have new realities in the external environment and in the internal workings of our organizations. But that is not all. We have new realities in safety and health also—in our beliefs about what causes an incident on the job. We used to believe incidents were caused by unsafe acts and/or unsafe conditions. Today we believe we have to reveal the root causes of unsafe conditions (a defect or defects in the management system) and, more important, the causes of human error, which are inevitable.

We have been studying the causes of human error since World War II. That's 80 years of research; we ought to know a lot. For instance, people err more when overloaded (physically, physiologically, psychologically). They err more when their workstations are poorly designed or when management has built in error traps (piece rates, wage incentives, early quits, etc.). It is normal for people to act unsafely when they are adhering to group norms and perceive a greater reward for productivity than safety.

When we shift our emphasis away from unsafe acts and conditions, we have had a paradigm shift. This requires us to question most traditional safety tools: inspections, investigations, JSAs, training, and so on. All of these tools search for symptoms, not for causes—that's like treating a brain tumor with an aspirin.

So, how do we deal with safety and health and accident prevention at the causal level?

Do the traditional "Three Es" of safety (Engineering, Education, and Enforcement) work?

The Three Es are hopelessly out of date unless we change their original meanings. Engineering has to be broadened to include ergonomics; the organization of work (scheduling, shifts, workflow layouts, work hours, etc.); the causes of disease, of stress, and so forth. As an example of this expansion, in 2018 the American Society of Safety Engineers changed its name to the American Society of Safety Professionals. We also must recognize that traditional safety education and enforcement are clearly not always valuable options in influencing behavior and will only be effective if we treat people maturely—using positive reinforcement—and invite their involvement and participation.

In all of this, we end up attacking our fundamental safety beliefs—Heinrich's "Axioms of Industrial Safety," which date back to the 1930s.

NEW PRINCIPLES

Heinrich's axioms, mostly untrue and never proven, have been our paradigms in safety. They are no longer. We have had a paradigm shift. What are the new principles? Safety people are now searching for and implementing them. They include:

- An emphasis on health (physical and mental) and well-being is increasing.

- Potentially violent behavior, such as verbal and physical abuse, bullying, harassment, and active shooters, is receiving more attention.
- The organization of work and its effect on employee stress and mental health is receiving more attention.
- Serious injuries and fatalities (SIFs), which continue to haunt major corporations with otherwise excellent safety and health processes, is a much researched and discussed topic. SIFs tend to occur in unusual and nonroutine work, where upsets occur, in nonproduction activities, where sources of high energy are present, when outside contractors are brought in to perform nonroutine jobs, and during plant construction operations.
- Occupational safety and health management systems, such as the recently released ISO 45001 standard and the ANSI/ASSP Z10: 2019 standard, are being operationalized by more companies.
- Human and operational performance (HOP), which recognizes the inevitability of human error, is a major topic at conferences, seminars, and summits; in books and articles; and in distance learning.
- Systems thinking is increasingly prevalent. Dr. James Reason asserts the best way to prevent workplace accidents is to take a system approach and look at "error traps" in the workplace that give rise to accidents, rather than taking a person approach and focusing on human fallibility, which is inevitable (Reason 1990).
- Human error is discussed, not in terms of humans being stupid or clumsy, although some of us are, but with the focus on management systems and designs that trap employees into error.
- It's recognized that employees err oftentimes because the work environment is incompatible with the individual's physique or with what they are physically used to; in other words, a bad fit exists. Another trap is workplace design that is conducive to human error, such as hard-to-read controls; a workstation that is cramped, dark, or otherwise difficult to operate in (poor human factors); and in changing weather/environmental conditions. Worker fatigue is a common factor in safety-related incidents, especially among individuals working rotating shifts, long shifts, and in long-haul trucking.
- The organizational culture is being seen as a potential trap by encouraging or discouraging certain behaviors. For example, does the culture promote the notion that workers should report signs of ergonomic distress early on, or does it reward them for hiding symptoms? Does the culture preach a concern for safety, but demonstrate the opposite in practice? Does the culture seek safety and health-related ideas and assistance from employees or reject their participation?

- Worker engagement is a priority in many companies. Get everyone involved. Let people know their opinion matters and they have a stake beyond just showing up for work every day.
- High-performing safety and health is recognized as the result of good relationships and a strong culture among hourly people.
- Emotions and feelings receive more attention today. How people feel about one another on the job is important to build a profitable, safe, and sustainable organizational culture.
- Developing safety as a personal value is a point of emphasis. When all employees accept safety as a personal value, the likelihood of unsafe behavior is minimized.
- Safety in the gig economy receives more attention. The safety of temporary workers, independent contractors, and part-time employees cannot be neglected. Any confusion must be straightened out regarding who is responsible for the safety and health training of temporary workers, hazard communication, recordkeeping requirements—the host/client employer or the temporary staffing agency. OSHA has concerns that some employers may use temporary workers as a way to avoid meeting all of their compliance obligation (OSHA n.d.). More than three million temporary and contract employees work for America's staffing companies during an average week. During the course of a year, America's staffing companies hire nearly 15 million temporary and contract employees (American Staffing Association n.d.).
- Contractor safety has increased in importance, and many companies are developing tighter oversight practices.
- Leading key performance indicators are being developed and used by many companies that realize the shortcomings of traditional lagging indicators.
- Technology disruption has created devices (smartphones, tablets, etc.) that can cause lethal distractions that must be managed.
- The "saying–doing" gap continues to be problematic in safety and health; what teams say and what they do (regarding safety, for example) are very often two distinctly different things. This misalignment affects/infects all teams and groups. It is the most common reason for poor teamwork. There are two causes: a team is conflicted about its (safety) commitments, and a team's commitments are out of step with the organization and the external environment. The "saying–doing" gap is also a trap that senior leaders fall into; what they say about safety and health often does not measure up to what they (and the organization) does about safety and health issues (Moussa, Boyer, and Newberry 2016).
- Leadership is seen as essential today. Leaders need to listen more than talk. Good leaders don't have egos. They enjoy listening to people and

encourage people to speak up. They pick up on what needs to be fixed, what needs to change. Effective leaders understand that they do not have all the answers. They involve their employees in developing solutions. Solutions and problem-solving are leadership constants.

ADDITIONAL REALITIES

The principles shown in figure 10.1 are mostly research-based. Needless to say, these principles will be replaced by others in the next paradigm shift.

PRINCIPLES OF SAFETY MANAGEMENT

1. An unsafe act, an unsafe condition, an accident: all these are symptoms of something wrong in the management system.

2. Certain sets of circumstances can be predicted to produce severe injuries. These circumstances can be identified and controlled:

    Unusual, nonroutine   Nonproductive activities
    High energy sources   Certain construction situations

3. Safety should be managed like any other company function. Management should direct the safety effect by setting achievable goals and planning organizing, and controlling to achieve them.

4. The key to effective line safety performance is management procedures that fix accountability.

5. The function of safety is to locate and define the operational errors that allow accidents to occur. This function can be carried out in two ways: (1) by asking why—searching for root causes of accidents, and (2) by asking whether or not certain known effective controls are being utilized.

6. The causes of unsafe behavior can be identified and classified. Some of the classifications are overload (improper matching of a person's capacity with the load), traps, and the worker's decision to err. Each cause is one that can be controlled.

7. In most cases, unsafe behavior is normal human behavior; it is the result of normal people reacting to their environment. Management's job is to change the environment that leads to the unsafe behavior.

8. Three major subsystems must be dealt with in building an effective safety system: (1) the physical, (2) the managerial, and (3) the behavioral.

9. The safety system should fit the culture of the organization.

10. There is no one right way to achieve safety in an organization; however, for a safety system to be effective, it must meet certain criteria. The system must:
    1. Force supervisory performance.
    2. Involve middle management.
    3. Have top management visibly showing their commitment.
    4. Have employee participation.
    5. Be flexible.
    6. Be perceived as positive.

Figure 10.1 Principles of safety management

There is more to today's safety and health realities, such as
- We know that we cannot use incident statistics to judge performance at almost any level, as they measure mostly luck. We can, however, use perception surveys and behavior sampling.
- Corrections resulting from incidents and injuries are a reactionary method of safety improvement. While investigating and implementing corrective actions resulting from incidents is a critical component of a comprehensive safety system, the effective use of proactive data (perception surveys, observations, behavior sampling, etc.) have proven to be a much more effective way to manage safety. Proactive approaches to safety management also yield greater opportunities to involve your employees in the day-to-day safety "work."
- Many (perhaps most) audits are invalid measures of system effectiveness.
- Audits also run counter to the philosophy of having a flexible system that allows employee ownership (today's parameters).
- Safety meetings are being replaced by one-on-one conversations.
- We believe that investigating all accidents is a waste of time. Certainly, some investigations are necessary (maybe using SPC tools), but not all.
- We believe that senior leaders should play a more significant role than simply signing policy. Management By Walking Around (MBWA) and other techniques can and are being employed by today's CEOs.
- We know that we must use activity measures to judge safety performance at lower organizational levels.
- We know that behavior change comes quicker and lasts longer by using positive reinforcement than with discipline and punishment.
- Many companies (or their workers serving as safety champions and leaders) are rewriting their safety and health rule books.
- We know from communication research that repeating the message is not the key to communication effectiveness. The keys lie in worker perception of management's credibility and in the meaningfulness of the message sent. It is what workers "see," not what they "hear" or "read" that works best.
- And most important, all of today's research on safety and health programming points to one fact: there are no magic pills or "essential ingredients" in a safety system.

The diversity of new principles only seems chaotic if we refuse to recognize today's realities in safety and health. If we recognize "the truth on the ground" (Scott 2002), it allows us to do almost anything with our safety and health processes. We can experiment and innovate. We can be creative.

There is nothing in OSHA law that says you cannot have a world-class safety and health system within the realm of these new realities.

SORT OUT YOUR PHILOSOPHY

Once you recognize that you are now at ground zero, you simply start upward. Start by sorting out your personal philosophy on questions such as "What's involved in incident causation?" "What do I believe are the safety and health elements best for my company?" "What is the culture of my company?" "Does my company accept injuries as part of doing business?" "What will the best safety and health elements look like ten years from now?" "What elements will protect us and get us to where we want to be?" And for the best input, bring in other people to assist your thinking and restructuring—executives, plant managers, middle managers, supervisors, and, most of all, hourly employees.

A number of safety and health professionals believe the total effectiveness of their efforts today is seriously reduced by an inability to integrate safety and health into the regular management systems and by an inability to effectively relate safety and health performance to corporate goals. Too often professionals still only ask for (or hope for) management support. And by "support" we mean "active, visible involvement."

Too often professionals are in this ineffective position because they have not demonstrated to management that safety and health is a management-controllable cost—controllable by planning, organization, and management direction. And more importantly, it is a controllable *value* that companies can build on.

Cultural consensus about the value of safety and health is the starting point for further agreements and advances regarding production, quality, customer service, supply-chain management, profitability, stockholder value, and brand reputation.

A study of companies that achieved "breakthrough change" (large improvements in workplace safety) found these common philosophies: responsiveness to occupational safety and health (OHS) concerns, positive social dynamics, a pattern of continuous improvement, simultaneous operational improvement (integration) and a supportive internal context (integration). Three elements are outcomes of breakthrough performance: integrated OHS knowledge, decreased OHS risk, and decreased injury and illness (Robson et al. 2016).

MANAGEMENT'S SAFETY BLIND SPOTS

There are reasons why the value of safety and health is a blind spot in the eyes of some, or even many, managers. As a supervisor you should know this, because it can affect the amount of unsolicited support you receive for your safety activities. Consider these as perhaps the main blind spots:

1. *We are not using (although they have been developed) the needed tools to quantify our objectives or our progress.* This weakness has been discussed in journal articles and conferences at length. While some

new techniques have been devised and tested, their use is still so limited in comparison to the use of incident statistics that we cannot really report much progress here. Most safety professionals agree that statistics are ineffective as a measure, as a diagnostic tool, or in communicating to management. Yet for many reasons (trade secrets, not taking time to understand new systems, etc.), the safety profession has not sufficiently improved its measures of performance, its communications to management, or its diagnostic tools.

2. *We are not relating safety and health goals to management objectives.* Some companies are succeeding at this today, but they are rare. Few companies set appropriate and achievable safety and health goals in the same manner they plan corporate goals. Few companies have adapted management's planning system to safety and health planning. Few safety techniques lend themselves to this kind of projection and planning. Again, a lack of integration and safety operating out of a distant silo might be among the impediments.

3. *We are not leveraging group resources.* We know employees' decisions regarding work are controlled by group norms more than any other single determinant of behavior. This was proven more than 85 years ago in Mayo's Hawthorne studies. The experiments took place at Western Electric's factory at Hawthorne, a suburb of Chicago, in the late 1920s and early 1930s. They were conducted for the most part under the supervision of Elton Mayo, an Australian-born sociologist who eventually became a professor of industrial research at Harvard. The Hawthorne Effect holds that increases in worker productivity will occur due to the psychological stimulus of being singled out and made to feel important. Other findings included: The workplace is a social system— the Hawthorne researchers came to view the workplace as a social system made up of interdependent parts; relations that supervisors develop with workers tend to influence the manner in which the workers carry out directives; and work groups tend to arrive at norms of what is a fair day's work (Big Dog 2010). Management today is coping with the phenomenon of group dynamics through participative sharing of decisions, improved communications, etc.

4. *We are not tapping the human resources in our organizations.* But there is progress. Modern management is incorporating knowledge from the behavioral sciences and neuroscience into its newer methods and techniques.

As a supervisor and leader, you should be familiar with business strategies used in companies.

Job Enrichment

Job enrichment is a concept based upon Frederick Herzberg's research, which bears out the fact that responsibility, achievement, and recognition are true motivators and should be built back into jobs if we really hope to excite employees about their work (Herzberg 1966).

Herzberg uses the term *motivation* to describe feelings of accomplishment, professional growth, and professional recognition that are experienced in a job that offers sufficient challenge and scope to the worker. He considers apathy and minimum effort the natural results of jobs that offer the worker no more satisfaction than a paycheck and a decent place to work. These factors may keep a worker from complaining, but they will not make the worker want to work harder or more efficiently. Offering still more prizes or incentive payments, produces only a temporary effect. According to Herzberg, these investments reach the point of diminishing returns rapidly and do not, therefore, represent a sound motivational strategy.

Employee-Centeredness

The most effective supervisors are "employee-centered." They create an atmosphere in which employees can work, and they remove the obstacles in the way, according to research from Rensis Likert (Likert 1961).

Likert found that most organizations can be given a numerical rating on a four-point scale that expresses the prevailing management system. This scale runs from System 1, an arbitrary, coercive, highly authoritarian management style that is seldom encountered any longer in its "pure form," through System 4, which is based on teamwork, mutual confidence and trust, and a genuine respect for the individuals who comprise the organization.

One of Likert's more significant findings is that the more closely a company's management style approximates System 4, the more likely it is to have a record of sustained high productivity, good labor relations, and high profitability. Similarly, the more closely an organization approximates System 1, the more likely it is to be inefficient and to suffer from recurrent financial crises. System 4 management holds high performance goals for itself and for all employees and makes it clear that management expects goals to be met. In other words, setting high goals for efficiency and productivity can be best attained by a system of management that is geared to satisfy real human needs.

Interpersonal Relations Improvement

Interpersonal relations training (leadership, coaching, communicating) is common today and is effectively (according to Chris Argyris's data) bridging the gap between mature people's needs for independence, sustained interests, and equality more than subordination, and management's historic principles that treat people like children (close supervision, specialization, etc.) (Argyris 1957).

The problems of the widely discussed, disengaged worker—exhibiting apathy and lack of effort—are not simply a matter of individual laziness. (In 2018, Gallup reported 34% of US workers were engaged in their jobs and 16.5% were actively disengaged—miserable in their jobs) (Gallup 2018).

Apathy and lack of effort are often healthy reactions of normal people to an unhealthy environment created by common management policies. More specifically, most adults are motivated to be responsible, self-reliant, and independent. These motives are acquired during childhood through the educational system, the family, and communications media, such as books, television, films, the Internet, and various social media platforms. But the typical organization confines most of its employees to roles that provide little opportunity for responsibility, self-reliance, or independence. Too many jobs are designed in ways that make minimal demands on the individual's abilities and place the responsibility for major decisions in the supervisor's hands.

In effect, such jobs create a childlike role for employees and frustrate their normal motivations for a more adult role. Argyris says that the common reaction of withdrawing one's interest from the job—treating it with indifference or even with a certain degree of contempt—is a necessary defensive move that helps individuals preserve their self-respect. Unfortunately, the cost to the organization of these reactions is heavy: minimal output, low quality, low morale, turnover, and excessive waste.

Job enrichment, employee-centered supervisors, and improvement in interpersonal relations are examples of many of the ways management is changing focus in the light of behavioral science and social science knowledge. These and many other areas indicate the marked changes that are and will be taking place in American industry. Safety and health management has not really begun to utilize this knowledge. There is little in the literature on safety techniques that is built on research, new safety principles, or handling today's employees. In general, management is now beginning to recognize that employees can contribute markedly to organizational effectiveness. Systematic techniques are being used to tap these human resources. So far, safety and health management has not developed comparable systematic techniques.

Safety management could be leading the way. Through employee participation in safety, job enrichment could be started. What better area is there than safety for a supervisor to begin to establish employee-centered attitudes and behaviors? Better interpersonal relations can often be attained in safety more easily than in production because of the unity of the purpose. Who can truly argue against the mission of safety? This is the philosophy Paul O'Neill applied with great success as CEO of Alcoa (Friedlander 2016).

TOTAL QUALITY MANAGEMENT (TQM) CONCEPTS

In most companies, quality of performance means initial quality of product and increased productivity. Some companies include quality of safety performance at a much later point, often as an afterthought.

Employee involvement has always been central to the TQM philosophy, which also includes these concepts:
- building a new organizational culture that embraces safety
- using new tools to solve problems
- continuously improving the process
- using upstream measures to monitor progress

Perhaps the best description of TQM is captured in Deming's "Obligations of Management." Although the total quality approach differs greatly from traditional safety concepts, the TQM philosophy works well when applied to safety.

If Deming's Obligations of Management were rewritten in safety jargon, they might read as follows:

1. Concentrate on the long-range goal of developing a world-class system, not on short-term, annual safety incident goals.
2. Discard the philosophy of accepting incidents—they are not acceptable.
3. Use statistical techniques to identify the two sources of incidents—system factors and human error.
4. Institute more thorough job skills training.
5. Eliminate dependence on incident investigation. Instead, use proactive approaches, such as behavioral sampling, fishbone diagrams, flowcharts, etc., to reveal system flaws and achieve continuous system improvement.
6. Provide supervisors (and employees) with knowledge of statistical methods (sampling, control charts, etc.) and ensure that these tools are used to identify areas needing additional study.
7. Reduce fear throughout the organization by encouraging all employees to report system defects without adverse consequences and to help find solutions.
8. Reduce incidents by designing safety into the process. Train research and design personnel in safety concepts.
9. Eliminate the use of slogans, incentives, posters, and gimmicks to encourage safety.
10. Examine work standards to remove accident traps.

Other aspects of TQM are valuable as well. In fact, the following measures are necessary in safety:
- Ask employees to define and solve company problems and identify system weaknesses.

- Provide employees with simple tools to solve problems. These include Pareto charts to determine problems; fishbone diagrams to help brainstorm problem causes; flowcharts to observe the system; and scatter diagrams to determine correlations.
- Replace incident-based statistics with other upstream measures (i.e., behavioral observations).
- Replace incident-based statistics with alternative downstream measures (i.e., employee perception surveys, employee interviews).

The ten safety obligations listed above represent a marked departure from traditional safety beliefs. Under these new corporate obligations:

- Progress is not measured by incident rates.
- Safety becomes a system or processes rather than a program.
- Statistical techniques drive continuous improvement efforts.
- Incident investigations are either reformed or eliminated.
- Safety sampling and statistical process control tools are used.
- Blame for "unsafe acts" is completely eliminated.
- Focus is on improving the system.
- "Whistle-blowers" are encouraged and supported.
- Employee involvement in problem-solving and decision-making is formalized via corporate procedures.
- Ergonomic well-being is designed into the workplace.
- Safety slogans and gimmicks are eliminated.
- Emphasis is placed on removing system traps that cause human error.

The move toward TQM in safety means refuting many traditional concepts, such as:

1. Irresponsible acts and conditions cause accidents.
2. The Three Es of safety—engineering, education, enforcement—are essential to safety programs.
3. Low compliance is sufficient.
4. The executive role is only to sign policy.
5. Management creates safety rules; employees follow them.

These beliefs should be replaced with the following axioms:

1. Incidents are caused by a defective management system and a weak safety culture.
2. Many methods can be used to shape behavior, not merely the Three Es.
3. No magic pill can be prescribed. Practitioners must determine which approaches will work best, depending on situational demands.
4. Low compliance has limited influence on safety results.
5. Executives must provide safety leadership.

6. Decisions made at the bottom—by affected employees—are most effective.
7. Safety must be integrated into Industry 4.0.

Real-time communication, Big Data, human–machine interactions, remote sensing, monitoring and process control, autonomous equipment, and interconnectivity are becoming major assets in modern industry. As the fourth industrial revolution (Industry 4.0) becomes the predominant reality, it will bring new paradigm shifts that will have an impact on the management of occupational health and safety. OHS consequences of Industry 4.0 transformations must be evaluated properly and given due consideration (Badri, Boudreau-Trudel, and Saadeddine 2018).

BEHAVIOR-BASED SAFETY (BBS)

Since the 1930s, it has been commonly accepted that most safety incidents are caused by human behavior (unsafe acts) and that, as a result, safety efforts should focus on reducing the probability of unsafe behavior.

Does this mean that most traditional approaches to safety can be called behavior-based approaches? Since the 1970s, regulations along with the fear of being fined have forced practitioners to concentrate on factors such as physical conditions, toxic exposures, health, recordkeeping, occupational diseases, and ergonomics. Defining such efforts as behavior-based is a stretch. However, training awareness campaigns and the use of media, which have continued during these years, do target employee behavior.

Behavior-based safety (BBS) started in the 1970s in companies such as Ford Motor Company and Procter & Gamble. It is important to note that BBS was part of a much larger safety and health program in these companies. BBS was never intended to be a stand-alone substitute for a comprehensive safety and health management system.

BBS peaked, thanks to a marketing barrage and charismatic advocates, in the 1990s. BBS has been tried by many companies, found to be successful in many companies, and when overrelied upon, discarded as a failure by many companies. Today, some former BBS advocates say it is time to move on from a strict focus on behavior to broader organizational and leadership performance issues. Others defend BBS, saying the underlying behavioral science principles are sound, but have too often been applied inappropriately (overrelied upon; just because employee behavior is now excellent doesn't mean the fire extinguishers no longer need to be maintained). Some say BBS is passé; others argue it has evolved into something more humanistic with an emphasis on empathy, emotional intelligence, and caring relationships.

What Is Traditional Behavior-Based Safety?

Behavior-based safety is still practiced by thousands of organizations. According to research, industry is distinctly divided in its opinion of BBS. About one-third (34%)

believe BBS is not as popular and effective as it once was. About one-quarter (26%) strongly disagree, saying BBS is still effective. Forty percent are on the fence, unsure of BBS's current effectiveness (Johnson 2017). BBS is a management system that defines precisely what behaviors are required from each organizational member (from shop employee to CEO), measures whether these behaviors are present, and reinforces desired behavior regularly (daily, hourly).

Behavior-based safety management systems do not turn safety over to any one level of the organization. Certainly, employee involvement is crucial. But eliminating or isolating management from the process is a problematic approach. Management is legally accountable for safety. To abdicate authority for safety, while retaining responsibility and accountability, is tricky at best, risky at worst.

A fundamental tenet holds that a safety system must meet two primary criteria.

1. Some system of accountability must define roles, ensure that individuals at all levels possess the knowledge to fulfill those roles, measure role fulfillment, and reward behavior based on role fulfillment.
2. The system asks for, allows, requires, and ensures participation at all levels.

Behavioral Measurement

A true behavior-based approach to safety requires behavioral measurements. For its upstream measure, the process requires a statistically valid observation/sampling process. (Are employees behaving more safely today than last week/month?) To achieve statistical validity, many observations are needed, with consistency over time (one sampler) looking at all unsafe behaviors, not just a select few.

Statistical validity is also required for downstream measures. For most practitioners, this means replacing traditional measures (frequency rates, incidence rates, and severity rates) with valid, meaningful measures (such as process improvements achieved and perception surveys).

WHY IS CHANGE NECESSARY?

Since many old-school beliefs must change to achieve successful performance, safety and health practitioners (and certainly supervisors) may ask: Why bother? How do today's realities affect me? Some answers are:

- Reality: Traditional top-down safety and health programs no longer work (if they ever did). Most are not based on fact (empirical scientific research), and they tend to conflict with both management and behavioral research.
- Reality: The safety and health system must be built into an organization's management structure. Historically, safety and health has been

kept separate from regular management—in its own silo as a compliance function. As management styles have evolved, safety and health has been suspended in the classical model: management mandates the rules, employees follow orders. As a result, safety and health remains a foreign subject to many managers and executives.

- Reality: As senior leaders' familiarity with safety and health fails to gain any traction, the external environment has increased both management and organizational vulnerability to significant regulatory fines, possible (but not likely) criminal liability, damage to brand reputation, damage to sustainability efforts and image, and so on.
- Reality: More "injuries" (e.g., musculoskeletal disorders, stress) are compensable today than ever before. Practitioners cannot address these problems via machine-guarding technology.
- Reality: The nation's workers' compensation (WC) system is not only in trouble, it is ill—perhaps terminally. WC carriers are withdrawing from some markets, a trend expected to continue. Subtle state law changes give employers more say over medical care, raising workers' burden of proof or limiting the scope of activities judges have deemed work-related.

These changes have had a comparable effect on cutting benefits, excluding people whose doctors say have legitimate work injuries—especially the costly musculoskeletal disorders, such as carpal tunnel syndrome that poultry workers are prone to. ProPublica and National Public Radio have examined how many states have been quietly dismantling their workers' comp systems, leading to serious consequences for injured workers. The cutbacks, often driven by business, have landed workers on public assistance and forced them to fight insurers for medical care their doctors recommended.

Since 2003, legislators in 33 states have passed workers' comp laws that reduce benefits or make it more difficult for those with certain injuries and diseases to qualify for them. Florida has cut benefits to its most severely disabled workers by 65% since 1994 (Grabell 2015).

REFERENCES

American Staffing Association. n.d. Staffing Industry Statistics. 2019 data. Accessed January 3, 2020. https://americanstaffing.net/staffing-research-data/fact-sheets-analysis-staffing-industry-trends/staffing-industry-statistics/.

Argyris, Chris. 1957. *Personality and the Organization.* New York: Harper & Row.

Badri, Adel, Bryan Boudreau-Trudel, and Ahmed Saadeddine Souissi. 2018. "Occupational health and safety in the industry 4.0 era: A cause for major concern?" *Safety Science* 109 (November): 403–411.

Big Dog & Little Dog's Performance Juxtaposition. 2010. "The Hawthorne Effect." http://www.nwlink.com/~donclark/hrd/history/hawthorne.html.

Condliffe, Jamie. 2019. "Smart Safety Checks for Smart Robots." *The New York Times*, Monday, March 25, 2019, page B7.

Friedlander, Adam. 2016. *Safety and Workers' Compensation Strategies*. CreateSpace Independent Publishing Platform.

Gallup News. 2018. "Employee Engagement on the rise in the U.S." Accessed January 3, 2020. news.gallup.com/poll/241649/employee-engagement-rise.aspx.

Grabell, Michael. 2015. "The Demolition of Workers' Comp," ProPublica.

Herzberg, Frederick. 1966. *Work and the Nature of Man*. Cleveland, OH: World Publishing.

Johnson, Dave. 2017. "The State of the EHS Nation." Reader Survey. *Industrial Safety & Hygiene News*, October 2017.

Kleiner, Anna. 2018. "Three Things Most Businesses Don't Know about Workers' Compensation." Concentra. February 19, 2018. https://www.concentra.com/resource-center/articles/3-things-most-businesses-dont-know-about-workers--compensation/.

Likert, Rensis. 1961. *New Patterns of Management*. New York: McGraw-Hill.

Mahdawi, Arwa. 2018. "We live in an age of anxiety—and we can't blame it all on Trump." *The Guardian*. August 7, 2018.

Moussa, Mario, Madeline Boyer, and Derek Newberry. 2016. *Committed Teams*. Hoboken, NJ: Wiley.

Occupational Safety and Health Administration (OSHA). n.d. "Protecting Temporary Workers." Accessed March 28, 2019. https://www.osha.gov/temp_workers/index.html.

Reason, James. 1990. *Human Error*. Cambridge, England: Cambridge University Press.

Robson, Lynda S., Benjamin C. Amick III, Cindy Moser et al. 2016. "Important factors in common among organizations making large improvement in OHS performance: Results of an exploratory multiple case study." *Safety Science* 86 (July): 211–227.

Schuetz, Rolf C., Jr. 2013. "Stressed at Work? You Might Have a Workers' Compensation Claim." American Bar Association, July 1, 2013. https://www.americanbar.org/groups/gpsolo/publications/gpsolo_ereport/2013/july_2013/stressed_at_work_might_have_workers_compensation_claim/.

Scott, Susan. 2002. *Fierce Conversations: Achieving Success at Work & Life, One Conversation at a Time*. New York: Viking.

Sorkin, Andrew Ross. 2017. "Navigating Uncertainty." *The New York Times*, November 14, 2017, page F2.

CHAPTER **11**

Today's Safety and Health Philosophy

Consider the many safety approaches that have been implemented since the early twentieth century.

- Physical condition approach (1911 to present)
- Industrial hygiene approach (1931 to present)
- "Unsafe act" approach (1931 to present)
- Human factors approach (1940s to present)
- Management approach (1950s to present)
- Noise control approach (1954 to present)
- Audit approach (1950s to present)
- System safety approach (1960s and currently)
- OSHA physical condition approach (1971 to present)
- OSHA industrial hygiene approach (1970s)
- Ergonomic approach, anticipating an OSHA standard that was withdrawn (1980s and 90s)
- Injury and Illness Prevention Plan (I2P2) approach, anticipating an OSHA standard that never materialized (2009–2015)
- Environmental approach (1960s to present)
- Total quality management thrust, using statistical process control (1920s to the present)
- Behavior-based safety (1970s to the present)
- Human and organizational performance (HOP), "the New View," Safety 2.0 (2010 to the present)

None of these were fads. They have all been real attempts to control losses. They are layers of things that must be done. But with smaller safety staffs and budgets, choices must be made (Petersen 2003).

We have been involved in industrial safety in an organized fashion since 1911 when the Triangle Shirtwaist Factory fire in New York City killed 145 female garment workers and triggered the founding of the National Safety Council and the American Society of Safety Professionals. The original emphasis was to improve physical conditions. Since the 1930s, we have also considered the unsafe acts of people, together with the many safety approaches listed at the beginning of this chapter.

In the early years of the safety movement, management chose to concentrate entirely on correcting the hazardous physical conditions that existed. This effort showed remarkable results during the first 20 years. In deaths alone, the reduction was from an estimated 18,000 to 21,000 lives lost in 1912 to about 14,500 in 1933. The death rate (deaths per million worker-hours worked) for that period would show an even better reduction. This reduction came largely from cleaning up working conditions. Cleaning up physical conditions came first—possibly because they were so obviously bad, and possibly because people believed that these conditions were actually the cause of injuries.

Overall injury and illness case rates have generally declined since the early 2000s. In 2018, the rate of total recordable cases (TRC) was 2.8 per 100 full-time equivalent (FTE) workers, according to the US Bureau of Labor Statistics (BLS) (US Bureau of Labor Statistics 2019a). This marked only the second year (also 2012) since 2004 that the TRC rate did not decline. In 2003, the TRC was 5.0 per 100 FTE.

Serious challenges remain in reducing serious injuries and fatalities. Cases involving days away from work (DAFW)—more severe injuries—have only declined from 1.5 per 100 FTE in 2003 to 0.9 in 2016. Since 2008, the DAFW rate has only dropped slightly from 1.1 cases per 100 FTE. In 2017, there were almost one million injuries requiring time off from work (882,730). Workers in manufacturing who sustained occupational injuries and illnesses resulting in days away from work in 2017 required a median of 8 days to return to work, 1 day less than in 2016, according to the BLS (US Bureau of Labor Statistics 2018).

A total of 5250 fatal work injuries occurred in 2018, a 2% increase from 2017, according to the Bureau of Labor Statistics (US Bureau of Labor Statistics 2019b)

Since the 1930s, we have built safety programs, built our techniques and our tools, on a set of principles that were first developed in 1930 and espoused by H.W. Heinrich in his text *Industrial Accident Prevention* (Heinrich 1931). He called his principles the Axioms of Industrial Safety.

COMMON AREAS OF SAFETY PROCESSES

By looking at five of the most common areas in our safety processes, we can quickly see how our programs were built upon his principles—and how they are changing. For example, in all of these approaches, the true cause of most injuries—human error—has just recently been studied in depth. Consider these types of errors: design errors; communications errors; management system errors, such as Bhopal, Chernobyl, the space shuttles, and others; and technological errors, such as the fatal crash of an Uber autonomous car (Petersen 2003).

Causation Theories

Incident investigations and inspections are integral to all safety and health processes. OSHA depends almost entirely upon this reporting and recordkeeping to target its enforcement. This approach is based on a Heinrich axiom that says: "The occurrence of an injury invariably results from a completed sequence of factors, the last one of these being the accident itself. The accident in turn is invariably caused or permitted directly by the unsafe act of a person and/or a mechanical or physical hazard." This is commonly known as the Domino Theory of Incident Causation. It suggests that if we remove the act and/or the conditions (that is, the middle domino), the incident and the injury will not occur (Heinrich 1931).

Newer safety theory disputes this domino theory and replaces it with a multiple causation theory. The multiple causation theory states that incidents are caused by the combination of a number of things, all wrong, that combine at one point in time and result in an injury. This theory suggests that the act, the condition, and the incident itself are all symptoms of something wrong in the management system. The role of safety—and supervisors—is not to remove the symptom, but to find out what is wrong with the system.

Along these lines, James Reason proposed what is referred to as the Swiss Cheese Model of system failure (described in detail in chapter 9) (Perneger 2005).

Employee Training

Employee training is a second area of safety processes. Our safety processes invariably include aspects such as safety orientation, employee training, and supervisory safety talks. These are based upon a Heinrich axiom that states, "The unsafe acts of persons are responsible for a majority of accidents." The underlying assumption of this axiom is that the employees do not know the difference between right and wrong, between safe and unsafe. We know that employees do know, in many cases, what is safe behavior and what is not. In such cases, training is not the solution to the problem.

Supervisory Training

Supervisory training is a third area. Safety systems are almost always heavy in the area of supervisory training. This is based on a Heinrich axiom that says, "The supervisor or foreman is the key man in accident prevention." One of the underlying assumptions here is that merely identifying the supervisor as the key man magically makes that supervisor do something about safety. This is often not the case. A second assumption is that the foreman automatically will do something about safety if he is made responsible for safety and if he knows what to do (that is, he is trained). We now know that this assumption also is often wrong.

Most supervisors today know that they are responsible for safety; some know what they should be doing, others do not. There is great variability in the safety training and skills development of supervisors. Among those supervisors who do know what to do regarding safety, there are many who do not follow through and execute their responsibilities.

Why? Because they usually are not held accountable. That is, they are not effectively measured in safety. Upper management's behavior often sends signals that they either do not know or do not care if supervisors do anything about safety incidents. If that's the case, why should foremen or front-line supervisors do much to prevent incidents? The "key man" axiom must be amended to recognize that "higher management holds the key chain."

Records

Fourth, our safety methodologies include recordkeeping and the analysis of these records. The belief is that if we find the most common kinds of incidents and attack them, automatically our costs and injury rates will come down. This thinking is based upon a Heinrich axiom that states, "The severity of an injury is largely fortuitous." We have interpreted this to mean that the causes of frequency and of severity are the same. Today we know that this is wrong. Severity is predictable in certain situations and under certain circumstances.

Safety Media

Fifth, safety in today's world includes the use of all kinds of safety media, such as social media —YouTube videos, text messaging, Instagram posts, Facebook posts, and Twitter alerts; posters; banners; videos; booklets; guides; and digital products, such as e-newsletters, e-books, digital editions of safety magazines, and webinars. This is based on a Heinrich axiom that says, "One of the four basic motives or reasons for the occurrence of unsafe acts is improper attitude."

Do posters, banners, YouTube videos, or Twitter posts do any good? We really do not know. To be more accurate, so far we know just a little bit about the answer to this question. Research tells us, in some cases these kinds of safety media help, in some cases they do harm, and in some there is absolutely no effect.

The above five areas fairly well describe the state of the art in safety programming. We do many things in our programs, almost all of which are based on the thinking of H.W. Heinrich in 1931.

OTHER MODERN PHILOSOPHIES

In 2019, we do have examples of more modern safety philosophies. One divides safety work into four aspects, without any one of them being more automatically legitimate or real than the others:

1. Social safety—affirming that safety is valued and achieved
2. Demonstrated safety—proving safety to external stakeholders

3. Administrative safety—establishing and following clear rules and requirements for safety
4. Physical safety—changing the work environment for safety

This view holds that safety management is a form of "institutional work" and that safety activity is as much ritual, routine, and dramatic performance as it is goal-directed. Actions are socially legitimized through their purported positive effects on safety outcomes but cannot be explained as strategic or tactical choices in pursuit of well-articulated goals. Safety performances are intentional, but their value comes primarily from the structures they maintain, and the beliefs and feelings that they reinforce, rather than from their ability to prevent accidents.

If organizations did not perform safety work, they would be unable to convince stakeholders that they were doing enough for safety, which would, in turn, prevent them from pursuing their core business (Rae and Provan 2019).

A second philosophy comes to us from Australia. Its thesis is: A common shortcoming with many existing OHS methods is that they are driven by events that stand out from the normal—which usually means that something has gone wrong.

Professor Erik Hollnagel divides safety into three steps (Safety Institute of Australia 2015):

1. Make safety productive rather than protective. "Safety is more than the absence of accidents and cannot be achieved only by eliminating hazards and by preventing things from going wrong. Safety management must also learn how things go right and find ways to make sure that it happens," says Hollnagel.
2. Realize that it is more important to learn from what happens all the time, even though the consequences may seem small, than to learn from what happens rarely, even though the consequences may be large. "It is also a lot easier, since there is an abundance of data that is readily available," Hollnagel adds.
3. Understand the importance of variability (approximate adjustments) for everyday performance. Hollnagel says variability is generally useful and should be controlled rather than eliminated.

A third philosophy integrates safety with Industry 4.0. Its thesis: If the technologies driving Industry 4.0 develop in silos and manufacturers' initiatives are isolated and fragmented, the dangers will multiply and the net impact on OHS will be negative. As major changes are implemented, previous gains in preventive management of workplace health and safety will be at risk. If we are to avoid putting technological progress and OHS on a collision course, researchers, field experts, and industrialists will have to collaborate on a smooth transition toward Industry 4.0 (Badri, Boudreau-Trudel, and Souissi 2018).

FOUR COMPONENTS OF SAFETY PROCESSES

Safety and health processes in some companies seem to expand gradually, incrementally: a training program added one year, safety sampling another, a recognition program, a contest or competition, and so on. But a closer analysis reveals the reasons behind the selection of safety and health process components:

1. *Knowledge and preference of the safety and health director.* Most corporate safety and health directors do the necessary developmental work and sell top management on the elements of a program. It is inconceivable that a safety director would install something that such a professional does not believe will work, or something they are not familiar with. The focus of corporate safety and health initiatives is, first of all, a reflection of the personality and knowledge of the safety director. For example, a technically sound safety professional with an inspection orientation leans toward the physical categories of safety programs. Another may be more system focused.
2. *Wishes of the boss.* Where top management involves itself in company safety efforts, or in the decisions on the elements of these initiatives, the manager's personality and style will show through. A good communicator at the top will lean toward safety processes built heavily on communications and training, for example. A senior leader who has had to call or visit the family of a seriously injured or killed employee can be deeply scarred and become an aggressive safety advocate, vowing "never again" will he have to go through that experience.
3. *Corporate climate.* How safety is administered and managed in a company reflects the safety climate of the organization. The paternal organization may well structure a safety system heavy on the attitudinal and awareness—cognitive—items. A company utilizing a Management by Objective (MBO) concept will tightly fix accountability and might be heavy in the behavior change category.

    A positive safety climate can improve hazard recognition performance. (Pandit et al. 2019). Remember, safety climate is a way to quantitatively measure what workers think about safety at any given time. It measures workers' *shared perceptions* of the company and their leaders' approach to safety (Geldart 2014).
4. *OSHA.* Obviously, OSHA has had a strong influence on safety and health processes since its inception in 1970. While the law makes substantial requirements for training and other attitudinal and behavioral activities, most safety professionals concentrate on the physical aspects of OSHA standards. The government's enforcement of the law seems to concentrate on physical aspects, too. This changed the look of safety processes: the trend is to reduce emphasis on the attitude influencers

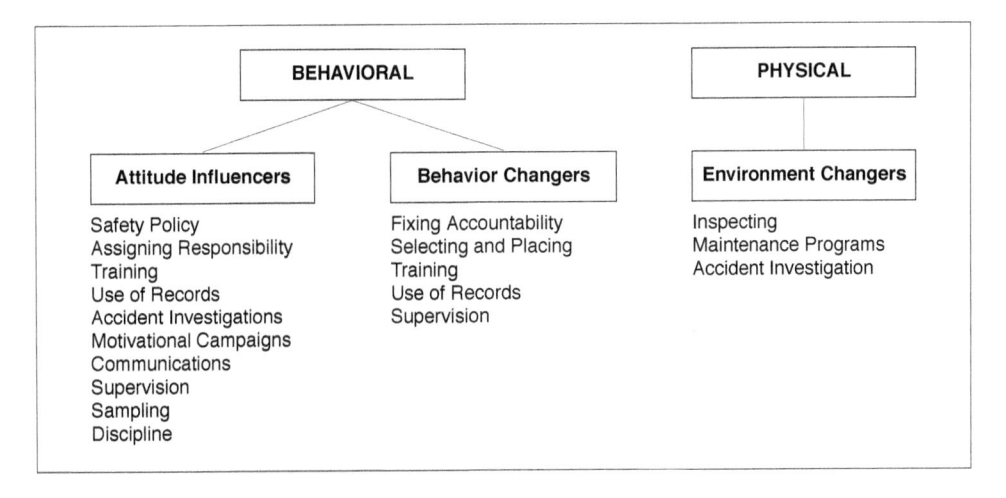

```
┌─────────────────────────────────────────────────────────────────┐
│              BEHAVIORAL                    PHYSICAL             │
│             ╱        ╲                        │                │
│  ┌──────────────┐  ┌──────────────┐   ┌──────────────────┐     │
│  │  Attitude    │  │   Behavior   │   │   Environment    │     │
│  │  Influencers │  │   Changers   │   │    Changers      │     │
│  └──────────────┘  └──────────────┘   └──────────────────┘     │
│  Safety Policy       Fixing Accountability   Inspecting         │
│  Assigning Responsibility  Selecting and Placing  Maintenance Programs │
│  Training            Training                Accident Investigation   │
│  Use of Records      Use of Records                             │
│  Accident Investigations   Supervision                          │
│  Motivational Campaigns                                         │
│  Communications                                                 │
│  Supervision                                                    │
│  Sampling                                                       │
│  Discipline                                                     │
└─────────────────────────────────────────────────────────────────┘
```

Figure 11.1 Common controls in safety programs

and behavior changers and to put more stress on environment changers (see figure 11.1).

Since OSHA was established in 1970, many companies have put the entire emphasis on the physical aspects of safety. Because processes reflect the safety director and the boss, this emphasis probably makes sense. Most senior leaders know about OSHA and would rather not be fined. (However unlikely that may be, given there are more than seven million workplaces in the United States.) Most safety and health practitioners, especially in small to midsize companies, are (or will be) judged by keeping the OSHA slate clean. Under these circumstances, it does not seem logical to place emphasis elsewhere.

However, it is important to understand that unsafe conditions by themselves do not, by and large, result in injuries. It is the unsafe act, or at-risk behavior, or uninformed decision of an employee, coupled with unsafe conditions and upstream factors, such as management decisions and safety budgets and staffing, that account for unwanted outcomes.

As this list of influences indicates, our safety and health systems today are a composite of what the safety and health director knows, what the boss likes, what the company likes, and what the federal government wants. Notably absent from the list are the needs of the company and employees.

What does your company need? What do your employees want in a safety and health process? These are tough questions to answer; many supervisors choose simply not to try. It is easier to do what they themselves know, what the boss likes, what fits the company, or what Uncle Sam says. Does this approach achieve the best possible outcomes? Probably not.

Of the above four reasons for safety program content, the fourth by far predominates today in small to midsize companies. Many large corporations consider

OSHA compliance a "floor" for better performance and have adopted sophisticated, unregulated practices that go "beyond compliance" for decades now. In one recent survey, almost half of safety professional respondents (48%) said OSHA is not the motivating force driving companies to protect employees that it once was. It was respondents in small firms who disagreed, stating OSHA still was a driving force (Johnson 2017).

Although some new regulations that were issued during the Obama administration (2008–2016) may not apply to every organization (silica, confined spaces in construction, electrical power generation), many will, some of which will be costly to an organization. One example is OSHA's 2016 walking/working surfaces standard for general industry fall protection. (From 2000 to 2008, during the George W. Bush administration, OSHA shifted focus to compliance assistance and almost totally away from standards setting.)

To comply with the provisions of broad-impact OSHA standards, such as the *Process Safety Management* standard and the *Hazard Communication* standard (plus laws such as the Americans with Disabilities Act), is not only expensive, it is likely that these costs will never be offset by reduced losses. In actuality, these regulations and pieces of legislation, and others, may move managerial time and corporate monies away from proactive safety toward compliance.

The state of the art in safety today is this: We do a number of things aimed at controlling the physical environmental conditions and the observed behavior of people, and we make other attempts at changing the attitudes of employees. In addition, proactive organizations are also taking steps designed to increase the visible involvement of senior management in the safety-related activities. We do these things even though they are, for the most part, based on principles that are dated and questionable in the light of modern thinking. We have done some rethinking of our principles, but our techniques still lag behind them.

ENDURING FUNDAMENTALS

In 1971, the first edition of *Techniques of Safety Management* was published. It questioned some of the fundamental tenets of safety of the 1960s (which were also the tenets of safety in the 1930s) and brought together a series of basic principles to guide safety efforts in the 1970s. Some of these were restatements or slight changes of Heinrich's axioms, and some were quite different from those axioms.

Here, quite briefly, are the principles outlined in that book (Petersen 1971):

Principle 1: An unsafe act, an unsafe condition, an incident: all of these are symptoms of something wrong in the management system.

We know that behind any incident are many contributing factors. Old theory, however, suggested that we select one of these as the "proximate" cause of the incident, or that we select one unsafe act and/or one unsafe condition. Then we were supposed to remove that condition or act.

This principle suggests not that we narrow our findings to a single factor, but rather that we widen our findings to as many factors as seem applicable. Hence, every incident opens a window through which we can observe the system, the procedures, etc. Also, the theory suggests that besides incidents, other kinds of operational problems result from the same causes. Production tie-ups, problems in quality control, excessive costs, customer complaints, and product failures are caused by the same things that cause incidents. Eliminating the causes of one organizational problem will eliminate the causes of others.

Principle 2: Certain sets of circumstances can be predicted to produce severe injuries. These circumstances can be identified and controlled.

This principle states that in certain conditions we can predict severity. We can attack severity instead of merely hoping to reduce it by attacking frequency.

Principle 3: Safety and health should be managed like any other company function. Management should direct the safety and health effort by setting achievable goals and by planning, organizing, investing, and controlling to achieve them.

Perhaps this principle is more important than all the rest. It restates the thought that safety and health is analogous with quality, cost, and quantity of production. It also goes further and brings the management function into safety and health (or rather safety and health into the management function).

Principle 4: The key to effective line safety performance is management procedures that fix accountability.

Any line manager will achieve results in those areas that management measures. The concept of accountability is important for this measurement.

When line managers are held accountable, they will accept the given responsibility. If they are not held accountable, they will not, in most cases, accept responsibility. They will place their efforts on whatever management is measuring: production, quality, cost, or wherever the current management is applying pressure.

Principle 5: The function of safety and health is to locate and define the operational errors that allow incidents to occur. This function can be carried out in two ways: (1) by asking why—searching for root causes of incidents and (2) by asking whether certain known effective controls are being utilized.

The first part of this principle is borrowed from W.C. Pope and Thomas J. Cresswell, in their article "Safety Programs Management" (Pope and Cresswell 1965). This article defines safety's function as locating and defining operational errors involving (1) incomplete decision-making, (2) faulty judgments, (3) administrative miscalculations, and (4) just plain poor management practices.

The second part of principle 5 suggests that a two-pronged attack is open to us: (1) tracing the symptom (the act, the condition, the incident) back to see why it was allowed to occur or (2) looking at the system (the procedures) that our company has and asking whether certain things are being done in a predetermined manner that is known to be successful.

Principle 6: The causes of unsafe behavior can be identified and classified. Some of the classifications are overload (the improper matching of a person's capacity with the load), traps, and the worker's decision to err. Each cause is one that can be controlled.

Principle 6 suggests that management's task with respect to safety and health is to identify and deal with the causes of unsafe behavior, not the behavior itself.

Principle 7: In most cases, unsafe behavior is not abnormal behavior; it is usually the result of normal people reacting to their environment (i.e., culture). Management's job is to change the culture that leads to the unsafe behavior.

Principle 7 is an extension of principle 6. It suggests that when people act unsafely, they are not dumb, are not careless, are not children who need to be corrected and changed to make them "right." Rather, it suggests unsafe behavior is the result of an environment or accepted, existing organizational culture that results from the actions, decisions, and priorities exhibited by senior management. In that environment, it is completely logical and normal to act unsafely. Corporate culture is simply defined as "What goes on when the boss isn't around."

Principle 8: There are three major subsystems that must be dealt with in building an effective safety and health system: (1) physical, (2) managerial, and (3) behavioral.

Principle 8 reemphasizes that our task is to change the physical and psychological environment that leads people to unsafe behavior.

Traditionally, "safety programs" dealt with the physical environment. Later we looked at management and attempted to build management principles into our safety and health processes. Today, we recognize the need to look at the behavioral environment as well—the climate and culture in which the safety system must live.

Principle 9: The safety system should fit the culture of the organization.

The way we manage has changed markedly. And the way we manage safety and health must also change to be consistent with other functions. To strive for an open and participative culture in an organization, but then to use a safety and health process that is directive and authoritarian, simply does not work.

Principle 10: There is no one right way to achieve safety and health in an organization; but for a safety and health system to be effective, it must meet certain criteria. The system must:
- force supervisory performance
- involve middle management
- have top management visibly showing their commitment
- have employee participation
- be flexible
- be perceived as positive

These ten principles, outlined earlier in figure 1.2, embody the underlying theme of this entire book.

For a number of years, probably starting in the mid-1960s or even before, we had observed the need for accountability systems in management as an essential to safety success. Prior to that, safety professionals had pushed for management to be responsible for safety, probably stemming back to the 1930s from one of Heinrich's axioms.

While we have recognized that accountability is the key, most organizations never created truly meaningful accountability systems for safety performance because they could neither accept nor sell the fact that to achieve accountability requires new measures of performance and new reward structures.

More recently, we have seen the "Behavior-Based Safety Era," the "Culture Era," the "Engagement Era," the "Human Performance Era," and the "Risk-Based Era." Some organizations are into culture-building (or talking about it); others are into some variety of behavior molding (or talking about it)—engaging employees (or talking about it), examining and modifying human factors to reduce human error (or talking about human factors and human and organizational performance—HOP), or basing priorities on risk assessments (or talking about it).

In all of these directions, there has seemed to be an unwritten law that one of these is *the* answer—nothing else is needed. The "Culture Companies" seem to jump to a belief that once the new culture is in place the "safety incident problem" will be solved—nothing else will be necessary. Culture articles, books, presentations, webinars, posters, and videos describe a new utopia that now exists. We no doubt need cultural reinforcers to convince employees they now live in an environment where safety and health is the key—a core value. Often management believes things have changed; managers believe their own writings. Often employees somehow miss the change—things are the same to them.

The "Culture Companies" seem to feel that since a positive safety culture exists, the old stuff is no longer necessary. Forcing managerial performance through accountability doesn't fit anymore—it's too out of step with the new culture.

The "Behavior-Based Safety Companies" focus on employees defining what safe behavior is and on employees observing each other in order to reach the conclusion that any safety problems obviously have been resolved. This belief allows their managers and supervisors or team leaders to concentrate on the truly important things like getting the product out the door, improving quality, filing reports, etc. These are the things they know to be important because these are the things they are being held accountable to accomplish.

The hot buttons for other companies can be human performance (HOP), or employee engagement, or risk-based thinking.

Not all companies have pursued these routes. Many keep going down their traditional routes, keeping the safety and health process as they've always done it—the path of least resistance. Others opt for traditional, condition-based processes as outlined by OSHA—an easier and less risky route. Some buy packaged processes. And many do nothing.

In all of these approaches to safety and health management, organizations say they have management responsibility, but happily, managers and supervisors or team leaders do not have to do anything about safety and health.

To compound the situation, we have fewer managers and supervisors today; larger spans of control; fewer aides to help; more reports to fill out; and, in many cases, supervisors must spend much more time in the office in front of a computer screen or scrolling through their smartphones or tablets.

THE REAL FORMULA

What is the real answer to safety and health system excellence? The behavior-based safety people are right—you cannot achieve safety excellence without proper behaviors. But the culture builders are also right, for you cannot get the proper behaviors without the right culture. Without employee engagement for that matter. And the right culture involves risk-based thinking and a new look at human error prevention (HOP). And here's the real hook—you cannot get the right culture without accountability. The real answer to achieving excellence in safety and health is not black and white, it has multiple dimensions.

Management accountability—a system of role definition, correct measures of performance, and adequate rewards contingent upon that performance—forces daily, proactive, managerial, and supervisory activities to take place. These actions build a culture that states, "Safety and health is so important around here that all managers and supervisors have to do something about it every day." When employees believe this, their behaviors will change—both behaviors such as working safe and behaviors such as becoming involved in helping the whole process.

Safety excellence can be achieved as long as we relearn our alphabet:

$$A \rightarrow C \rightarrow B \rightarrow E$$

Accountability builds a Culture that begets Behaviors resulting in Excellence. And today, this equation also must include employee engagement, risk-based thinking, and human and operational performance.

And in large organizations, all of the above is impossible to do consistently long term without an effective management system that includes safety and health.

WHERE DO WE GO FROM HERE?

There is probably no better time than the present in most companies to launch a new safety and health system or build a fire under the present one. Physical conditions are probably at the best (safest) level they have ever been. Management's spending on safety and health has remained steady or increased slightly in most companies since the Great Depression of 2008, according to research (*ISHN* magazine surveys, 2008–2017). In 2017, safety and health budgets increased slightly in

41% of companies surveyed, remained the same in 43%, decreased slightly in 11%, and decreased significantly in only 3% (Johnson 2017). Employees today are seeing improvements happening before their eyes, a steady stream of money being spent on their safety. Why not capitalize on this?

Well, there are barriers. Safety and health programming conducted in a traditional manner incurs some very distinct drawbacks and difficulties.

1. Traditionally, safety and health as a separate function has not been integrated into management's goal-setting and achieving process. Safety and health simply has not been a regular, normal part of the management process. It has been separate and distinct, a system superimposed on the management structure and purpose. Therefore, safety and health has not necessarily been results-oriented or results-producing.
2. Safety (whatever that might mean to line people) has not been a "known" supervisory skill. Supervisors seldom have known specifically what it is they were to do to achieve "safety" and have spent precious little time on it.
3. Safety and health historically has had few real measures of performance at the supervisory level. Without measurements, little is ever accomplished.
4. Safety awards and recognition efforts (if they have existed at all) have almost never been in any way tied to safety performance for the line manager. Usually, if there are rewards and recognition, it is for good luck more than for actual performance.
5. Safety and health training historically has involved more preaching and exhorting ("do the right thing") than real teaching of skills to achieve results. It has been almost totally ineffective in terms of getting results for the line manager.

Some of these difficulties are being addressed using existing techniques described earlier. Others are addressed with new processes in use today in safety and health management.

Here are a few examples, briefly summarized:

"Safety Differently: Highly Reliable Organizations"—Safety is not the absence of incidents; it is the presence of capacity, according to Todd Conklin. Capacity refers to the power of early hazard identification—the ability to access knowledge from the field and the floor to discover or identify problems before they cause incidents. This requires a shift away from audits and investigations that focus on employee behavior and toward placing emphasis instead on event context, local rationality (what the employee was thinking when the event happened that led the employee to believe the next activity would be safe), and the holistic nature of an event (Conklin 2016).

Human error/error control—The principles of human error control are synonymous with the principles of safety management. "As an industrial engineering undergraduate, I studied work simplification, plant layout, and motion study, not for the purpose of reducing error, but rather to increase productivity. Years later I became acquainted with human factors concepts in graduate work in psychology. It seems that this was a natural for the safety profession. That was 1971. For some reason, the profession found OSHA and its standards to be considerably more interesting. From a human factors standpoint, it seems safety has lost 30 years of possible progress in reducing human error" (Petersen 2003).

From Safety-I to Safety-II—Safety-I is defined as avoiding things that go wrong. One way to do this is by finding errors when something has gone wrong and then trying to eliminate them. This is the find-and-fix approach. A second way is to prevent a transition from a normal state to an abnormal state by controlling and reducing variability using barriers—physical barriers, functional barriers (locks, etc.), symbolic barriers (signs, alarms, etc.), and internalized knowledge barriers (rules, regulations, laws, etc.).

Safety-II is defined as a condition where as much as possible goes right. It emphasizes resilience—the ability to succeed under expected and unexpected conditions alike. This safety management principle is proactive, continuously trying to anticipate developments and events. The purpose of an investigation is to understand how things usually go right as a basis for explaining how they occasionally go wrong. Humans are seen as a resource necessary for system flexibility and resilience. Performance variability should be monitored and managed (Hollnagel 2014).

Risk-centric Safety—The prevention focus in many companies should expand beyond OSHA compliance to leverage effective practices and include a more robust understanding of and emphasis on risk. For example, some companies define an acceptable level of risk for the enterprise and calibrate standards, procedures, and behaviors accordingly. Managing risk in this manner requires more than focusing just on specific hazards and controls, understanding the organizational context in which employees work with hazards is also critical.

Experts agree that risk is heavily influenced by organizational characteristics and human factors. Yet these are often overlooked when an incident occurs. It seems much easier to "fix" an employee who seemingly made a misstep than to address the organizational issues that lie at the heart of the problem.

A new approach to assessing risk must be promoted that focuses on ensuring the effectiveness and vitality of controls in place and on addressing the organizational and human factors that are often key contributors to an incident (Lally, Newell, and Woodhull 2017).

Human and organizational performance (HOP)—"HOP is a risk-based operating philosophy which recognizes that error is part of the human condition and that organizational processes and systems greatly influence employee actions and the likelihood of success." Companies that have embraced HOP and incorporate HOP principles and concepts into the design and management of their workplaces and systems have not only realized significant reductions in their injuries and illnesses, but have also seen significant improvements in "employee engagement, work quality, system reliability, and overall operational excellence" (ORCHSE Strategies 2018).

Preventing Serious Injuries and Fatalities (SIFs)—Processes are evaluated to identify precursors to SFIs. Once precursors are identified, different approaches are used for risk assessment and risk management:

1. Safety and health professionals engage leaders to proactively shift focus from "outcomes" (often limited to tracking OSHA data) to the risks that drive them.
2. These hazards must then be inventoried, assessed, and managed. Related human and organizational factors that could activate or intensify the hazard or undermine controls must be identified and managed.
3. Identified precursors should be evaluated based on the potential severity of the hazard (severity), the degree of control (likelihood), and the number of workers exposed (magnitude).
4. Be proactive to ensure operational consistency in these steps. Promote the use of checklists for key aspects and anticipate mistakes.
5. Cultural and organizational norms, management policies and practices, process conditions, and human factors impact safety and health performance—and the SIF rate. Flawed incident investigations and a culture that assigns blame and concentrates on the last factor in a chain of events leading up to the incident ignore these issues. It's critical to incorporate human and organizational performance (HOP) issues into precursor recognition and assessment strategies.
6. Cultural and organizational improvements are keys to sustaining SIF prevention efforts over the long term. To sustain and drive continuous improvement, changes must be made in ongoing management system requirements, particularly regarding learning. Changes also must be made in the metrics used to measure prevention efforts and evaluate performance. Leading indicators can be developed to drive and assess key organizational and system improvements (Lally, Newell, and Woodhull 2017).

Total Worker Health—In June 2011, NIOSH launched the Total Worker Health (TWH) program as an evolution of the NIOSH Steps to a Healthier U.S. Workforce and the NIOSH WorkLife Initiatives. The TWH approach integrates workplace interventions that protect safety and health with activities that advance the overall well-being of workers.

TWH explores opportunities to both *protect* workers from hazards and *advance* their health and well-being by targeting the conditions of work. Scientific evidence now supports what many safety and health professionals, as well as employees themselves, have long suspected—that risk factors in the workplace can contribute to health problems previously considered unrelated to work.

For example, there are work-related risk factors for abnormal weight fluctuations, sleep disorders, cardiovascular disease, depression, and other health conditions. In recognition of these relationships, some newly observed and others based on well established scientific evidence, the TWH approach focuses on how environmental and organizational factors related to work can diminish or enhance overall worker health (NIOSH 2018).

System 1 and System 2 Thinking—System 1 thinking is "fast" brain processing. Move first, think second, as in running to the exit in an emergency. System 1 thinking can be logical and useful, but often wrong, taking very little information and making decisions on how to act and behave. It is short-term, instinctive, here-and-now thinking. It is more selfish and self-centered.

System 2 thinking is what separates us from animals. It is "slower" brain processing, more reflective and introspective. It is a deliberate type of thinking involving focus, deliberation, reasoning, and analysis. Despite being conscious and deliberate, System 2 thinking can produce poor, sometimes irrational decisions.

Supervisors should bear in mind the distinct traits of System 1 and System 2. Mapping mental skills (and the mini-skills they consist of) onto those labels can clarify your thinking about thinking (Kahneman 2011).

Safety information networks (or "the connected worker")—The network is an interoperable system of smart applications, accessible through multiple devices and taking advantage of secure cloud storage to maintain and organize data security. Smart networks using numerous sensing devices can provide information about the duration and intensity of workers' exposure to hazards; the long-term effects of hazards for individuals and groups of workers; and, by linking to smart PPE, can track information about different exposure types for each worker, including noise, electricity, and heat. Networks grant workers real-time, individualized information about exposures, equipment, access, and training. When something goes wrong, a system can send automated alerts to all parties involved and offers real-time reporting on accidents (Kolkey 2017).

Mindfulness—Carl Weick and his associates argue that what characterizes high reliability organizations is their "collective mindfulness" of danger. Weick introduced the term into the safety literature in an article in 1999 entitled "Organizing for high reliability: processes of collective mindfulness." The term *mindfulness* is most often used to describe the mental state of individuals, but Weick's innovation is to transfer this idea to the organizational context. Mindful individuals and organizations possess an alert form of situational awareness that enables them to better notice the unexpected, normalization of deviation, and various cognitive biases in real time and halt their development (Hopkins 2002).

REFERENCES

Badri, Adel, Bryan Boudreau-Trudel, and Ahmed Saadeddine Souissi. 2018. "Occupational health and safety in the industry 4.0 era: A cause for major concern?" *Safety Science* 109 (November): 403–411.

Conklin, Todd. 2016. *Pre-Accident Investigations: Better Questions—An Applied Approach to Operational Learning*. Boca Raton, FL: CRC Press.

Geldart, S. 2014. "Health, Safety and Environmental Issues." *Comprehensive Materials Processing*.

Heinrich, H.W. 1931. *Industrial Accident Prevention*. New York: McGraw-Hill.

Hopkins, Andrew. 2002. "Safety Culture, Mindfulness and Safe Behavior: Converging Ideas?" December 2002. https://openresearch-repository.anu.edu.au/bitstream/1885/41764/3/WorkingPaper7.pdf.

Hollnagel, Erik. 2014. *Safety-I and Safety-II: The Past and Future of Safety Management*. Farnham, England: Ashgate Publishing.

Johnson, Dave. 2017. "State of the EHS Nation." Reader Survey. *Industrial Safety & Hygiene News*, October 2017.

Kahneman, Daniel. 2011. *Thinking Fast and Slow*. New York: Farrar, Straus, and Giroux.

Kolkey, Jason. 2017. *How a Safety Information Network Transforms the Safety Function*. Honeywell.

Lally, Rosemarie, Stephen Newell, and Dee Woodhull. 2017. "Getting Serious About Preventing Fatalities and Serious Injuries." *Industrial Safety & Hygiene News*, June 2017.

National Institute of Safety and Health (NIOSH). 2018. "NIOSH Total Worker Health." December 18, 2018. https://www.cdc.gov/niosh/twh/totalhealth.html.

ORCSHE Strategies. 2018. "ORCHSE Strategies." Accessed March 28, 2019. https://www.eventbrite.com/e/2018-hop-summit-fundamentals-conference-registration-34495720629#.

Pandit, Bhavana, Albert Alex, Yashwardhan Patil et al. 2019. "Impact of safety climate on hazard recognition and safety risk perception." *Safety Science* 113 (March): 44–53.

Perneger, Thomas, V. 2005. "The Swiss cheese model of safety incidents: are there holes in the metaphor?" BMC Health Services Research 5: 71. https://doi.org/10.1186/1472-6963-5-71.

Petersen, Dan. 1971. *Techniques of Safety Management*. New York: McGraw-Hill.

Petersen, Dan. 2003. "Human Error: A closer look at safety's next frontier." *Professional Safety*, December 2003.

Pope, W.C., and Thomas J. Cresswell. "A New Approach to Safety Programs Management." *Journal of the American Society of Safety Engineers*, August 1965.

Rae, Andrew, and David Provan. 2019. "Safety work versus the safety of work." *Safety Science* 111 (January): 119–127.

Safety Institute of Australia. 2015. "How to shift from reactive to proactive OHS." July 1, 2015. https://www.safetysolutions.net.au/content/business/article/how-to-shift-from-reactive-to-proactive-ohs-1276975754.

US Bureau of Labor Statistics. November 7, 2019a. "Employer-Reported Workplace Injuries and Illness–2018." Accessed January 3, 2020. https://www.bls.gov/news.release/pdf/osh.pdf.

US Bureau of Labor Statistics. 2018. "Census of Fatal Occupational Injuries, 2017." December 18, 2018. https://www.bls.gov/news.release/cfoi.nr0.htm.

US Bureau of Labor Statistics. 2019b. "Census of Fatal Occupational Injuries Summary, 2018." December 17, 2019. Accessed February 27, 2020. https://www.bls.gov/news.release/cfoi.nr0.htm.

CHAPTER **12**

Industrial Hygiene and Health

One might ask why a chapter on industrial hygiene (IH) and health is included in a book on safety supervision.

Dan Petersen foresaw the blurring of the lines between safety and industrial hygiene and other allied environmental, health, and safety fields of professional practice. In an interview with *Industrial Safety & Hygiene News* in 2003 (Petersen 2003), when asked what advice he had for young pros coming out of college, Dan said, "Study not only safety but organizational psychology, organizational management. Broaden your background with industrial hygiene, safety, environmental."

In fact, one of Dan's first jobs in the foundry industry in the late 1950s was training employees about the hazards of lung disease (Petersen 2007). His focus was on respiratory exposures more than injury prevention. "The lung, that was the only thing we were worried about," he said. "We would send a letter and say, 'Get over there and get your pulmonary function (lung capacity and performance) test done.'"

Almost 70 years later, work-related lung diseases are having a resurgence (Mining Editor 2017). "This resurgence in occupational lung diseases should have clinicians, tradespeople and industry on alert. These are diseases we thought had almost been eradicated, but thanks to exposure to high levels of dust and poor control measures they're resurfacing," said Professor Allan Glanville, president of the Thoracic Society of Australia and New Zealand, at the Asian Pacific Society of Respirology Congress 2017, where international experts discussed the spike of new silicosis cases in relatively young tradespeople.

Pneumoconioses (which include silicosis and coal mine lung dust diseases) are progressive, irreversible, and sometimes fatal lung diseases caused by prolonged exposure to crystalline silica, quartz, and coal dusts. There is no known treatment or cure, but they can be prevented with proper workplace dust controls (Mining Editor 2017).

In 2018, 19,200 cases of respiratory illnesses were reported to the US Bureau of Labor Statistics. The number one occupational illness reported in 2018? Skin diseases and disorders, with a reported 25,100 cases. Hearing loss was the second most frequent occupational illness reported, with 17,500 cases. There were 2900 poisoning cases and a huge number of "all other illnesses" reported—111,800 (US Bureau of Labor Statistics 2017).

Many work-related illnesses have long resisted protective measures because symptoms often are considered minor annoyances (itchy skin, watery eyes, blisters, etc.) and go unreported. Plus, more serious illnesses caused by work exposures, such as lung diseases and repetitive motion strains, sprains, and nerve damage, have long latency periods and can take years if not decades to manifest into physical diseases or illnesses requiring days away from work.

And the fact remains that many preventive solutions/controls to lower disease risks are not thought to be needed or are considered more difficult or even not feasible to implement. Personal protective equipment (PPE) becomes the adequate short-term and less expensive default option, although many employees have been found not to wear gloves, respirators, hearing protectors, and other PPE (when not being closely watched) either because they are uncomfortable or inconvenient, or because workers have not been effectively trained or otherwise understand how or why to use the PPE.

Let's look at the most common types of job-related illnesses.

Skin diseases and disorders are caused by work exposure to chemicals, paints, or other substances. Contact dermatitis (allergic and irritant) is overwhelmingly the most common cause of occupational skin diseases, according to NIOSH (1996a), accounting for 15–29% of all reported occupational diseases. There is virtually no industry or occupation without potential exposure to some of the many diverse agents that cause allergic and irritant dermatitis. The more serious, irritant contact dermatitis, more common than allergic skin reactions, usually results from a variety of human reactions to chemical irritants, such as solvents and cutting fluids. However, some pesticides are known to trigger severe allergic (delayed hypersensitivity) reactions. Numerous substances can cause both irritant and allergic dermatitis as well as hives. In particular, latex (a common component of gloves) has been found to cause allergic reactions.

The hands, arms, face, and legs are the most common areas where contact dermatitis occurs. During a flare, contact dermatitis inflames the skin surface, making it look red and scaly. Sometimes tiny water blisters develop, and these leak fluid when scratched. Other symptoms include skin that burns, extreme itching, and sun sensitivity. Allergic contact dermatitis reactions can happen 24 to 48 hours after contact. Once a reaction starts, it may take 14 to 28 days to go away, even with treatment. Nickel, perfumes, and dyes also frequently cause allergic contact dermatitis, according to NIOSH.

How do you get rid of dermatitis? Wash your skin with mild soap and cool water right away, if you can. That may get rid of all or most of the problem substance, according to www.healthline.com. It could help cut back on symptoms. When the rash covers only a small area, a hydrocortisone cream may be all you need for relief.

Prevention, including engineering controls to minimize exposures and the use of hand protection—gloves—as well as possibly face shields and long-sleeve shirts, is frequently important, because one study found 75% of patients with occupational contact dermatitis developed chronic skin disease, according to NIOSH (1996a). In recent years, due to a spike in latex allergic reactions, glove manufacturers have developed many models of nonlatex worker gloves.

Hearing loss, also known as noise-induced hearing loss for OSHA recordkeeping purposes, is a change in hearing threshold relative to the baseline audiogram of an average of 10 decibels (dB) or more in either ear at 2000, 3000, and 4000 hertz, and the employee's total hearing level is 25 dB or more above the audiometric zero (also averaged at the same hertz levels) in the same ear(s).

Occupational hearing loss can result from a single, traumatic exposure to extremely deafening noise, but it's far more likely to develop gradually as a result of chronic exposure to agents that damage the ear or hearing process. Noise is by far the most common of these agents, but some solvents, metals, asphyxiants, and heat may also play a role.

Unfortunately, occupational hearing loss is so common that it is often accepted as a normal consequence of employment. More than 30 million workers are exposed to hazardous noise, according to NIOSH (1996b). NIOSH laments that it has not been possible to create a sense of urgency about work-related hearing loss. Preventive efforts have been hindered because the illness is insidious and occurs without pain or obvious physical abnormalities in affected workers. Nonwork-related causes, such as loud music and ear buds, frequently contribute to this aspect of our society's ills as well.

The consequences of hearing loss go beyond workers' compensation payouts. Victims can suffer reduced quality of life due to social isolation and unrelenting tinnitus (ringing in the ears), and impaired communication with family members, the public, and co-workers. They also are at risk of a diminished ability to monitor the work environment and hear warning signals and equipment sounds. This impaired communication and isolation can cause lost productivity and increased accidents.

Respiratory conditions may result from breathing hazardous chemicals, biological agents (think healthcare industry or laboratories, agriculture), dust, gases, vapors, or fumes at work. There are many examples of respiratory disease: silicosis; asbestosis; pneumonitis; rhinitis or acute lung congestion; farmer's lung; beryllium disease; tuberculosis; occupational asthma; chronic obstructive pulmonary disease (COPD); and toxic inhalation illnesses, such as metal fume fever, chronic obstructive bronchitis, and other lung diseases.

Occupationally related airway diseases, including asthma and COPD, are of particular concern today. Cigarettes, of course, without a doubt are the primary cause of pulmonary disease in the United States, but many occupational exposures—by themselves or in combination with smoking—are known to contribute to COPD. More than 20 million US workers are exposed to substances that can contribute to airway disease, according to NIOSH (1996c). Perhaps as much as 30% of COPD and adult asthma cases may be somehow attributable to or complicated by occupational exposure. Nearly nine million workers are occupationally exposed to known sensitizers and irritants associated with asthma, according to NIOSH. Occupational asthma is now the most frequent occupational respiratory disease diagnosis among patients visiting occupational medical clinics. Many workers are unaware that preexisting asthma conditions may be worsened by the work environment.

Occupational agents, such as coal dust, grain dust, and cotton dust, have been shown in some studies to cause COPD. Again, smoking remains a major factor. But individual genetic variance is increasingly recognized as being a factor. Investigations of particulate exposure in the general environment, where exposure levels are far lower than those found in the workplace, suggest that some individuals with allergies might be impacted by conditions not otherwise considered to be dusty or otherwise polluted. Workers with existing lung disease from other causes may be especially vulnerable to excessive occupational respiratory hazards.

Poisoning includes illnesses evidenced by abnormal concentrations of toxic substances in blood, other tissues, other bodily fluids, or the breath that are caused by ingesting or absorbing toxins into the body. Examples include poisoning by lead, mercury, cadmium, arsenic, other metals; poisoning by carbon monoxide, hydrogen sulfide, other gases; poisoning by benzene, benzol, carbon tetrachloride, and other organic solvents; poisoning by insecticide sprays; and poisoning by other chemicals, such as formaldehyde.

Musculoskeletal disorders (MSDs)—low back pain, wrist pain (carpal tunnel syndrome), rotator-cuff tendinitis in shoulders, neck pain, and other soft tissue MSDs of the fingers, wrist, hand, elbow, neck, shoulder, and back may seem to be *injuries*, not *illnesses*. Injuries are due to a singular event or incident; indeed, you can throw your back out with one inappropriate (or too heavy) lift, twist your neck with one sudden motion, or twist your wrist and elbow to the point of severe pain with one awkward movement. But when MSDs occur cumulatively, over time, due to repetitive motions, they are not single-incident injuries but take on the characteristics of other gradually developing disorders, such as hearing loss, skin diseases, and respiratory illnesses.

For OSHA recordkeeping purposes, if any of your employees experiences a recordable work-related musculoskeletal disorder (MSD), you must record it on the OSHA 300 Log. There is no separate column to report or check off MSDs on the OSHA 300 logs. They are lumped in with "all other illnesses."

According to OSHA, MSDs, like other workplace injuries and illnesses, must be recorded if an "event or exposure in the work environment either caused or contributed to the resulting condition or significantly aggravated a preexisting injury or illness." When the Clinton administration designed the new OSHA 300 Logs, there was a separate column for MSDs on the form. However, in the early 2000s, OSHA eliminated the column for recording MSDs. MSDs, which include back injuries, tendonitis, and carpal tunnel syndrome, still must be recorded, but now they are lumped in with "all other illnesses."

OSHA (n.d.) defines musculoskeletal disorders as disorders of the muscles, nerves, tendons, ligaments, joints, cartilage, and spinal discs. MSDs do not include disorders caused by slips, trips, falls; motor vehicle accidents; or other similar accidents. Examples of MSDs include carpal tunnel syndrome, rotator-cuff syndrome, De Quervain's disease, trigger finger, tarsal tunnel syndrome, sciatica, epicondylitis, tendinitis, Raynaud's phenomenon, carpet layer's knee, herniated spinal disc, and low back pain.

Back disorders account for 27% of all nonfatal occupational injuries and illnesses involving days away from work, according to NIOSH (1996d). As many as 30% of Americans are employed in jobs that routinely require them to perform activities that could increase the risk of developing low back disorders. Male construction laborers, carpenters, and truck and tractor operators are nearly two times more likely to experience a low back disorder than all other male workers, according to NIOSH.

MSDs of the neck and upper extremities due to work factors affect employees in every type of workplace and include food processors, automobile and electronics assemblers, carpenters, office data-entry workers, grocery store cashiers, and garment workers. The highest rates of these disorders occur in the industries with a substantial amount of repetitive, forceful work. The most frequently reported upper-extremity MSDs affect the hand and wrist region. According to NIOSH (1996e), carpal tunnel syndrome requires the longest recuperation of all conditions resulting in lost workdays, with a median 30 days away from work.

All other illnesses is one of five occupational illness columns on the 300 Log. This category includes cumulative MSDs for OSHA recordkeeping purposes. "All other illnesses" cover a wide range of occupational illnesses. These include heatstroke; sunstroke; heat exhaustion; heat stress; freezing; frostbite; decompression sickness; effects of ionizing radiation (such as x-rays); effects of nonionizing radiation (welding flash, ultra-violet rays, lasers); anthrax; bloodborne pathogenic diseases, such as AIDS, HIV, hepatitis B, or hepatitis C; and malignant or benign tumors.

WHAT TO DO

Many of these occupational illnesses involve (1) hazards that are not easily identified; (2) symptoms not readily or commonly associated with work activities; and (3) often complex prevention control measures that are above the pay grade and beyond the scope of knowledge of front-line supervisors. So what should we do?

First, you should know many exposures associated with the risks of occupational illnesses are already covered by OSHA standards. Respiratory protection, hearing protection (the Hearing Conservation Amendment), and specific substances, such as benzene, silica, lead, and asbestos, are covered by US exposure standards that are among the strictest in the world. Most, if not all, require exposure controls and employee training and health monitoring.

HAZCOM

One very important standard is OSHA's hazard communication rule, which mandates that employers maintain on-site safety data sheets (SDSs), formerly called material safety data sheets, that identify the hazardous components, give information on their composition and ingredients, tell you how to identify associated risks with the substances, and provide first-aid measures. SDSs contain 16 information categories, which also include fire-fighting measures, accidental release measures, handling and storage, exposure controls/personal protection, physical and chemical properties, stability, and reactivity.

Chemical manufacturers and importers are required to evaluate the hazards of the chemicals they produce or import and prepare labels and safety data sheets to convey the hazard information to their downstream customers. All employers with hazardous chemicals in their workplaces (which is essentially every workplace by today's standards) must have labels and safety data sheets for their exposed workers and train them to handle the chemicals appropriately. Workers must be able to access SDSs because it is their "right to know."

Permissible Exposure Limits (PELs)

OSHA sets enforceable permissible exposure limits (PELs) to protect workers against the potential health effects that might result from excessive exposure to hazardous substances, including limits on the airborne concentrations of hazardous chemicals in the air. Most OSHA PELs are eight-hour time-weighted averages (TWAs), although for some materials there are also ceiling and peak limits, and some chemicals include a skin designation to warn against skin contact. Approximately 500 PELs have been established.

Threshold Limit Values (TLVs)

Unfortunately, many PELs date back 40 or 50 years and have not been updated. Many companies have set their own in-house permissible exposure levels, and most use the ACGIH Threshold Limit Values (TLVs). The American Conference of Governmental Industrial Hygienists (ACGIH) has established TLVs for more than 600 substances and more than 30 biological exposure indices. TLVs are updated regularly, new ones established, and OSHA requires SDSs to list TLVs as well as PELs. OSHA has conceded that most of its PELs are out of date, and in Appendix D of the PEL standards, the agency lists "recommended" exposure limits set by California OSHA and NIOSH, as well as the TLVs.

You might be surprised at the type of substances covered by TLVs. They include time-weighted averages for nuisance dusts, talcum powder, lead solder, turpentine, carbon dioxide from your breath or dry ice, and hundreds of other common and mundane, yet potentially hazardous, substances if exposed to a sufficient dose. You can obtain the latest copy of the TLV list from www.acgih.org.

According to the ACGIH, Threshold Limit Values (TLVs) and Biological Exposure Indices (BEIs) are developed as guidelines to assist in the control of health hazards. Determinations are made by a voluntary body of independent, knowledgeable individuals. These are recommendations or guidelines intended for use in the practice of industrial hygiene (IH), to be interpreted and applied only by a person trained in the IH discipline. They are not developed for use as legal standards, and ACGIH does not advocate their use as such. In using these guidelines, industrial hygienists are cautioned that the TLVs and BEIs are only one of multiple factors to be considered in evaluating specific workplace situations and conditions. TLVs are generally considered to be the level to which nearly all workers may be exposed day after day for their entire careers without adverse effect. Since TLVs and BEIs are based solely on health factors, there is no consideration given to economic or technical feasibility.

OSHA A–Z INDEX

A third source of information is OSHA's A–Z Index (osha.gov/a-z). Here you'll find detailed information and precautions for many hazardous substances, such as anthrax, asbestos, asphalt fumes, benzene, cadmium, chromium, diesel exhaust, formaldehyde, latex allergy, nail salon exposures, silica, and the zika virus.

INDUSTRIAL HYGIENE

So who are these industrial hygienists that the ACGIH says are qualified to use its TLVs? Industrial hygiene is the science of anticipating, recognizing, evaluating, and controlling chemical, physical, biological, and ergonomic stressors. The term *industrial hygiene* has seen a broadening in recent decades to include community health; environmental hygiene; occupational health; environment, health and safety (EHS); and even sanitarians, who were among the first hygienists a century ago. In fact, today there is a distinct overlap between the work of industrial hygienists and safety professionals. Safety professionals identify acute hazards and evaluate them for the potential to cause injury or illness. Industrial hygiene pros anticipate, recognize, evaluate, and control chronic exposures to eliminate levels of known risk posed by hazards. At times, industrial hygienists and safety professionals work together to identify and mitigate unacceptable workplace conditions.

For more detailed information on industrial hygiene, visit the American Industrial Hygiene Association (AIHA) website (www.aiha.org). AIHA has a membership of more than 10,000. For more information on safety professionals, visit the American Society for Safety Professionals (ASSP) website (www.assp.org). ASSP (formerly the American Society for Safety Engineers—ASSE) has more than 39,000 members.

In 2018, the association officially changed its name to the American Society of Safety Professionals.

One distinction between industrial hygienists and safety professionals is their respective certifications. If you encounter a hazardous condition, unexplained illnesses either in individuals or in clusters, or employee complaints or concerns beyond your scope of knowledge, and especially if you have no in-house safety and health, full-time department staff, you might consider bringing in a Certified Industrial Hygienist (CIH) or a Certified Safety Professional (CSP).

The American Board of Industrial Hygiene (www.abih.org) certifies industrial hygienists through a rigorous credentialing process. In 2016, there were 6844 CIHs worldwide in active status. The test to become a CIH is not an easy one, with a percent passing rate of about 46%. CIHs must pursue continuing education to maintain their credentials.

The Board of Certified Safety Professionals (BCSP) (www.bscp.org) sets standards for professional, technician, technologist, and supervisory-level safety practices; administers examinations; and issues certificates to candidates who meet qualifications and pass the exam(s). Recertification requirements are mandatory.

There are no legal restrictions on who can be called a "safety professional" or an "industrial hygienist." That's why, if you are in need of professional expertise, seek out a CIH or a CSP. Many qualified individuals today have both the CIH and CSP certifications. Consider, if you had financial troubles, wouldn't you feel most confident in using a Certified Public Accountant? The same logic holds true if you encounter safety and/or health challenges beyond your knowledge as a supervisor. Health and industrial hygiene hazards, illnesses, and solutions are very often complex and can involve mixtures of substances. These are serious, potentially life-altering or life-threatening cases far beyond simply going to your first-aid kit. The AIHA website offers listings of CIH and CSP certified consultants.

Consultative Services

OSHA's On-Site Consultation Program offers free and confidential safety and occupational health advice to small- and medium-sized businesses in all states across the country, with priority given to high-hazard worksites. On-site consultation services are separate from enforcement and do not result in penalties or citations. Consultants from state agencies or universities work with employers to identify workplace hazards, provide advice on compliance with OSHA standards, and assist in establishing injury and illness prevention processes. For more information visit www.osha.org.

Safety & Health Achievement Recognition Program (SHARP)

The Safety & Health Achievement Recognition Program recognizes small business employers who have used OSHA's On-Site Consultation Program services and operate an exemplary injury and illness prevention process. Acceptance of your worksite into SHARP from OSHA is an achievement of status that singles you out among your business peers as a model for worksite safety and health. For more information, visit osha.gov/consultation.

Voluntary Protection Program (VPP)

OSHA's Voluntary Protection Program requires employers to submit an application to OSHA and undergo a rigorous on-site evaluation by a team of safety and health professionals. Union support is required for applicants represented by a bargaining unit. VPP participants are reevaluated every three to five years to remain in the program. VPP participants are exempt from OSHA programmed inspections while they maintain their VPP status. In VPP, management, labor, and OSHA work cooperatively and proactively to prevent fatalities, injuries, and illnesses through a system focused on hazard prevention and control, worksite analysis, training, management commitment, and worker involvement. Employers and workers in private industry and federal agencies who have implemented effective safety and health management systems, such as VPP, ISO 45001, and ANZI/ASSP Z10: 2019, maintain injury and illness rates below national Bureau of Labor Statistics averages for their respective industries.

AIHA's Consultants Listing

This is a searchable print and online directory of the association's consultant members. The directory lists consulting firms and individual consultants engaged in a wide variety of customized services in the EHS arena. It's available to anyone free of charge. You can browse the printed directory or use the directory's online search at www.aiha.org.

TECHNOLOGY TODAY

Today, we obviously live in a techno world. There seems to be a tech device for every application. And that holds true for occupational safety and health. Front-line supervisors can make their lives easier by accessing a number of free apps and tools.

OSHA Hazard Identification Training Tool

You can download this interactive, online, game-based training tool for small business owners, workers, and others interested in learning the core concepts of hazard identification. After using this tool, users will better understand the process to identify hazards in their own workplace. This tool is intended to (1) teach small business owners and their employees the process for finding hazards in their workplace and (2) raise awareness on the types of information and resources about workplace hazards available on OSHA's website.

NIOSH Ladder Safety

This is an app that provides employers, workers, and those doing home improvement projects with the following tools:
- *Angle Measuring Tool*—uses visual, sound, and vibration signals to make it easier for users to set an extension ladder at the proper angle of 75.5 degrees
- *Decision Tool*—offers tips to plan your job using a ladder while considering time, materials, and tools required
- *Selection Tool*—provides a procedure to select the appropriate ladder size and the minimum, required ladder duty rating corresponding to user characteristics and task
- *Inspection Tool*—includes a comprehensive checklist for ladder mechanical inspection
- *Proper Use Tool*—presents a set of rules for safe ladder use in a user-friendly format
- *Accessories Tool*—describes a number of available extension ladder safety accessories

NIOSH Pocket Guide to Hazardous Chemicals

This mobile web app works with an HTML5-compliant web browser. The app can be used offline when no internet or cell-phone connection is available. Features include 634 chemical entries and appendices; links to immediately dangerous to life and health (IDLH) substances, as well as NIOSH and OSHA Methods (requires a data connection); search chemical by name and synonym, DOT number, CAS number, RTECS number; "type ahead" technology to quickly find chemicals; "preferences" menu to select information to display; and "favorite," commonly used chemicals.

OSHA-NIOSH Heat Safety Tool

The OSHA-NIOSH Heat Safety Tool is a useful resource for planning outdoor work activities based on how hot it feels throughout the day. The device features a real-time heat index and hourly forecasts, specific to your location, as well as occupational safety and health recommendations from OSHA and NIOSH.

NIOSH Lifting Equation App

This is a tool to calculate the overall risk index for single and multiple manual lifting tasks. This application provides risk estimates to help evaluate lifting tasks and reduce the incidence of low back injuries in workers.

NIOSH Sound Level Meter App

This is a tool to measure sound levels in the workplace and provide noise exposure parameters to help reduce occupational noise-induced hearing loss.

Download the NIOSH apps from NIOSH's Mobile Applications (Apps) web page at https://www.cdc.gov/niosh/pubs/apps/default.html. You can find other available apps, such as Octave Band Analyzers, in the app stores for Android and Apple. The NIOSH App is noted as validated for the accuracy of occupational noise readings, whereas others might not be.

Online Courses

ASSP's online courses are fully online courses that provide you with a flexible, engaging, and immediately applicable learning experience. Topics are many and include hazard identification; laws, regulations, and standards; risk assessment; risk management; safety management; education and training; safety culture; organizational culture; and communication engagement and influence. To learn more, visit https://www.assp.org/education/online-learning.

REFERENCES

Mining Editor. "Work-Related Lung Diseases Making a Resurgence." 2017. *Australasian Mine Safety Journal*, December 28, 2017.

National Institute for Occupational Safety and Health (NIOSH). 1996a. *National Occupational Research Agenda*, DHHS (NIOSH) Publication Number 96–115. "Allergic and Irritant Dermatitis." Accessed February 27, 2020. https://www.cdc.gov/niosh/docs/96-115/diseas.html#Allergic%20and%20Irritant%20Dermatitis.

National Institute for Occupational Safety and Health (NIOSH). 1996b. *National Occupational Research Agenda*, DHHS (NIOSH) Publication Number 96–115. "Hearing Loss." Accessed February 27, 2020. https://www.cdc.gov/niosh/docs/96-115/diseas.html#Hearing%20Loss.

National Institute for Occupational Safety and Health (NIOSH). 1996c. *National Occupational Research Agenda*, DHHS (NIOSH) Publication Number 96–115. "Asthma and Chronic Obstructive Pulmonary Disease." Accessed February 27, 2020. https://www.cdc.gov/niosh/docs/96-115/diseas.html#Asthma%20and%20Chronic%20Obstructive%20Pulmonary%20Disease.

National Institute for Occupational Safety and Health (NIOSH). 1996d. *National Occupational Research Agenda*, DHHS (NIOSH) Publication Number 96–115. "Low Back Disorders." Accessed February 27, 2020. https://www.cdc.gov/niosh/docs/96-115/diseas.html#Low%20Back%20Disorders.

National Institute for Occupational Safety and Health (NIOSH). 1996e. *National Occupational Research Agenda*, DHHS (NIOSH) Publication Number

96–115. "Musculoskeletal Disorders of the Upper Extremities." Accessed February 27, 2020. https://www.cdc.gov/niosh/docs/96-115/diseas.html#Musculoskeletal%20Disorders%20of%20the%20Upper%20Extremities.

Occupational Safety and Health Administration (OSHA). n.d. "Ergonomics." Accessed February 27, 2020. https://www.osha.gov/SLTC/ergonomics/.

Petersen, Dan. 2003. Interview by Dave Johnson. *Industrial Safety & Hygiene News enewsletter*, July 22, 2003.

Petersen, Dan. 2007. Interview by Mike Williamsen. *Professional Safety*, March 2007.

US Bureau of Labor Statistics. 2018. "Employer-Reported Workplace Injuries and Illness – 2018." November 7, 2019. Accessed January 3, 2020. https://www.bls.gov/news.release/pdf/osh.pdf.

US Bureau of Labor Statistics. n.d. Supplemental News Release "Table SNR07. Nonfatal occupational illnesses by major industry sector and category of illness, 2017." Accessed December 5, 2019. https://www.bls.gov/iif/oshwc/osh/os/snr07_00_2017.xlsx.

PART V

Appendices

APPENDIX A

Executive Safety Leadership

By Dan Petersen and Kyle Dotson

On Nov. 8, 2006, over a lunch of burgers and fries, Dan Petersen and I talked about the good old days and where the safety of business—and the business of safety—might be headed. While we both enjoyed talking about the history of safety and health management, Dan in particular was never one to stop looking toward the future.

On that day, I was more interested in gaining his assistance in tapping a famous friend of his for a donation to the American Industrial Hygiene Foundation. At age 72, and after having suffered a mild stroke, he was more interested in discussing the book that I had been writing on my own for too long and that we were to finish together.

As most of you know, Dan passed away a short time later, and I feel the need to share with other safety, health, and environment professionals a few of his thoughts on safety leadership as best practiced by executives. These thoughts reflect some of our dialogue over the years on my longstanding fondness for management systems and his well-experienced view of the wide range of reasons for failed industrial safety programs. But by and large, these thoughts share what Dan felt was right—and wrong—about one of my previous articles, "How to Coach Senior Managers: Ten Roles Executives Should Assume for Safety."

When (if?) I finish our book, it will be dedicated to Dan, my teacher, mentor, and friend, as he was known to so many of us in the occupational safety and health management professions.

HEALTH AND SAFETY MANAGEMENT SYSTEMS

Management systems will be critical to achieving long-term safety and health excellence in the large organizations of the future. The publishing of the ANSI/ASSP Z10.0-2019 *Occupational Health and Safety Management Systems* standard that accepts variance in individual company approaches is a significant step forward for everyone. The resulting systems may vary from simple to complex but will only work if implemented well. Like many safety programs sitting on the shelf collecting dust at organizations of decades past, it often matters more how they are executed than how comprehensive they may be in design. However, poor design of safety systems, such as a foundation in common practices based on incorrect theories, is a recipe for failure. Preventing some of these frequently designed-in failures may be where a consensus standard such as ANSI/ASSP Z10 will contribute the most. To be sure, behavioral scientists have a different perspective than most. Behavioral science holds that consequences (such as recognition or corrective actions or feedback based on observations) motivate behavior and related attitudes. "People do what they do because of what happens to them when they do it," writes psychologist Dr. E. Scott Geller (Geller 1996).

Systems Can Get Everyone Involved, Including Senior Managers

Only senior managers can ensure safety as an organizational value and part of the company culture. Therefore, senior management engagement is crucial for long-term safety success. One way that standardized safety and health management systems help safety staff is to provide a template for getting people at all levels of the organization involved in the safety management process, including senior management. Safety and health professionals are perhaps wisely shy about telling chief executives what they should be doing to lead safety in the organization. Yet that is exactly what a safety and health management system does—it defines and maps the role and safety participation of senior management along with those at all other levels in the company.

On the Safety Commitment of Executives

Most senior managers value and want to actively support safety and health but are pulled in so many directions that they feel they simply must focus only on what strategically is in the way of the company's success. Frankly, occupational safety and health is, and historically has been, something that, unless obviously out of control, has been easy to assume to be under control. This is not only logical, but as a pure intent, represents good corporate governance.

    I have been known to say that I have never met a manager who wanted anyone to get hurt. Dan believed he had met a few. Since we always agreed that it was more realistic for SH&E professionals to influence the activities rather than the core values of individual managers, we agreed that rather than asking a manager to commit to a role that s/he is unlikely to routinely fulfill in the long term, it is better for today's professional staff to help the executive in three leadership activities: (1) saying the right things about safety and health, (2) measuring the right things, and (3) holding his/her lieutenants accountable.

On the Safety Commitment of Employees

Despite the fact that safety is among the most fundamental of human needs, safety and health risks in the workplace and elsewhere in life are adapted to and quickly become familiar and accepted. Various practices have encouraged risk-taking. One example is hazard pay, a concept still well accepted by many industries, governments, labor unions, and workers around the world. Perhaps the safest worker is one educated in the hazards and risks, adequately motivated by personal factors, and continually coached by superiors and peers in the workplace to be rewarded for safe behaviors and held accountable for unsafe behaviors in a wide variety of financial and emotional ways.

On the Measurement of Safety in Large Organizations

There is likely no single best measure of safety performance, but the standardization of some measures is critical to ensure benchmarking of performance. Part of measuring the right things means understanding that different measures are appropriate at different levels of large organizations. The "behavior-based processes" that define critical behaviors measure the percent behavior achieved and provide feedback for corrective action. They are tools for the measurement of one leading indicator of safety at the employee level.

Other measures, such as the percent implementation of all appropriate elements of a corporatewide safety management system, may be appropriate at a business-unit level. At the top of an organization, the results of leading indicators such as a high-quality safety perception survey that includes worker satisfaction together with long-term health indicator results and short-term lagging indicators of bottom-line injury results may be a perfectly appropriate combination of measures.

Eight Executive Habits for Safety Leadership

1. Executives must lead by example in the area of safety as well as every other aspect of ethical business. This includes, for example, the correct wearing of appropriate PPE in the workplace. One minor lapse observed by persons two levels down in the organization will undo untold other positive efforts to achieve excellence in workplace safety.
2. Executives must verbally communicate about safety in meetings with other managers. While what people do is sometimes more telling than what they say, it is the rare executive who can effectively lead without verbal articulation of his position on the matter. What executives say to each other one on one about safety while safety staff or other support staff is not present speaks volumes and has the greatest effect on crucial aspects of company culture.

3. Executives must put their money where their mouths are and fund safety adequately. This does not mean employing arbitrarily large staffs of SH&E professionals. Instead, it means that in all business decisions executives seek to treat the safety of all employees as the ethical right thing to do—a prudent act that uses corporate funds and corporate governance and an intangible factor of business relationships that is almost always also a good investment.
4. Executives must hold their subordinates accountable for managing safety and must require that subordinates report on safety matters. Make sure that the roles and responsibilities for safety and health are defined (in writing and in practice). Doing so is part of treating safety just like any other important part of the business. Safety should be simply part of an overall performance measurement process.
5. Executives must provide appropriate feedback regarding safety performance. Monitor the results of management system audits and provide feedback. Personally praise exceptional performance, ignore average performance, and confront substandard performance on the part of subordinate operations managers/supervisors. Realize that human exposure to injury risk has an element of randomness and may not be well described by current statistical analysis methods, such as the frequency rate of recordable, reportable or lost-time injuries. Therefore, acknowledge and appropriately reward efforts in risk-reduction even if short-term injury results are poor.
6. Executives must make sure that the risk profile of the organization is continuously improved. New hazards and potential risks to the business (not just safety or health) are introduced continuously, and large corporations that are good managers of risk will be successful in the long term. When something bad happens—and it will—get to the root cause and try to systemically build in whatever must be feasibly done to ensure that it won't happen again.
7. Executives of organizations that use potentially toxic materials must ensure that there is long-term support for the anticipation, recognition, evaluation, and control of industrial hygiene in the organization. The past actions or inactions of corporations in the developed world are judged today by a society with extremely high expectations as compared to even the recent past. One can safely assume that societal norms for a safe and healthy work environment will continue to increase in the future in all countries of the world.
8. Executives must ensure that safety and health processes are being fully integrated into the primary management system processes of the business. Safety and health cannot be effectively managed long term separate from the management of the routine affairs of the business.

In today's companies, this includes the deep integration of safety and health matters into systems such as the enterprisewide management software and process control systems.

ABOUT DAN PETERSEN

From the 1950s into the 21st century, Dan Petersen richly interpreted the rapidly developing management and social science of the time and applied this body of knowledge to the field of safety management. Through his prolific writings that span 30 years, he created a body of safety management literature unmatched by any other single contributor.

His teaching on the need to focus on the actions of people as the ultimate avoiders of industrial accidents, as well as to guard the machines, is a concept that is likely to be even more true in the future. The increasing complexity in future workplaces, ranging from biotech to nanotech, will require the anticipation of risk and the building of safety into the physical, chemical, and biological "machines" in ways that cannot yet be imagined. The recognition of the human factor in perhaps overriding what is intended by designers to be fail-safe machine processes will ensure that Petersen's work remains a critical factor of safety management for decades to come.

DAN PETERSEN RESOURCES

OSH professionals can learn more about Dan's philosophies and vision for the profession in his many books and videos.

Analyzing Safety Performance (1979, Garland STPM Press).
Analyzing Safety System Effectiveness (1996, Van Nostrand Reinhold).
Authentic Involvement (2001, National Safety Council).
The Criteria for Safety Excellence. Dan Petersen's Safety Management Series, Part 1 (1990, distributed by CoreMedia Training Solutions).
Dan Petersen's The Challenge of Change (1993, CoreMedia Training Solutions).
Dan Petersen's The Challenge of Change: Creating a New Safety Culture Resource Manual (1993, CoreMedia Training Solutions).
Evaluating Your Safety System. Dan Petersen's Safety Management Series, Part 2 (1990, distributed by CoreMedia Training Solutions).
High Participation Safety—A Case Study. Dan Petersen's Safety Management Series, Part 5 (1990, distributed by CoreMedia Training Solutions).
"Human Error Reduction and Safety Management" (thesis) (1980, University of Northern Colorado).
Human Error Reduction and Safety Management (1996, Van Nostrand Reinhold).
Industrial Accident Prevention: A Safety Management Approach (coauthored with H.W. Heinrich, N.R. Roos, J. Brown, and S. Hazlett; 1980, McGraw-Hill).

Measurement and Reward. Dan Petersen's Safety Management Series, Part 3 (1990, distributed by CoreMedia Training Solutions).

Measurement of Safety Performance (2005, ASSE).

The OSHA Compliance (1975, McGraw-Hill).

Readings in Industrial Accident Prevention (coauthored with J. Goodale; 1980, McGraw-Hill).

Safe Behavior Reinforcement (1989, Aloray).

Safe Behavior Reinforcement. Dan Petersen's Safety Management Series, Part 4 (1990, distributed by CoreMedia Training Solutions).

Safety Accountability (1999, CoreMedia Training Solutions).

Safety by Objectives, SBO (1978, Aloray).

Safety by Objectives: What Gets Measured and Rewarded Gets Done (1995, Van Nostrand Reinhold).

Safety Management: A Human Approach, 2nd ed. (2001, ASSE).

Techniques of Safety Management: A Systems Approach, 4th ed. (2003, ASSE).

Appendix B

The "New View" of Safety*

FOCUS MORE ON POSITIVE OUTCOMES & SYSTEMS,

LESS ON BUREAUCRACY AND HUMAN FAILURE

By Dave Johnson, *ISHN* Editor

How can we do safety differently?

Do we need to do safety differently?

It's long overdue, according to Dr. Sidney Dekker, who in 2014 wrote an essay on "The 'Failed State' of Safety." Yes, says Corrie Spitzer, who is giving a talk, "Safety at a Dead End" at the American Society of Safety Professionals' annual conference this June [2019].

ISHN asked more than 20 safety professionals, consultants, academics, and authors for their opinions about six tenets of the so-called "new view" of safety. It's also referred to as "Safety Differently," "Safety-II," and includes human and organizational performance (HOP) practices.

By any name, the "new view" is more a philosophy and mindset than any single program. New safety tactics and strategies are flowing out of this new mental model. It is anything but another "flavor of the month" program or slogan—something here today, gone tomorrow.

The "new view" or doing safety differently has been written about in books, discussed at workshops, and even made into YouTube documentaries. But US safety and health pros—and companies—are just beginning to get wide exposure to the differences between traditional safety and safety v2.0.

So what do our survey respondents have to say about six of the pillars of this new way of thinking about safety?

---

*Published in *ISHN*, June 2019, Vol 53, No. 6, pages 17–19.

1 Safety is at a dead-end and is a "failed state."

Proponents of doing safety differently make several arguments here. Safety and health performance in the United States is stagnating. Both in terms of metrics and fresh ideas. Even companies with excellent EHS performance are frustrated by their inability to reduce the most serious injuries and workplace fatalities.

In millions of US workplaces, especially smaller businesses, the focus remains as it has for decades: rulebooks; compliance; policing; PPE as the first line of defense; and command and control, top-down, "do-as-I-say" safety bureaucracies. These practices, the argument goes, continue to leave too many safety and health departments isolated and detached from mainstream business imperatives.

Not surprisingly, some pros see marketing-driven shock value in proclaiming safety a failed state and at a dead end. "I absolutely and unequivocally disagree with this," says Ryan Gilmore, human resources and safety director for B&B Fabricators, Arlington, WA. "Just because safety is not easy, we don't give up. We work together and do everything to steer our safety programs in a positive direction.

"The safety profession is replete with its share of pessimists," says Mark Hansen, director of risk management, Contek Solutions LLC. "Safety success is a marathon, not a sprint."

"Quite the opposite; I believe emerging technology will result in even greater reduction in injuries over the next several years and decades," says Aaron Rowland, an EHS supervisor.

2 Safety is more than identifying and managing things that go wrong. The focus should be on the 99.9% of the times things go right, and learn from these successes.

"New view" advocates are distressed by the profession's decades-old embrace of recordable incidents as the measure of performance—in many companies the only measure that counts. This overemphasis on the numbers leads to unethical management, suppression of incidents and injuries, and overspecified and overprescribed rules, they claim. Plus, traditional recordkeeping numbers give safety a negative image. Top management think of safety in terms of accidents, risks, hazards, OSHA violations, human error and unsafe acts, because that's the language many safety pros speak.

A key principle of doing safety differently is that this focus on negative outcomes results in most of organization life going unexamined. Safety and health departments need to identify and learn from things that go well. What makes for successful confined space entries, lockout-tagout procedures, and safe work at heights? What makes most work come off without a hitch? Study and learn from how normal work processes get the job done—almost always without incident. Communicate these positive learnings up the chain of command to show top managers the value and advantages of safe work.

Many professionals are coming around to a proactive, positive attitude toward their work. They "get it." Safety needs to pivot away from fishing for faults and the goal of finding and mitigating errors. "Safety is much more than identifying and managing the things that go wrong," says Gilmore. "Focus on successes and positives."

"To increase teammate ownership, focus on the actions people take to protect themselves and others," says Rowland. "Show off their successes, give them positivity, and they will keep working on the goal of incident prevention."

3 Safety too often views humans as a weak link, a liability or a hazard.

Blaming the injured victim is the path of least resistance in many investigations. Concluding that human error or unsafe acts are the culprits, the primary cause of failure, saves time, wraps up incident analyses quickly, and gives management the easiest of answers. Just discipline, retrain, or terminate.

Again, more safety and health pros are seeing the fallacy in this approach. "We are 'human beings,' not 'human doings,'" says Deborah Grubbe, owner and president of Operations and Safety Solutions. "We get it right much of the time."

"It's easy to blame the worker. It's harder and ultimately more beneficial to analyze an incident to find multiple systemic breakdowns," says Abby Ferri, CSP, president of The Ferri Group LLC.

Systems thinking in safety is nothing new. Same with complexity theory, human factors, high reliability organization theory, and resilience engineering. But safety v2.0 emphasizes that today these approaches are more relevant than ever. Technology, robotics, artificial intelligence, the Internet of Things, and smart factories make operating systems and process more complex and shape-shifting than ever.

Posters, safety slogans and songs, compliance controls, a rush to do observations at the end of the month are not going to uncover how conditions, systems, upstream decisions and complexities influence behavior, say new view proponents. They stress looking for sources of variability—frustrations; constraints; unrealistic time pressures, schedules, goals; too many rules; poor communication; lack of resources; inadequate defenses; design shortcomings; degraded, poorly maintained processes—and enable workers to respond to system variabilities positively and safely. Developing and sustaining situational awareness is a key.

Rather than focusing on individual workers and conditions, pros should expand their view and identify drivers, complexities, and the entire context of the system as causes of incidents and failures.

4 People inevitably make mistakes. Human error is normal. Obtaining and sustaining zero incidents is impossible.

The new view of safety is not particularly vested in the goal of zero incidents. Zero incidents is oriented around numbers, cases and recordables. Doing safety differently means pivoting away from these lagging indicators of performance—getting away from an obsession with numbers.

Zero incidents is akin to the idea of "safety first." Workers know the truth. Profits come first. And achieving zero incidents is possible for a period of time, but "impossible for any length of time," says Dr. Timothy Ludwig, psychology professor at Appalachian State University. "Instead of counting down to zero we should be counting up all the safe actions as we adapt our human behavior and safety systems."

"Zero injuries is a wonderful goal, but we need to be forgiving when an injury does occur," says Dr. Krista Geller, president of GellerAC4P. "Find out the contributing factors, the error precursors and anything else that might have contributed to the event."

5 Punishment fails as a tool for improvement. It suppresses reporting, speaking up, and learning.

If people inevitably make mistakes and human error is normal, punishment is not a tool for improvement, holds the new view. But "punishment" comes off as cold, even cruel, as opposed to "corrective feedback" and "progressive discipline." Many pros make this distinction in definitions.

"No question punishment promotes a culture in which reporting is nonexistent," says Gilmore. "Speaking up about safety issues is completely discouraged; there's no incentive to learn."

An equal number of pros will add a "but" here, a caveat.

"But I have had to dismiss a handful of individuals who simply refused to come on board with the safety program," says Gilmore. "These were cases that leaned to the extreme and are the exception."

"Disciplinary and accountability actions, if used the right way, can result in improvement. The key phrase is: used the right way," says Rowland.

6 It is more useful to know how an accident happened than knowing why it happened.

Doing safety differently shifts attention from "why" an incident occurred to "how" it happened. Learning is a fundamental tenet of the new view, and gaining insight and understanding to prevent incidents requires close study of how work actually gets done—in reality—not work as imagined or drawn up in a playbook. How do workers successfully adapt to changing conditions? How do they get the job right 99.99% of the time? How are successful outcomes achieved?

"Researchers or scientists typically avoid 'why' questions, and focus on 'how'," says Dr. Scott Geller, psychology professor at Virginia Tech. "How" uncovers the environmental factors, past or present, that enabled or motivated the occurrence of an event, behavior, or attitude, says Geller. "In my view, clinicians and spiritual leaders deal with answers to the 'whys' of life and death."

Many pros, while no longer so wedded to the old "5 Whys" line of root-cause analysis, are pragmatic. "We need to know both 'how' and 'why' equally," says Hansen. Knowing one without knowing the other leaves pieces of the puzzle missing, he says.

This is an example of how the new view or doing safety differently have no intent of tossing traditional safety practices in the dust bin. Advocates are quick to point out new philosophies and models complement tried-and-true staples—not supersede or eliminate them. Continue to write rules and enforce procedures. Just don't write tomes. Continue to audit, find and fix hazards, train employers, and analyze incidents.

But don't put it all on the safety department. The new view holds that safety is a system of interactions involving leadership, culture, processes, training, supervision, design, and more. Safety is not housed in one department. It's integrated into almost all areas of the business—procurement, contractors, maintenance, operations, engineering, human resources, legal, and senior leadership.

Some pros see this as a threatening diffusion of their power. For others, integration, alignment, and making safety invisible has been their thinking all along. And they will tell you, in essence, that they have been doing safety differently for years.

"AN IDEA WHOSE TIME HAS COME"

ISHN interviewed by email Dr. Sidney Dekker, professor, Safety Science Innovation Lab, Griffith University, Brisbane, Australia, and author of *The Safety Anarchist* among other books. Dr. Dekker posts regularly at www.safetydifferently.com and is one of the founding fathers of the new view of safety.

"Over the past two decades, we have not seen any progress in reducing fatalities across many industries. Yet during those same two decades the amount of safety bureaucracy (petty rules, a growing clutter of procedures and checklists. and invasive surveillance of front-line work through technologies everywhere) has doubled or even tripled. The problem is not going away. It is staying stubbornly the same.

"All these new ideas are pointing to us interfering less with how work is actually accomplished, and instead asking operational front-line people what they need to get it done safely (rather than safety professionals telling them what to do through all kinds of compliance). Safety professionals can actually feel a bit threatened by all this. It might have consequences for the relevance and importance of their role, after all.

"There is a groundswell of adoptions of these kinds of approaches. You can see this in incident reports, for instance, where it is increasingly illegitimate to say that 'human error' was the cause: people are demanding more explanation than that. How did the organization set the worker up for failure? Not many organizations have figured out yet how to learn from things going right, but we do see progress there.

"The greatest obstacles to progressing to Safety Differently include a fear of regulatory authorities that demand compliance (like OSHA), the opposition from safety professionals themselves who might see their influence diminished, and the fears of boards and managers of losing control over 'accountability' in their organization."

"NOTHING MUCH FOUNDATIONAL HAS CHANGED"

ISHN interviewed by email Corrie Pitzer, CEO of SAFEMap International.

"Safety has been at a dead end before, or so claimed Dan Petersen, way back in 1975, when he stated that the 'human era' is (was) upon us. Yet, for the past few decades, maybe even since the 1970s, nothing much foundational has changed in safety management. We still set up a manual of policies and rules of work, set performance standards and require compliance—all with the same focus: to control and/or modify behavior, especially that of the front-line workers.

"The way we define and measure safety has NOT changed. That executives and management are still rewarded for safety, as measured by accident rates, and we still show trendy graphs on injury rates, even at board meetings! I have not yet seen a business, any business, that defines safety in any other way.

"Safety is killing business. We are the millstone around the operation's neck because it goes against everything we want the business to be: To be more efficient, smarter, leaner, more profitable. We want an agile production system that allows risk-taking and experimentation, in order to innovate, to prosper, to change and improve. We need people to be adaptable, operational systems to be flexible, and performance goals to be stretched to the limit.

"Henry Ford famously said: 'If I asked people what they wanted, they would have said, a faster horse.' If he asked the safety directors what they wanted, the answer would have been: 'A slower horse.'

"Sadly, we are not part of the success, reach, or stretch of the business, we are part of its restraint, its containment, its failures."

"THE OSHA STUFF DOES NOT HELP SMALL ORGANIZATIONS"

ISHN interviewed by email Dr. Todd Conklin, author of *Better Questions*, among other books. He is a retired senior advisor at Los Alamos National Laboratory and one of the foremost authorities on human factors and human performance.

"If you ask bad questions you get bad answers. So one way to be better (that is more effective and meaningful) is by pulsing, validating, asking, looking at the right stuff. Our questions traditionally have been very focused on worker behavior—because we believed that worker behavior was the problem. Those questions always lead us to the same damn stuff. And that damn stuff does not make for long-term, sustainable improvement.

"The push is to get industry off the outcome bias. Safety is never (nor never will be) an outcome to be achieved. Safety is never over—you know that. Every day the clock starts again, so to speak.

"Shift the question from 'who failed' to 'what failed'? Don't look down and in but look up and out. You will find new stuff to fix, and that is really refreshing.

"For way too long we have treated the workers as if they are the problem with safety. That is crap. The workers create safety all the time in all types of conditions. Pursuing the context of how work is done is vital to understanding how both success and failure happen."

APPENDIX C

ANSI/ASSP Z10.0-2019
Occupational Health and Safety Management Systems

By Dave Johnson

HISTORY

Approved August 22, 2019. Effective January 1, 2020.

The Z10 committee began its work in 1999, and the standard was originally approved in 2005, revised in 2012, reaffirmed in 2017, and significantly revised in 2019.

SCOPE

To encourage the use of management system principles and guidelines for occupational health and safety among American organizations.

This is a voluntary consensus standard on occupational safety and health (OSH) management systems. It uses recognized management system principles in order to be compatible with quality and environmental management system standards such as ISO 9001, ISO 14001, and ISO 45001. The standard also draws from approaches used by the International Labor Organization's (ILO) *Guidelines on Occupational Health and Safety Management Systems* and from systems in use in organizations in the United States.

While it is not the intent of this document to duplicate requirements covered in ISO 45001, this standard provides a level of alignment and interpretation of those requirements relative to a US perspective on the ISO standard.

ANSI/ASSP Z10.0 focuses primarily on the strategic levels of policy and the processes to ensure the policy is effectively carried out. The standard does not provide detailed procedures, job instructions, or documentation mechanisms. Each organization must design these according to its needs.

The design of ANSI/ASSP Z10.0 encourages integration with other management systems to facilitate organizational effectiveness using the elements of the Plan-Do-Check-Act (PDCA) model as the basis for continual improvement. PDCA was popularized by Dr. W. Edwards Deming and is used as a framework by most management system standards.

KEY CONCEPTS

- Context of the organization – strategic considerations
- Understanding the needs and expectations of workers and other interested parties
- Management leadership
- Worker participation
- Education, training and competence
- Awareness and communication
- Risk assessment
- Hierarchy of controls
- Occupational health
- Monitoring, measurement and assessment
- Incident investigation
- Audits
- Corrective actions
- Feedback and organizational learning

CHANGES TO ANSI/ASSP Z10.0-2019

As the publication of ISO 45001 accounts for the greatest development in the field of occupational health and safety standardization since the previous publication of ANSI/ASSP Z10.0 in 2012, ANSI/ASSP Z10.0-2019 underwent significant updates to better align it with the high-level structure of ISO 45001.

The changes made to ANSI/ASSP Z10.0-2019 to synchronize it with ISO 45001:2018 include:

- The addition of Section 4, "Context of the Organization – Strategic Considerations" (this also helps organizations consider internal and external issues when planning their OHSMS).
- The replacement of the definition of "employee" with a definition of "worker." This potentially broadens the coverage of the management system to include certain workers who are not employed by the organization.
- New Section 7, "Support," which features resources, education, training and competence, communication, and document control process.

- The conversion from the traditional two-column format to single column. This facilitates electronic access, and most of the previous right column explanatory material was either converted to notes or added to Annex A.

However, not all changes to the standard resulted from harmonization with the international standard for OHSMS. ANSI/ASSP Z10.0 dates back to 2005, and its most recent revision was completed in 2019. Throughout this time, there have been numerous advancements in the field of occupational health and safety, which are reflected in the ANSI/ASSP Z10.0-2019 standard. Changes to ANSI/ASSP Z10.0-2019 to reflect this include:
- The inclusion of worker input and involvement in determining an acceptable level of risk.
- New section 8.2, Identification of OHSMS Issues.
- New occupational health information in 8.8 to emphasize the importance of occupational health in the overall OHSMS.
- New emphasis on organizational learning and feedback in 9.5. These two concepts are critical to successful management system implementation.
- Updates throughout regarding the integration of the OHSMS with business systems.

Users should be aware that ANSI/ASSP Z10.0-2019 revises ANSI/ASSE Z10-2012, and the removal of ASSE in the standard designation resulted from the American Society of Safety Engineers (ASSE) changing its name to the American Society of Safety Professionals (ASSP) in 2018.

COMPARISON WITH ISO 45001

The ANSI/ASSP Z10-2019 revision is structured to be compatible with ISO 45001 to help users achieve conformance with both standards. However, North American users will find ANSI/ASSP Z10 to be easier to understand and implement because some of the terms and concepts in ISO 45001 do not translate easily across countries. A separate implementation manual, ASSP GM-Z10.100-2019, *Guidance and Implementation Manual for ANSI/ASSP Z10.0-2019 Occupational Health and Safety Management Systems*, was published by ASSP that users of both ANSI/ASSP Z10 and ISO 45001 will find useful. ASSP also published ASSP GM – Z10.101-2019, *Guidance Manual: Keep Your People Safe in Smaller Organizations*, to help small- and medium-sized organizations adopt the basic principles, if not all the details, of the standard.

The Z10 revision drops the word employee in favor of worker to reflect changes in workforce arrangements and to be consistent with ISO 45001. Section 4 on strategic considerations and context helps the user understand the needs and expectations of the organization, its workers, and other interested parties, including regulatory agencies.

Z10 GUIDANCE AND IMPLEMENTATION MANUAL

The manual contains cutting-edge thinking on a variety of health and safety topics:

- The manual promotes a new view of health and safety as active, not passive. This concept expands beyond the historical view of safety as merely the absence of injury or freedom from unacceptable risk. Organizations should see health and safety not as outcomes to be achieved but as dynamic processes to be managed, resulting or emerging from the interactions of the management system's components. For example, building error-tolerant systems and learning from work as performed are key elements of health and safety.
- The guidance manual has a chapter on integrating occupational health—including medical issues, industrial hygiene, and total worker health—into the OHSMS.
- A separate chapter discusses prevention of fatal and serious injuries and illnesses, or FSII. Companies with effective safety programs as measured by most traditional indicators may still experience FSII. Because these events are typically infrequent, their causes and precursors may sometimes be overlooked. The chapter explains how FSII prevention activities require a greater focus on a set of risk-based tools and techniques that need to be integrated into an effective OHSMS.
- The metrics and measurement chapter provides helpful information on leading and lagging indicators. Lagging indicators, including many of the familiar injury and illness statistics, are measures of outcome, while leading indicators can be predictive or can drive activities that lead to better performance. The chapter explains how metrics can be used to manage and improve health and safety, and not merely to monitor outcomes.

REFERENCE

Slavin, Thomas. n.d. "Active Health and Safety: Looking Forward to the New American Standard for Occupational Health and Safety Management Systems." *The Synergist*. Accessed March 4, 2020. https://synergist.aiha.org/201903-active-health-and-safety.

Index

A

Accident proneness, 61–63, 65–66
Accident repeater, 45, 61
Accidents and injuries
    causal factors, 63–66
    precursors, 99–100
Accimap, 113
Accountability, defined, 76, 80, 86
Accountability ladder, 115
Accountability systems, 119–127
    Balanced Scorecard, 126–127
        Kodak, 126
        Navistar, 126
        Procter and Gamble, 126
    Menu, 4, 122–126
    Safety by Objectives (SBO), 4, 120–122
    System of Counting and Rating Accident Prevention Effort (SCRAPE), 4, 119–120
American Conference of Governmental Industrial Hygienists (ACGIH), 250–251
American Industrial Hygiene Association (AIHA), 252, 253
    consultants listing 253
American Management Association (AMACOM), vii, xi
American National Standards Institute (ANSI), 98, 107
    Z16.2-1995, *Information Management for Occupational Safety and Health*, 107
American Society of Safety Professionals (ASSP), vii, 211, 251, 275
    ASSP GM-Z10.100-2019, *Guidance and Implementation Manual for ANSI/ASSP Z10.0-2019 Occupational Health and Safety Management Systems*, 275

ASSP GM-Z10.101-2019, *Guidance Manual: Keep Your People Safe in Smaller Organizations*, 275
Americans with Disabilities Act, 63, 234
ANSI/ASSP Z10-2019 *Occupational Safety and Health Management Systems*, 108, 212, 259–260, 273–276
ANSI/ASSP/ISO 31000-2018 *Risk Management—Guidelines*, 168
ANSI/ASSP/ISO 45001-2018 standard, 107–108, 212
Argyris, Chris, 34–35, 38, 218–219
Asian Pacific Society of Respirology Congress 2017, 245
As low as reasonably practical (ALARP), 187
Australian Transport Safety Bureau (ATSB), 202

B

Baer, Walter, 56–57
    "Discipline: When an Employee Breaks the Rules," 56
Baker III, James A., 185
Bayesian statistics, 187
Behavior-based safety (BBS), 74, 81, 83, 140, 222–223, 227, 237–238, 261
Behavior Observation System (BOS), 85
Biological Exposure Indices (BEIs), 251
Board of Certified Safety Professionals (BCSP), 252
Boeing 737 Max 8 jet crashes, 209
Bowtie analysis, 187

C

Canadian Centre for Occupational Health and Safety, 170, 171–172, 201
Castlight Health, 64
Cause Map, 113

Certified Industrial Hygienist (CIH), 252
Certified Safety Professional (CSP), 252
Coaching, 89, 97, 119, 136, 151–156
Collective mindfulness of danger, 242
Conflict management, 15
Conklin, Todd, 239, 270
    Better Questions, 270–271
Contracts, 141–142
Corporate climate, 144–145, 232
Corporate culture, 3–4, 36, 100–101, 134, 141, 145, 212, 216, 236, 237–238
Cost/benefit analysis, 187
Culture survey, 82

D

Dalton, Melville, 13–14
Decision tree, 187
Dekker, Sidney, 265, 269
    "The 'Failed State' of Safety," 265
    The Safety Anarchist, 269
Dekra, 151, 181–182
Delphi method, 186
Deming, W. Edwards, 220, 274
    Obligations of Management, 220
Deschamps, Didier, 136
Direct employer accountability, 129
Domino Theory of Incident Causation, 102–103, 229
Dual Factor Theory, 38–39

E

Earnest, Gene, 83
Emotional intelligence, 153
Employee(s)
    behavior change, 141–142, 215
    communication and engagement, viii, 76, 89–91, 133
    observation, 76, 80, 85, 97–98, 156–159
    poor performance, 64–65
    safety commitment, 261
    screening and training, 71, 73, 76, 91, 119, 141, 229
Employee assistance program (EAP), 66
Environmental Protection Agency (EPA), 181
    Risk Management Plan (RMP) rule, 181
Ergonomic analysis (EA), *see* Hazard identification and assessment
Ergonomics, defined, 97–98
Event tree analysis, 187

F

Facebook, 20
Failure Modes and Effects Analysis (FMEA), 113, 179–181, 187
Fatal and serious injuries and illnesses (FSII), 276. *See also*: Serious and fatal injuries
Fault Tree Analysis (FTA), 113, 181, 187
Ferri, Abby, 267
Fishbone Diagram, 113, 192, 194, 203, 221
5S system of work organization, 100–101
5-Why Problem-Solving Process, *see* Root-Cause Analysis
Flat organization, 20, 78, 79–80
Flowchart, 192, 193, 194, 221
    defined, 192
Ford, Henry, 270
Ford Motor Company, 222
Frito-Lay, 85–87
Front line, defined, 3–4
Function Analysis Diagram, 113

G

Gap analysis, 82, 201, 203
Geller, E. Scott, 33, 43, 260, 268
Geller, Krista, 268
General Electric (GE), 86–87
Gibb, Gerry, 202
Gilmore, Ryan, 266, 267
Glanville, Allan, 245
Group, 47–50. *See also*: team
    defined, 47–48
    formation, 48
    influence, 47, 49
    norms, 48–49
    peer pressure, 49
Grubbe, Deborah, 267

H

Hajaistron, Michael, 151
    "Helping Mining Superintendents Become Effective Safety Coaches," 151
Hannaford, Earle, 40–41
    Supervisor's Guide to Human Relations, 40
Hansen, Mark, 266
Harvard Business Review, 13
Hawthorne Effect, *see* Mayo, Elton
Hazard analysis and critical control points (HACCP), 186

Hazard and Operability (HAZOP) study, see Hazard identification and assessment
Hazard Control Plan, 100
Hazard Hunt (HH), see Hazard identification and assessment
Hazard identification and assessment, 71, 75, 89, 91–98, 167–174, 181–183
    Ergonomic analysis (EA), 97–98, 177–180
        checklist, 180
        overview, 179
    Hazard and Operability (HAZOP) study, 181–182, 186
    Hazard Hunt (HH), 98, 174–176
    Job Safety Analysis (JSA), 98, 169–174
        worksheet, 170, 173
    major categories of hazards, 168–169, 182–183
    Process Hazard Analysis (PHA), 181
Hazard prevention and control, 98–102, 168–174
    emergency controls, 102, 169
    implementing controls, 75, 100–102
    OSHA *Hazard Prevention and Control*, 168
    OSHA's six action steps, 168
    OSHA sources for information on hazards, 168
    selecting controls, 99–100
    validating controls, 101
Heinrich, H.W., xi, 80, 102–103, 211, 228–229, 230, 234, 237
    Axioms of Industrial Safety, 211
    Domino Theory of Incident Causation, 102–103, 229
    Industrial Accident Prevention, 228
Herzberg, Frederick, 38–39, 218
Hollnagel, Erik, 231
Holmes and Rahe Stress Scale 138
Horizontal organization, 20, 79–80
Human and Organizational Performance (HOP), vii, 86–87, 162, 212, 227, 238, 240, 265
Human error, 86–87, 140–141, 202, 211–212, 220, 228, 238–240, 267–268
    decision to err, 140
    traps in the workplace, 141, 212, 211, 221
    worker overload, 140, 211
Human factors concepts, vii, 141, 263, 270
Human learning, 155–156
Human reliability analysis (HRA), 187

I

Incident(s)
    catastrophic, 124, 126
    causation theories, 228–229
    cause identification methods, 113, 194–203
    cost, 109, 111–112
    investigation, 79, 89, 102, 103, 107–108, 185–203
        Safety Sampling, 188–191
        Statistical Safety Control (SSC), 192–194
    key facts, 107–109
        checklist, 110
    rate, 84, 85, 106
    report forms, 104–106, 112, 198
Incident Cause Analysis Method (ICAM), 202–203
Incident Recall Technique (IRT), 113, 195–200
    worksheet, 200
Incongruence Theory, 34–36
Industrial hygiene, 83, 245–255
    defined, 251
    elements, 83
    hearing loss, 247
    musculoskeletal disorders (MSDs), 248–249
    occupational illnesses, 249
    other illnesses, 249
    poisoning, 248
    respiratory conditions, 245, 247–248
        COPD, 247–248
    skin disorders, 246–247
Industrial Safety and Hygiene News (*ISHN*), vii, 74, 87, 245, 265, 269, 270
Industry 4.0, 222, 231
Inspecting work practices, 97
Institute for Corporate Productivity, 13
Integrated safety, 28, 29, 30
Intelex, 203
International Labor Organization (ILO), 273
    Guidelines on Occupational Health and Safety Management Systems, 273
International Organization for Standardization (ISO), 98, 107–108, 167
    ISO 9001, 273
    ISO 14001, 273
    ISO 31000 *Risk Management—Guidelines*, 167
    ISO 45001, 273, 274

ISHN, *see* Industrial Safety and Hygiene News
ISO/IEC Standard 31010:2009 *Risk Assessment Techniques*, 186–187
Interpersonal relations, 218–219
Inverse Performance Appraisal (IPA), *see* Leadership, tools
Issue-Based Information System, 113

J

James, Muriel
    five-step process for making contracts with employees, 141–142
    The OK Boss, 141
Job
    behavior, 33, 40–42
    enlargement, 39
    enrichment, 38–39, 218, 219
Job Safety Analysis (JSA), 98, 138, 169–174
    OSHA compliance worksheet, 171
    procedure, 173
    worksheet, 170, 173
Job Safety Observation (JSO), 156–159
    worksheet, 159

K

Key element rating (KER), 84, 85, 86
Klee, Ann R., 86–87
Kotter, John
    eight-step process for leading change, 135
    Leading Change, 135

L

Lawler, Edward E. and Lyman W. Porter, 118
Layers of Protection Analysis (LOPA), 181, 187
Leadership, 133–147, 213–214, 259–263
    styles, 133
    transformational, 133–134
    tools, 138–147
        Climate Analysis (CA), 144–147
            survey, 145
        Inverse Performance Appraisal (IPA), 142–143
        Safety Improvement Teams (SITs), 144
        Worker Safety Analysis (WSA), 138–140
Leung, Jade, 210
Life change unit (LCU), 138
Likert, Rensis, 36, 218

M

Mager, Robert, 42–46
    Developing an Attitude Toward Learning, 42
Maier, Normand, 57–58
    Psychology in Industry, 57
Management by Objective (MBO), 232
Management By Walking Around (MBWA), 215
Markov analysis, 187
Mayo, Elton, 217
    Hawthorne Effect, 80, 217
MENU, *see* Accountability systems
Metrics Task Force of Organization Resources Counselors (ORCHSE Strategies), 126
Mid-level managers, 4, 124–125, 127
Modeling, 40, 43, 46
Monte Carlo simulation, 187
Motivation, 15, 33, 36–37, 40, 73, 117, 155–156, 218
Mueller, Paul, 194
Multicriteria decision analysis (MCDA), 187
Multi-employer worksites, 129
Multiple Causation Theory, 103, 107, 229
Musculoskeletal disorders (MSDs), 98, 177–178, 248–249

N

National Fire Protection Association (NFPA), 98, 181
    Standard for the Prevention of Fire and Dust Explosions, 181
National Institute for Occupational Safety and Health (NIOSH), 98–99, 241–242, 246, 247, 249, 254–255
    ladder safety app, 254
    lifting equation app, 254
    Pocket Guide to Hazardous Chemicals app, 254
    sound level meter app, 255
    Total Worker Health (TWH) program, 241–242
National Public Radio, 224
National Safety Council (NSC), 9, 41, 64, 72–74, 91, 94–95, 110, 111, 227
    Injury Facts, 9

O

O'Neill, Paul, 219
One-minute contact (OMC) system, 161

One-on-one contact (OO), 2, 127, 152, 160, 215
Organization(s)
    characteristics, 35–36
    high-performance, 5, 80–85, 239, 242
    management style, 218
        employee-centered, 218, 219
    roles 3–5
OSHA
    A–Z topic index, 9, 176
    compliance emphasis, 101, 210, 232–234
    Hazard Communication (HAZCOM) standard, 234
    Hazard Identification Training Tool, 253–254
    Hazard Prevention and Control, 168
    Occupational Safety and Health (OSH) Act of 1970, 129, 208
    On-Site Consultation Program, 252
    Process Safety Management standard, 181, 234
    "Recommended Practices for Safety and Health Programs," 74–75
    Safety & Health Achievement Recognition Program (SHARP), 252–253
    Severe Violator Enforcement Program (SVEP), 208
    standards and guidance documents, 90, 98
    Voluntary Protection Program (VPP), 53, 253
OSHA Compliance Check (OCC), 98, 176–177
OSHA-NIOSH Heat Safety Tool, 254
OSHA 300 and 301 logs, 168, 248, 249
Ouchi, William
    Theory Y: How American Management Can Meet the Japanese Challenge, 38
Oxford University Center for the Governance of Artificial Intelligence, 210

P

Paradigm, defined, 201
Paradigm shift, 207
    new principles, 211–214
Pareto Chart, 192–193, 194, 221
Perception surveys, 82, 126
Permissible exposure limits (PELs), 250
Personal protective equipment (PPE), 46, 89, 96, 97, 99, 101, 242, 242, 246, 261, 266

Petersen, Dan, 234, 245, 259, 270
    Analyzing Safety System Effectiveness, xii
    "Human Error Reduction and Safety Management," ix
    Human Error Reduction & Safety Management, xii
    Industrial Safety & Hygiene News interview, 245
    "Organizational Behavior and Management," ix
    reading resources, 263–264
    Safety by Objectives—What Gets Measured and Rewarded Gets Done, xii
    Techniques of Safety Management, 29, 96, 127, 234–236
Peters, Tom, 13
    In Search of Excellence, 13
Pitzer, Corrie, 270
Plan-Do-Check-Act (PDCA) model, 274
Pope, W.C. and Thomas J. Cresswell, 235
    "Safety Programs Management," 235
Positive Organizational Scholarship (POS), 36–37, 43
Predictive analytics, 108–109
Prejob and postjob briefings, 162
Preliminary hazard analysis (PHA), 186
Probabilities of failure on demand (PFD), 182
Problem worker, 61–66
Process Hazard Analysis (PHA), *see* Hazard identification and assessment
Process Safety Information (PSI), 182
Procter and Gamble Company (P&G), 82–85, 126, 222
Professional Safety, viii
ProPublica, 224
Punishment and safety, 55–61, 215, 268

Q

Quest Diagnostics study, 63–65

R

Reason, James, 202, 212, 229
    Swiss Cheese Model of system failure, 202, 229
Recordkeeping, 73, 228, 230, 266
Report of the BP US Refineries Independent Safety Review Panel, 185–186
Risk assessment techniques, 186–187
Root-Cause Analysis, 113, 186–187, 194–203

Gap Analysis, 201, 203
5-Why Problem-Solving Process, 201, 203
Incident Recall Technique (IRT), 195–200
Technique of Operations Review (TOR), 194–195
techniques, 186–187
Root causes, 167, 186, 195, 203, 235
    defined, 103
Rowland, Aaron, 266, 267

S

Safe Behavior Reinforcement (SBR), 160–161
Safety
    as a dead end, 266, 270
    attitude, 40–46, 78–79. 115, 137
    director, 232
    information networks, 242
    in the gig economy, 213
    management, 214, 237–238
        accountability systems, 237–238
        blind spots, 216–217
    media, 230
    modern philosophies, 230–231
    "New View," 227, 265–271
    processes, 228–238
        common areas, 228–230
        components, 232–234
        fundamental principles, 234–238
    risk-centric, 240
    supervision elements, 14–15, 83
Safety 2.0, 227, 267
Safety-I, 240
Safety-II, 240, 265
Safety and health professional, 76, 115, 124
Safety and health staff, 5, 127, 187
Safety and health system *See also*: Supervisor, responsibilities
    aversives, 44–45
    common controls, 233
    components, 71
    criteria for effectiveness, 236
    defined, 28–30
    drawbacks of traditional programs, 239
    effective, 61
    group norms, 50
    major areas, 72–75
    management principles, 76, 214, 234–236
    new realities, 207–224. *See also*: Paradigm shift
        external environment changes, 207–210
        internal environment changes, 210
    organizational participants, 71–82, 127
        middle management, 71–73, 75–76
        staff personnel, 72–73, 76–77
        supervisor, *see* Supervisor, responsibilities
        top management, 71–75
    positives, 45–46, 89–90, 97
    subsystems, 236
    tasks, 89
    team principles, 80
    twentieth-century approaches, 227
Safety by Objectives (SBO), *see* Accountability systems
Safety Data Sheet (SDS), 90, 168, 250
Safety Differently, 239, 265, 268–269
Safety Instrumented Systems, 181
Safety matrix, 175
Safety Performance Model, 116–120
    rewards, 116–117
    supervisor role perception, 118
Safety Sampling (SS), 113, 188–191, 220
    number of observations needed, 191
    worksheet, 190
Samuel, Mark, 128
    "Unleash the Power of an Accountable Organization," 128
Sayles, Leonard, 77–78
    Managerial Behavior, 77
Schleh, Edward C., 14–15
Schultz, Howard, 209
Schulzinger, Morris, 62
Scott, Susan, 44, 56, 57, 60, 115
    Fierce Conversations: Achieving Success at Work & Life, One Conversation at a Time, 44, 115
Senior leaders, 3–4, 36, 55, 71–75, 124, 126, 127, 209, 215, 259–263
    eight executive habits, 261–262
    first-level manager's safety report, 123
    saying–doing gap, 213
Serious injuries and fatalities (SIFs), 74, 99, 212, 241, 276
Sherif, Muzafer, 52

Index

Society of Automotive Engineers (SAE), 180
Space Shuttle Columbia Accident Investigation Board (CAIB) independent review, 185–186
Spitzer, Corrie, 265
    "Safety at a Dead End," 265
Standard operation procedures (SOPs), 127
Statistical Process Control (SPC), 192
    tools, 192–194
Statistical safety control (SSC), 113, 192–194
Stress Assessment Technique (SAT), 162–164
Stress-related illness, 66, 138, 207, 208, 209
Structured What If Technique (SWIFT), 186
Substance abuse, 63–65
Substance Abuse and Mental Health Services Administration (SAMHSA), 65
Supervisor(s)
    ability, 118
    accountability, 24–28, 86, 122–123, 128, 129–130
        types of measurement, 24–25
    attitude, 78–79, 115, 137
    authority, 16, 18–24, 40
    coaching 151–164
        the individual, 152–155
        the team, 155
    disempowered, 58
    effort, 116, 118
    ineffectiveness, 8
    job-centered versus employee-centered, 30, 37, 218
    leadership, 13, 89, 133–138, 153
    performance, 113, 116–120
    personal philosophy, 216
    poor practices, 33–34
    promotion, 13–14
    responsibilities, 1–2, 15–18, 72–74 77–79, 89–113, 127
    rewards for performance, 116–117, 121
    role perception, 118, 134
    status, 6–8
    training, 9, 58, 71, 73, 74, 118, 121, 229–230
    traits, 13
    use of discipline, 55–61
Swiss Cheese Model of system failure, *see* Reason, James
System 1 and System 2 Thinking, 242

System of Counting and Rating Accident Prevention Effort (SCRAPE), *see* Accountability systems
Systems-Theoretic Accident Model and Process (STAMP), 113

T
Team(s)
    building, 50–54
        strong, 50–54
        weak, 51
    cohesiveness, 52–54
    competing with enemies, 53–54
    developing symbols, 53
    high-performance concept, xi, 80–85
    leadership roles, 53
    member, 5
Technique of Operations Review (TOR), 113, 194–195, 197, 199
    Cause Code, 194, 196–197
    worksheet, 199
Thaler, Richard and Cass Sunstein
    Nudge, 33
Theory X versus Theory Y versus Theory Z, 38
Three Es of Safety, 80, 211, 221
Threshold Limit Values (TLV s), 250–251
Time-weighted averages (TWAs), 250
Total Quality Management (TQM) concepts, 220–222, 227
Triangle Shirtwaist Factory fire, 227

U
Uber autonomous car crash, 210, 228
Unsafe practices, 92–96
US Bureau of Labor Statistics (BLS), 228, 245
US Department of Agriculture, 65
US Department of Health and Human Services, 65
    "Dietary Guidelines for Americans 2015–2020," 65

W
Weick, Carl, 242
Workers' Compensation (WC), 207–208, 224
World Health Organization (WHO), 109, 209
    International Statistical Classification of Diseases and Related Health Problems (ICD), 109

Y
Yale University secluded camp, 52–54

Z
Zappos, 20

Zenger and Folkman survey, 135
    top eight leadership skills, 135
Zero incidents, 87, 100–101, 267–268
Zion Market Research, 209